A Whaler's Dictionary

A Whaler's Dictionary

Dan Beachy-Quick

MILKWEED EDITIONS

(800) 520-6455
www.milkweed.org

Published 2008 by Milkweed Editions
Printed in the United States of America
Cover design by Christian Fünfhausen
Cover art: Nantucket Historical Association
Author photo by Sergio Vucci
Interior design by Wendy Holdman
The text of this book is set in Sabon.
16 17 18 19 20   7 6 5 4
First Edition

Library of Congress Cataloging-in-Publication Data

Beachy-Quick, Dan, 1973–
    A whaler's dictionary / Dan Beachy-Quick. — 1st ed.
       p.   cm.
    ISBN 978-1-57131-309-6 (pbk. : acid-free paper)
       1. Melville, Herman, 1819–1891. Moby Dick. 2. Philosophy in literature.
    I. Title.
    PS2384.M62B43 2008
    813'.3—dc22

                                                              2008028797

This book is printed on acid-free paper.

For Kristy—

Let be be finale of seem

& for Hana—

Little whale, little ghost,
　　　　The world grows quiet
　　When you speak it most—
　　When you see it most
It grows blank as ocean
　　　　Grows blank at noon—
No boat but a coffin,
　　And horizon for a coast.

I'd like to thank the editors of the following journals who kindly published sections of this book: "Experience," "Imagination," "Silence," and "Writing" at *GutCult*; "Coffin," "Etching," "Inscribe," and "Reading" at *Identity Theory*; "Hero," "Reciprocity," and You/Thou" at *Paper & Carriage*. Thank you, too, to the editors of *New American Writing*, where the poem in the dedication was first published as "Lullaby."

I owe a great debt to the friends whose advice and patience made this book possible. Thank you Fawn Trigg, Srikanth Reddy, Suzanne Buffam, and Sally Keith. Thank you Rebecca Beachy. Thank you Mai Wagner and Lou Robinson and Leila Wilson. Thank you Alex Jovanovich. Thank you Fran Benson, for so much advice. Thank you to my mother, Ruth Ann Quick. Thank you to my father, R.C. Quick. Thank you to the students at The School of the Art Institute of Chicago whose discussions in our *Moby-Dick* seminar inspired this book. I'd also like to thank Zach Barocas for creating a beautiful broadside on behalf of this book. Thank you, in abundance, to the wonderful people at Milkweed Editions. For the time and freedom given me by the Lannan Foundation and The School of the Art Institute's Roger Brown Residency which allowed me to begin writing *A Whaler's Dictionary*—thank you.

Call the world if you Please "the vale of Soul-making" Then you will find out the use of the world (I am speaking now in the highest terms for human nature admitting it to be immortal which I will here take for granted for the purpose of showing a thought which has struck me concerning it) I say '*Soul making*' Soul as distinguished from an Intelligence— There may be intelligences or sparks of the divinity in millions—but they are not Souls till they acquire identities, till each one is a personality itself. . . . I can scarcely express what I but dimly perceive—and yet I think I perceive it—that you may judge the more clearly I will put it in the most homely form possible—I will call the *world* a School instituted for the purpose of teaching little children to read—I will call the *human heart* the *horn Book* used in that school—and I will call the *Child able to read, the Soul* made from that *school* and its *hornbook*.

—John Keats, *Letter to the George Keatses,*
14 February–3 May 1819

The hermit does not believe that any philosopher—assuming that every philosopher was first of all a hermit—ever expressed his real and ultimate opinions in books: does one not write books precisely to conceal what one harbors? Indeed, he will doubt whether a philosopher could *possibly* have "ultimate and real" opinions, whether behind every one of his caves there is not, must not be, another deeper cave—a more comprehensive, stranger, richer world beyond the surface, an abysmally deep ground behind every ground, under every attempt to furnish "grounds." Every philosophy is a foreground philosophy—that is a hermit's judgment: "There is something arbitrary in his stopping *here* to look back and look around, in his not digging deeper *here* but laying his spade aside; there is also something suspicious about it." Every philosophy also conceals a philosophy; every opinion is also a hideout, every word also a mask.

—Friedrich Nietzsche, *Beyond Good and Evil*

. . . intelligence is impossible without soul . . .

—Plato, *Timaeus*

Apology

"I can scarcely express what I but dimly perceive—and yet I think I perceive it—" writes John Keats. I hope to give fair warning to the reader, before this book is begun, that its pages are full of dim perceptions scarcely expressed. What follows is the result of the mad task I found within myself after more than a decade spent reading the same novel. I meant not to exhaust *Moby-Dick* of meaning, but to exhaust myself of the meaning I found in it. Perhaps this is every attentive reader's absurd hope when thinking about a book he or she loves: to write a loving response that includes every thought—coherent or ambiguous, true or frivolous—that the book engendered. It is an almost erotic entanglement. The book exists between the author and the reader as a private room where the mind of one consummates meaning with the mind of the other. The pages of a book are those sheets between which two minds enter one another to think the same thoughts. But every margin is Lethe, and to cross it is to begin to forget.

This book is written from such a margin: attempting to record what glimmers remain of thinking impossibly realized before the thought is vaguely lost, as if a jewel, once apprehended, had somehow turned into fog in the hand. As such, I feel an apology is in order. This book is not responsible. It is not thoroughly researched. It merges vastly different disciplines and influences into a single expression; it asks contraries to be one. It does not mean to be an addition to the field of scholarship.

This book's aims are both more humble and more audacious. I am not the first to say much of what follows, but I have written nothing that I have not thought myself. Such is the great promise in reading. One might say of a book the same Thoreau says looking up at the night sky: "The stars are the apexes of what wonderful triangles!" Except the image must be slowed and changed. We do not look up at but rather up from the book. The book gives us not the star but the ground, and so the angle that finds the brilliant height. To read is to look up by casting eyes down. Both reader and writer see the same star. This book is the inevitably marred attempt to write by such light. It is a dim light—and yet I think I see—

Introduction (or, How to Use This Book)

Submerged within *Moby-Dick* lurks an unfinished dictionary, specific to the science and art of whaling. In it Ishmael attempts to classify and define every whale a whaler may encounter. The effort is more touching than pedantic. Whales, of course, pose a great problem to the would-be lexicographer: they are always diving down. One might as well define evanescence by noting the horizon line.

A Whaler's Dictionary does not finish Ishmael's failed cetological endeavor—it simply repeats the failure in a different guise. No whale is defined, unless we consider the book itself a kind of whale, its meaning always plumbing down past thought's reach. As Ishmael's dictionary was meant to allow a whaler to know what kind of beast he was chasing, so *A Whaler's Dictionary*'s highest hope is simply to allow a reader to gain a greater sight of what this leviathan *Moby-Dick* itself might be, and in doing so encourage a closer reading. As Ishmael's dictionary let a whaler name his danger, *A Whaler's Dictionary* offers a series of interlaced meditations to bring a reader near to the white squall of meaning that is *Moby-Dick*.

Some words of advice and warning: *A Whaler's Dictionary* is not meant to be read from first page to last. This dictionary is not concerned with sequence so much as consequence. A reader is encouraged to thumb through the book until an entry seems of interest. At the bottom of every entry, then, is a list of cross-references that build upon, expand, tangentially link, or contradict the entry just read, that allow the reader to recognize the elements of his or her own interests, the direction of his or her own interpretation. As with any dictionary, this book has the humble hope not of being read, but of making more possible the reading of a book outside itself.

Some Gams (with Books, Not Boats)

Although *A Whaler's Dictionary* is not truly academic or scholarly in nature, certain texts have contributed their deep and broad influence to my smaller meditations. I mean the list much as one of the mates aboard the Pequod might have kept in the logbook a list of the ships met on gams at sea. These are the books that by chance I found floating and whose gracious thinking guided me in my pursuit: John Keats, *Selected Letters*; Frederich Nietzsche, *Beyond Good and Evil*; Emerson, in particular "Experience" and "The American Scholar"; Montaigne, *Essays*; Charles Olson, *Call Me Ishmael*; *Early American Writing,* edited by Giles Gunn, in particular selections by Ann Hutchinson and Mary Rowlandson; Plato, *Phaedrus*; Tzvetan Todorov, *The Conquest of America*; Michael Paul Rogin, *Subversive Genealogy*; K.L. Evans, *Whale!*; Maurice Blanchot, *The Space of Literature*; Ludwig Wittgenstein, *Tractatus Logico-Philosophicus*; Emmanuel Levinas, *Totality and Infinity*; Martin Buber, *I and Thou*; Thomas Hariot, *A Brief and True Report of the New-found Land of Virginia*; Walter Benjamin, "On the Origins of Human Language and Language as Such"; Gottlieb Frege, "The Thought" and "Sense and Reference"; Gilles Deleuze and Felix Guattari, *1000 Plateaus*; Pascal, *Pensees*; Jose Ortega y Gassett, *Meditations on Quixote*; Roland Barthes, *A Lover's Discourse*; Martin Heidegger, "The Origin of the Work of Art" and "What is Called Thinking"; Avivah Gottlieb Zornberg, *The Beginning of Desire*; Mircea Eliade, *Rites and Symbols of Initiation*; and the writings of Simone Weil, among others that have seeped, now anonymous, into the cargo hold of my own experience.

Epigraph

The weaver-god, he weaves; and by that weaving is he deafened, that he hears no mortal voice; and by that humming, we, too, who look on the loom are deafened; and only when we escape it shall we hear the thousand voices that speak through it.

—Herman Melville, *Moby-Dick*

A Whaler's Dictionary

Accuracy

Accuracy and experience are betrothed, but it's a marriage on the rocks. Ishmael's basic project is not to tell the indelible tale of Captain Ahab's vengeful demise. *Moby-Dick* is ours to read because Ishmael failed in writing the book he thought could capture the experience of the whale—of whaling—accurately. The failure of Ishmael's cetological dictionary (Chapter XXXII) occurs with as great a weight, as great a consequence, as Ahab's failure. In many ways, Ishmael's failure is more unnerving. For he gives us a dictionary that is meant to be a model of utmost semantic honesty. He tries to name the whales he has seen. And he fails.

Ahab chases the white whale; Ishmael chases accuracy. Ishmael's question, which is to say his quest, is the very same as his captain's: How to catch the white whale? But Ishmael's quest, occurring upon a different plane, begs a different means of capture. Ishmael's harpoon is a lexicon—not a tool of piercing, of deadly wounding, but a language-net cast into the sea, drawing into sight what it catches. Ishmael's tale is this net.

Language functions with greater mercy than does Ahab's blood-forged blade. Ideally, what language pulls up is still alive. The accuracy language promises provides a means by which one can speak of the world without killing the world. A honed description is not murder.

Language allows one to record the world accurately before one of two possibilities occurs: the whale dies or the net breaks. Both outcomes are accuracy's failure. One records the lifeless form of the slain creature caught, the other lets the living creature descend back into the depths.

Ishmael's deepest humanity lies in his understanding that the whale can be described only in the encounter with a living whale—not a place of language but prior to language, and an encounter that language, in its most humble effort toward accuracy, tries to recapture after it has passed.

See also:

Classification
Description
Dictionary
Duplicates
Etching
Imagination
Inscribe
Plato
Silence
Skin
Writing

Adam

Ahab inherits Adam's fallen world. The loss of paradise also costs Adam, and the generations born after Adam, God's immanence in the world. Sensing God's absence, one might choose a stone and carve an image of the departed. Ahab's name alludes to such idolatry: idols of Ba'al placed in the Temple. But Ahab's connection to Adam goes deeper.

To understand that depth one must see the Fall in relation to language. Saint Augustine offers a model:

> . . . This, I since learned, Thou, through these Thy gifts, within me
> and without, proclaiming Thyself unto me. For then I knew but
> to suck; to repose in what pleased, and cry at what offended my
> flesh; nothing more.
>
> Afterwards I began to smile; first in sleep, then waking: for
> so it was told me of myself, and I believed it; for we see the like
> in other infants, though of myself I remember it not. Thus, little
> by little, I became conscious where I was; and to have a wish
> to express my wishes to those who could content them, and I
> could not; for the wishes were within me, and they without;
> nor could they by any sense of theirs enter within my spirit. So
> I flung about at random limbs and voice, making the few signs
> I could, and such as I could, like, though in truth very little like,
> what I wished.

This description of the infant coming into language offers a strange parallel to the loss of paradise. He describes the inevitable sorrow of moving from a state in which all needs are foreseen by those who can (and do) fulfill them to one in which desires must be communicated in order to be fulfilled. Language erupts out of the sense of lack that occurs when one comes to self-consciousness. Augustine's description suggests the subtle difficulty of the crisis: "a wish to express my wishes." The cost of having desires, of suffering lack, is that one must desire *desire,* want *want,* wish *wishes.* One must cipher distinct words to call out distinct needs from the shapeless neediness of one's being. To name one wish never satisfies the overwhelming sense that one wishes. Language erupts from the child's separation from parents and world, and language opens in each a further division. The self scrutinizes the self's desires, wishes to wish. The infant's dilemma exists at no far remove from the adult's, whose vocabulary but masks the same desperation. Language makes an outside of the inside, and expresses itself in loss. And when, despite it, we aren't understood, we flail, and by our flailing hope to receive the comfort for which we could not find the words.

Eden is the archetype of such loss. Adam and Eve must leave the paradise in which every wish was granted without being articulated in words—and though Adam does talk to God, and ask favors of God, his language isn't essentially expressive of such wishes, for Adam's needs would be known without a single word.

Adam's relationship to language is fundamental. Adam names all the creatures and things of the world. This naming is not an arbitrary process (in the way, for example, Saussurean semiotics is an arbitrary process) but an essential. In naming the creatures of the world, Adam attempts to express what they themselves do: the name that carries forward what they are. This language does not refer, does not sign. There is no separation between name and named. That which is named discloses the immanence that is its word.

The eating of the fruit of the tree of knowledge of good and evil results in a linguistic fall that parallels the expulsion from paradise. Words contain the distance they express. Words must move across the incommensurable abyss of desire in order to fill the lack that sparks their utterance. The loss of paradise, painful though it may be, is the formation of consciousness: one he does not wish, but wishes to wish. Paradise ceased to be paradise the moment Eve and Adam bit into the fruit. The first result wasn't merely the realization of their nakedness but the possibility of such a realization. To be ashamed Adam and Eve had to be separate from the God in whose identity they earlier dwelled. They knew they were naked because they recognized themselves.

Inherent in that awful moment is the seed expressed in Descartes' cogito: "I think, therefore I am." For what is haunting in the phrase is the vague sense that the first "I" is not the same as the second. A self is an I thinking about an I that thinks. We fall into a world in which words but signify what they embodied in paradise, and when we speak of ourselves we replay the same trauma. For we are not only separate from paradise, we are also separate from ourselves.

~

"Adam" appears five times in *Moby-Dick*. Ishmael, in trying to explain Ahab's hatred for the white whale, says of his captain, "He piled upon the whale's white hump the sum of all the general rage and hate felt by his whole race from Adam down." This giant blankness of a whale that no harpoon or knife, no nib or cipher can kill nor account, represents for Ahab the blank-dread work of consciousness itself, the sign that the world we dwell in is itself already some distance from itself, and all is homeless, as in the mind every thought is anchorless, strangely doubled, and afloat. To conquer the whale, perhaps, is to end the timeless consequence of Adam's appetite: to speak so as not to mean, but to be.

Ahab, whose acuteness of mind has been far more honed by his madness than dulled by it, is as aware as Saint Augustine of language's inherent loss, and as sensible as Saussure of language's semiotic doubleness. Ahab is a captain whose loss, like Adam's, resulted in doubleness. Ahab speaking to the carpenter:

> Look ye, carpenter, I dare say thou callest thyself a right good
> workmanlike workman, eh? Well, then, will it speak thoroughly
> well for thy work, if, when I come to mount this leg thou makest,
> I shall nevertheless feel another leg in the same identical place

with it; that is, carpenter, my old lost leg; the flesh and blood one,
I mean. Canst thou not drive that old Adam away?

That "old Adam" refers to the time before Ahab fell into the sea and suffered the wound from Moby Dick's scythelike jaw, when his body and his mind were whole. Ahab walks upon a linguistic torture: he feels the whole nerve alive by virtue of the leg carved of bone to replace it. The referent refers, but Ahab is not fooled. He knows the replacement never replaces the living connection with what has been lost. The point holds true for world and leg, paradise and word.

These Adam allusions progress curiously. The first is made authorially: an observation, an act of interpretation, spoken of Ahab rather than by him. The second is a metaphysically pointed allusion leaping out of Ahab's wit. The last is the most intimate and harrowing. Speaking to Starbuck the day before the chase begins, Ahab says, "I feel deadly faint, bowed, and humped, as though I were Adam, staggering beneath the piled centuries since Paradise." Whatever multiple torments of world and self sum themselves up in Ahab's mindful rage, a large portion of his pain is his ocean-deep sense of his own wordless consciousness, called into mortal urgency by Moby Dick's blank nearing. There is no language to alleviate the fundamental lack of a whaler's existence—a whaler hunts. One is alone—an *isolato*. The world is not recompense for all that has been lost, but rather reminder. When we seek to save ourselves by naming, to near the world by speaking it closer, we find that the word pushes away the world as a ripple pushes away a leaf from the hand that sweeps forward to pull it from the water. Yet one remembers the tree from which the leaf fell, and the garden in which the tree stood, as vividly as Ahab remembers the leg he no longer walks on. Language gives us a ghost and tells us it's alive.

See also:
Duplicates
I / *I* / "I"

Jonah
Pyramid
Saying / Said
Vishnoo
Whale (Ghost)

Ahab

STARBUCK: "Aye, and say'st the men have vow'd thy vow; say'st all of us are Ahabs."

〜

CARPENTER: "Seems to me some sort of Equator cuts yon old man, too, right in his middle. He's always under the Line—fiery hot, I tell ye!"

〜

AHAB: "Is Ahab, Ahab?"

See also:
Corpusants
Death
Hero
I / *I* / "I"
Idolotry
Leg (Ghost)
Line
Magnet
Quest / Question
Reciprocity
Thought (Ahab)
Wound
You / Thou

ALEPH

The first letter of the Hebrew alphabet possesses no sound. *Aleph* bears the sound of any letter it is put against. *Aleph* carries breath, inspires—a livingness that comes to no life without the consonant obstructing breath's freedom. *Aleph*'s power can come to no use in the world, for it remains too close to the infinity that inspires it. *Aleph* is possibility unlimited by potential, if we understand potential as a power that can be manifested in form. It makes possible without becoming possible. *Aleph* is a beginning that cannot cease from beginning, a commencement outside time, cause's shapeless cause. *Aleph* is not ontology, for it precedes being. *Aleph* is that from which being must spring, and yet it can never be included in or reduced to the being it engenders. For the Infinite to come into form, it must be housed by another form. So Isaac encloses Abraham's love in fear, and so love dwells in the world—the bountiful residue of Isaac's horrific experience on Mount Moriah. So *bet,* with which letter Torah begins, contains *aleph's* infinite breath.

See also:

Bet
Breath (Thought)
Chaos
Fear
Inspiration
Silence
Tzimtzum
Void

AMBERGRIS

Stubb feels humiliated when Ahab kicks him, feels treated like a cur. But in a dream that night, a sperm whale hobbles up to Stubb to tell him that he should be honored by the kick, that the wise Ahab has, by virtue of the boot from the bone-leg, made of Stubb a wise man too. But what is the nature of Stubb's wisdom? Certainly he and Ahab share no similar enlightenment. Ahab's wisdom—if we can call him wise— occurs in the singular act of the chase after Moby Dick. Wisdom does not equal action. In fact, the wise often do not act, for wisdom implies the ability to contemplate the world from without the world—an impossibility at which Ahab would scoff, if he'd even recognize it worth the comment.

Ahab's wisdom is inseparable from the chase after the "inscrutable thing" that lurks behind the mask of the white whale that wounded him. Stubb has no set rails of purpose whereon "his soul is grooved to run." Stubb has no force that exerts itself through him so overwhelmingly as to almost unravel the warp and weave of body and soul that entwine a given self. Stubb's wisdom bodies, Ahab's wisdom souls, and one cannot add them together to form a whole. Stubb speaks to himself (a quality he shares with his captain): "Well, Stubb, *wise* Stubb—that's my title—well, Stubb, what of it, Stubb? Here's a carcass. I know not all that may be coming, but be it what it will, I'll go to it laughing."

Stubb's wisdom shows him a carcass—a valuable toll aboard a vessel that hunts for its livelihood. Stubb sees a carcass and says it's a carcass. In this, his body shares with every other body. To Stubb, all of it—whales and men and world—is a carcass. His jolliness occurs within the inevitable recognition not only of his own mortality, but of all mortality. Such a dark comedy allows one to eat one's whale raw, by the light of the same beast stuck on one's fork, the same beast filling one's mouth. And Stubb, of course, is a man who speaks with his mouth full.

↵

Stubb's is a comic wisdom, not a foolish one. Unlike Pip, whose madness derives from deepest wound, the affliction brought about by infinity's boundless approach, Stubb's wisdom comes from recognizing the uselessness of any thinking, any purpose, against a mortal fate that none can avoid. His wisdom is in his arse—bruised by Ahab's ivory heel. Stubb knows a man falls down; comedy is standing back up, even if only to fall again. Gravity of all sorts is the wise comedian's straight man: the natural law that assures the slip upon the oil on the deck will result in the guffaw of every onlooker; likewise, the gravitas of a captain whose fearful intensity seems to suffocate a laugh before it starts. Such wisdom resulting from such mortal recognitions—one who sees a carcass instead of reading a book—does have its deep, and unexpected, use.

↵

When Stubb sees the French ship Bouton de Rose alongside two dead whales, his comic wisdom prevails. Stubb, knowledgeable whaleman that he is, knows not "to turn his nose up at such a whale as this," regardless of the stink wafting about it. Stubb knows that hidden within the putrid mortal stench may lie the source of "a faint stream of perfume," which flows through "the tide of bad smells without being absorbed by it, as one river will flow into and then along with another, without at all blending with it for a time." Stubb knows that in the plaguey bowels of the desiccated whale may lurk an abundance of ambergris, a substance found only in such fetid sources, and of great monetary worth.

In order to gain it, though, Stubb must convince the French captain to heave away from his bounty. He hatches a plan, concocted with the first mate aboard the Rose-Bud, who only wants to leave the nauseating whales behind. The mate will act as interpreter, telling the captain whatever he wishes as he pretends to translate the insults Stubb hurls at the besotted man. Stubb "diddles" him by creating a confusion that seems to clarify information rather than misdirect it. Language, put through the comic subterfuge of false translation, achieves its end by masking its purpose. The body of the words is recognized only by the man whose wisdom is bodily; the sense the words connote applies to nothing, a phantom he speaks into truth, a miasma he makes into a fact. Speech masks intention. The comic doesn't lie so much as convince of an already existing belief, not yet acted upon, within the person being fooled. Stubb knows the French captain would seek any excuse to be excused from his malodorous "duty," and so he offers it to him, and the Rose-Bud's captain cuts both whales loose.

When the Bouton de Rose has sailed far enough away, Stubb drops his subterfuge and his men row back to the desiccated whale. Plunging a knife into its bowels, he smells a perfume amidst the decay and shit. And so Stubb proves the nature of his wisdom: not one who finds salvation, but one who finds salve. Stubb does not end pain, he pulls easement from ailment. He does not rage against nor mourn the mortal limits and aches all living bodies are subject to. He finds within the unalterable fact a jollity born of death's inevitability. Hidden in every worthless substance—rotten flesh, full bowels, dead fish—lurk riches unforeseen. The fatal laugh that responds to death, the shocked recognition of the vast nothingness that encompasses life, finds worth in the humor that reconfirms the substantial meaning of the body. There is a body and there is death; for Stubb, the hand willing to plunge equally deep into both emerges perfumed.

See also:

Fear
Fool
Hunger

Imagination
Joke
Profit
Prophet
Pyramid

Babel

Babel's "great stone mast," knocked down by God's fury, presaged the whaler climbing the masthead. Between those biblical lookouts and the modern whaler on the crosstree, his weather eye keen to spot a spout, are the historical Egyptians, that "nation of mast-head standers," who from pyramid's apex charted the night sky to "sing out" for new stars. Beneath Ishmael's charmingly pedantic discourse lurks an implication that all three towering cases share the same venture—all that removes the pyramids and the mastheads from Babel's fate is an inevitable lack of outrageous altitude.

The pyramids and the whale ship are built in the aftermath of Babel's curse. No nation will ever again speak to another nation, no person to another person, of the ambition to build a tower that threatens heaven. Babel's threat, more than piercing the heavenly vault and so undoing the cosmic balance that separates an upper from a lower realm, is in gaining height in order to see all the higher, not to steal into heaven so much as to sing out at what one sees there. The trespass was in wanting to name the world never seen by human eyes and, by naming it, to bring it down into sight. The curse of Babel was not blindness, as would befit the sin of blasphemous seeing, nor the loss of legs to climb or arms to build; the curse was the loss of the chance to speak in a common language. Babel's curse condemns us to language's opacity, to the solitude of thoughts one cannot speak. And the deeper the thought, the higher its aspirations, the more confused language grows. Belief becomes bafflement.

John Donne's beautiful conviction aside, each man is but an island to himself. "How it is, there is no telling, but Islanders seem to make the best whalemen. They were nearly all Islanders in the Pequod, *Isolatoes* too, I call such, not acknowledging the common continent of men, but each *Isolato* living on a separate continent of his own." A man—a whalingman, that is—may be defined in simple terms: a continent balanced on a pole, and singing out, when he sings, in a tongue of his own.

See also:
Accuracy
Expression
Jonah
Lightning
Plato
Pyramid
Saying / Said

BET

The Torah begins the story of creation and all that ensues with the letter *bet*. *Bet* allows the world to be spoken, pushed through the stop of the lips. The first sound from which all meaning is consequent. Inspiration fills the mouth but does no work until, pivoting in the depth of the lungs, it rises back to the mouth, whose air the lips punctuate: "buh," beginning.

The possibility can be seen in the letter's graphical structure: a foundation with a house upon it. The sound in which one dwells.

See also:

Aleph
Dictionary
Tzimtzum

Brain

Twenty feet behind the mountainous bulk of the sperm whale's forehead, behind the vast tun that holds the spermaceti, lies the brain. A sailor can hold in both hands the meager girth: ten inches deep by ten inches wide. Some sailors, though, "peremptorily deny that the Sperm Whale has any other brain than that palpable semblance of one formed by the cubic-yards of his sperm magazine." If the latter are right, then perhaps the whale's brain—and the mind the brain makes possible—functions far differently than the wrinkled gray mass in a human head.

Perhaps it functions differently because it is formed differently. Rather than a physical substance through which thoughts electrically pulse, the whale's brain is wholly fluid. The whale's brain is not electrically lit, as when an idea suddenly glows, but rather a flammable liquid whose thinking occurs before illumination is struck. In the sperm whale's brain there are no channels forged of habit, no physical links that limit the connections between one sphere and another—it is its own illimitable possibility, in which the substance of thought takes no final shape, its furthermost point in instantaneous connection with every other point, as the liquid sphere denies partition, makes center and circumference one.

Only upon death does that liquid mind—exposed to the air—begin to solidify, "sending forth beautiful crystalline shoots, as when the first thin delicate ice is just forming in water." Form is evidence and proof of its own mortality. Form is not thinking, but having had a thought—the spar of ice that does not thaw in warmest waters, but cools the water around it, turns the lake to ice.

~

Other whalers say the handheld mass behind the spermaceti's tun is the brain. Ishmael doesn't commit. But he suggests, if the sperm whale's is as ours, that one should count the spinal cord into the whole mental equation. Indeed, by both direct observation and scientific survey, Ishmael suggests that the vertebrae can be regarded as "a strung necklace of dwarfed skulls." And if each vertebra is but an undeveloped skull, so the cord within it is a lengthening of brain. The sperm whale's brain cavity "is continuous with the first neck-vertebra; and in that vertebra the bottom of the spinal canal will measure ten inches across, being eight in height, and of a triangular figure with the base downwards." That is, the spinal cord maintains an astonishing girth for almost the entire length of the whale's body. And if so, the intelligence of the whale may not be located within its forehead but expressed by its entire material existence. The sperm whale's motion is likewise its thinking, as if its whole physical being embodied thoughtfulness—as if to dive down were its philosophy, to breach its ethics, to flee its will, to attack its justice.

See also:

Eyes
Hands
Justice
Phrenology
Scroll
Skin
Spermaceti
Tongue
Thought (Ahab)
Thought (Hunt)
Truth

Breath (Thought)

Among the ongoing inaccuracies, unresolved mysteries, and indefinable anatomy that mark, or fail to mark, the nature of the sperm whale belongs the enigma of its spout. No whaler knows whether the whale spouts water or air. But we do know that the whale is vulnerable to a blade because it needs to breathe—and to breathe, it must rise.

Unlike a human in whom one breath serves "for two or three pulsations," the sperm whale "only breathes about one seventh or Sunday of his time." Rumors, as always, abound in vaster numbers than facts. The scientific resolution to such rumors requires one to observe more closely, to get nearer the subject under evaluation. But could one—whaler or scientist or he whose occupation combines both fields—ride atop a sperm whale as it breathes to complete his study? Even then, among plainest things, mystery asserts itself. The pursuit of knowledge exposes those who would know to grave danger:

> For even when coming into slight contact with the outer, vapory shreds of the jet, which will often happen, your skin will feverishly smart, from the acridness of the thing so touching it. And I know one, who coming into still closer contact with the spout, whether from some scientific object in view, or otherwise, I cannot say, the skin peeled off from his cheek and arm. Another thing; I have heard it said, and I do not much doubt it, that if the jet is fairly spouted into your eyes, it will blind you. The wisest thing the investigator can do then, it seems to me, is to let the deadly spout alone.

The spout's deadliness, symptom of the indecipherable mystery of the whale's breath, spurs consideration at the very point it advises one to let the question go. The sperm whale's respiratory danger warrants its own inquiry.

The elements of the mystery highlight the oddity of the problem. The whaler-scientist does not want a chemical breakdown of the elemental components of the spout; he wants to know whether the creature spouts air or water. The absolute dichotomy of the confusion speaks to the depth of the question. The whale exhales a vapor that entwines to the point of indecipherability two of the four basic elements of the world. The sperm whale's life confuses the same two elements—it lives in water but lives on air. Subtly, Ishmael is revealing a metaphoric quality in breath: its nature reflects our own. Pneuma and soul occupy a similar realm of investigation. Indeed, etymologically "soul" ties back, through the Proto-Germanic, to "coming from the sea, belonging to the sea." The sea both denies breath and makes its need conscious—as for a drowning man a next breath is a last thought. The sperm whale, who lives within an element (water) that opposes the element it lives on (air), must bear an intelligence uniquely tuned to the need to breathe, for it must act consciously to do so.

The sperm whale thinks as it breathes. The mental and the physical do not necessarily play out in opposing realms. Of this, Ishmael is vitally aware:

> My hypothesis is this: that the spout is nothing but mist. And besides other reasons, to this conclusion I am impelled, by considerations touching the great inherent dignity and sublimity of the Sperm Whale; I account him no common, shallow being, inasmuch as it is an undisputed fact that he is never found on soundings, or near shores; all other whales sometimes are. He is both ponderous and profound. And I am convinced that from the heads of all ponderous profound beings, such as Plato, Pyrrho, the Devil, Jupiter, Dante, and so on, there always goes up a certain semi-visible steam, while in the act of thinking deep thoughts. While composing a little treatise on Eternity, I had the curiosity to place a mirror before me;

and ere long saw reflected there, a curious involved worming and undulation in the atmosphere over my head.

The mist scalds because it is steam—air and water combined into a single, boiling-hot, vaporous substance. The heat creating the steam results from the intense depth of the sperm whale's thoughts. The thoughts that caused a similar heat in our author revolved around a short "treatise on Eternity." The evidence given allows us—we reader-scientists—to conclude that similarly eternal considerations have heated the whale's breath to a boil. Eternal considerations within a mortal life speak even more profoundly to the confusion of opposing elements that describes the problem of the sperm whale's spout. The sperm whale embodies the crux of the eternal and the mortal, the infinite and the definite. And the collision of these opposites—a collision that never results in the annihilation of either extreme but rather the coexistence of them—causes its indefinite, unspeakable, unpaintable nature.

Ishmael here makes a claim, too, upon the nature of thought. For thought shares in the same crisis the sperm whale's breath exemplifies. Thought, if tied to truth, is a process that involves the collision of an eternal principle with a mortal one. The young student learning Euclid, and so thinking what Euclid thought, grasps via thought a geometric truth that would be as true had he never learned it. Ishmael understands: "For unless you own the whale, you are but a provincial and sentimentalist in Truth. But clear Truth is a thing for salamander giants only to encounter." To think truly, which is to encounter truth, belongs only to those amphibious creatures capable of living in two realms at once. To live in water and air both reveals a parallel capacity to dwell simultaneously in thought and on earth. It is perhaps out of some universal reverence—as Ishmael claims a pod of sperm whales has been seen praying to the setting sun—that the whale's breathing occurs in a continual Sabbath. For the Sabbath is the day of the week in which the limit between the earthly and the all, the mortal and the immortal, dissolves, and breath—the very proof of our mortality—is one with eternity.

See also:

Chaos

We tend to think of the chaotic as the noisome, but in doing so betray the deeper chaos the word brings: a yawning gape or abyss, a child's mouth before a tooth has broken through the gums. That original chaos, that state of being that exists within or immediately prior to the creation of the universe, has not a single harsh sound, not a consonant's glottal stop, but merely, as in the child's mouth, vowels carried upon the breath that voices them.

And, as important, the implicit connection made in the chasm both mouth and abyss contain: that to speak materializes word into world, the nothing of the wordless mouth a repetition of the worldless universe. The deep set, still-mystical notion—the grammar in the abyss—that to speak is to found upon nothingness a phenomenon. That we dwell in such wording, such worlding.

To trace back chaos to its source is to be in the open mouth of an absolute silence in which the first sound spoken sets into motion the world soon to be. The ontological urge is an urge back toward silence—the nothing that posits being before being can be. This search is not for language, but done in language. There is no word by which to reach back to origin, no sacred chant. One senses in every word a hidden silence that informs the word, that silence that seems its essence. It is a silence that theories of semantics, of sense and reference, are helpless to touch, to explain or explain away.

~

Why does Ahab chase a "dumb brute"?

Imagine the silence Jonah heard, in the mouth of the whale deep in the ocean. Do you hear silence double and dwell in silence? Why?

To find an answer, a child must open her mouth.

See also:
Aleph
Child
Crisis
Etymology
Experience
Inspiration
Nothing/ness
Silence
Storm
Void
Wound

Child

The day before the chase begins, a mild wind blows. The wind moves through Ahab's hair as through an aeolian harp, conjuring a bittersweet music whose notes he cannot control. Ahab—for the first time in our experience of him—is a man played upon. What he hears within himself as he stares overboard into the ocean affects him so deeply that when this man in whom hell's furnace burns drops a tear into the ocean, "nor did all the Pacific contain such wealth as that one wee drop."

That tearful wealth is a sentimental salt. It might not be scientifically true, but it is symbolically true to suppose that the composition of Ahab's tear and the composition of the Pacific's salt water are identical. By one tear, Ahab adds himself back into a wider element that in his mad singularity he had seemingly forsaken—the wider element of human experience. The ocean functions as a complex, almost incomprehensible symbol. Simultaneously, the Pacific is fury and calm, rage and meditation, mimicking the motion of the heart gently soothed as well as the conscience-stricken, gale-driven, turbulent mind. The ocean confuses heart and head in one pulsing thought. The ocean is origin and death. The ocean is the place of work that separates origin from death. Each wave marks a moment in time, and then the ocean is timeless. What is the worth of Ahab's tear? It is Ahab's unwilled self-recognition that he is not inhuman, that his eye is still a human eye.

This moment, this mild moment, almost staves Ahab's purpose. And it is within this moment that Starbuck finally senses that he might sway his captain back to sense, back to safety. Starbuck does so in a noble way (if Starbuck is ever noble): he listens. Ahab speaks to him of a weariness so heavy he feels as if he were Adam beneath "the piled centuries since Paradise." When Ahab looks in Starbuck's eye, he seems to see his own wife and child. To Starbuck's ear, this admission signals a means of manipulation by which he could use Ahab's affections against his pursuit:

> "Oh, my Captain! my Captain! noble soul! grand old heart, after all! why should any one give chase to that hated fish! Away with me! let us fly these deadly waters! let us home! Wife and child, too, are Starbuck's—wife and child of his brotherly, sisterly, playfellow youth; even as thine, sir, are the wife and child of thy loving, longing, paternal old age! Away! let us away!—this instant let me alter the course!"

Starbuck mistakes Ahab's nature because Starbuck, unlike Ahab, is a man always willing to deceive himself, if the deception gains a desired end. Starbuck attempts to dangle Ahab's heart in front of his eyes as a bauble before a child—to swerve the child with the promise of a momentary pleasure and, once the child is calmed, to put the toy away. We do this for the child's own benefit—to re-focus his attention on an acceptable object. Between Ahab's gaze and the whale, Starbuck would dangle Ahab's family, a portrait in a locket, and then slowly, imperceptibly, turn Ahab's gaze homeward by moving the locket behind his captain's head. But Starbuck mistakes the nature of Ahab's affection, mistakes what, for Ahab, the memory of his wife and child means.

The whale and the child are not opposing forces within Ahab. The memory of his child, and the imagined present tense the memory awakens in him (seeing his child wake from his noontime nap to listen again to stories of "cannibal old me"), does not signal for Ahab a choice between pursuit and return. The whale and the child pose the same problem.

Whatever ceaseless enigma Moby Dick embodies, or whatever mystery Moby Dick is mask of, the white whale is a creature whose nature blurs the line between matter and spirit. The white whale rises to the surface to breathe and, breath taken, sounds down into fathomless depths, only by breath's need to rise again.

At the point of inspiration, a whaler can pierce the whale. If the harpoon strikes, the line follows the whale in its frantic dive down. The tension of that line, the speed at which the line descends, can sever a hand from the man who holds it. But that knifelike friction isn't the only explanation for the danger of the line. Ahab knows that the deeper source of threat is that the line binds together two separate realms, and the whaler's work is to preserve the connection.

That tarred and hempen line enters into an other almost wholly Other. As the whale dives down, it eclipses imagination, it betrays fact, it ceases to be body as mere matter and becomes this more frightening possibility—body as perimeter of spirit. What we think of when we say "whale" has no relation to the whale beneath the waves; it is a safe and hollow comfort to think otherwise. The terror of the line—as much a terror to the transcendental whaler—is that it holds as fast in spirit as it does in body, and drags from the unseen, limitless source an eternal figure back to the surface, back to the day, in whose light the Whale becomes again merely whale.

Ahab does not hunt Moby Dick as the crew of the Pequod hunts whales. He does not hunt to capture or kill. Ahab hunts to approach, his madness is named Proximity. In Ahab, pursuit serves no higher purpose than nearing that which one pursues, to reencounter the wounding Other and, within that reencounter, to participate—via hate or love, vengeance or self-sacrifice, blasphemy or belief—in that mystery the Other places before him.

When we stop thinking of love as an emotion governed by certain conditions that make our feeling "love" possible—a euphemistic lust, an excretion of a gland—and see it instead as an essential condition of human experience, it is easier to accept that love is not a defined quantity in the human heart. Love is not a rational light; love is not reason. Love opens within us that murky region from which the deepest motivations exert their dark pressure. And only by seeing love so can we accept that hate—for instance, Ahab's hate—is not an opposite of love (even if he himself describes it so). For love and hate inform human experience from a place in which opposition does not apply. They are in us primordial, before time, inseparable—the dark matter by which the human universe maintains its existence without ever revealing its shape.

Love does not oppose hate but blurs into it, exists near it, at times within it, not because any event occurs that changes one feeling into the other, but because no event can occur that affects the region in which love and hate dwell in us. We do not choose to love or to hate. We love and we hate—and the force by which either love or hate moves does not serve to distinguish one from the other. Ahab can hate the white whale, he can love his little boy, and Ahab's love and his hate are the same.

⌁

Starbuck hopes to awaken in Ahab a sentiment, a heart tug that will rouse him from his vengeful trance and into reason's clear light. Ahab will see it is wisest to turn home. Such is Starbuck's profitable wisdom: heart and hearth as the reward to which one returns after a bloody journey. But Ahab has no home; he has a motion, a pursuit. To return home to his boy would be to pursue, though in different degree, in different body, what he pursues in the whale. For Ahab—and Starbuck cannot understand such a truth—the child and the whale are one. At least, the child and the whale, if not one, represent for Ahab the same pasteboard mask, the same wall, he'll strike through with his hatred. One can strike out in love and pierce to the same marrow hate pierces to. The same hand that cups a cheek casts a harpoon. The gestures differ not in intent but in speed—the first fills an empty hand, the latter empties a full one. But the end of both gestures is to draw near that which has emerged out of—and in emerging from become mask of—mystery.

The child, like the white whale, is the embodiment of such mystery.

The child arrives through love. One sees in a child's face a blank preface to a book that cannot be written, the unmarked mind before experience has yet inked in the owner's own name. There are no words in the world-less. No means by which to read back into that origin from which the child just emerged, save to strike though the page, and so reach into that profound blank which makes blankness possible. The page and the child and the whale are white. One can write a meaning on them, as-cribe a meaning to them, but such inscription does not pierce into that possibility that takes on form. Ahab knows that origin is undefined. A word dropped on a page creates the distance it defines. Ahab intuits the worldless, wordless realm from which both child and whale emerge. Both emerge and take a breath—but only the white whale grows inspired, then dives back down.

See also:

Adam
Aleph
Brain
Chaos
Death
Fate
Fear
Infinite / Indefinite
Line
Loomings
Other
Time

CLASSIFICATION

Ishmael divides his dictionary into three books—The Folio Whale, The Octavo Whale, and The Duodecimo Whale. The books classify the whales as books, each in descending size: sperm whale, grampus, and porpoise. Beneath the pleasurable wit lurks a claim that has nothing to do with his attempt to define the varieties of whales: A whale is a book, and a book a whale. Ishmael's writing of *Moby-Dick,* if we take the implications of his analogy as literally as it suggests we do, is itself an act of whaling. The book is Leviathan, a creature that escapes our definition because it already defines itself. We can but read it, ask our questions, and wonder.

That wonder results from a book's whalelike nature. It emerges from underneath the world, wordless, unfathomable, and indefinite. As it nears the surface one suspects its form. It breaches the waves to take a breath, and each page opens like a billows inhaling. Each book mimics for its whole length a depth that shallows as one reads and grows on its opposite shore deep again—the depth that has been read. Each page that comes to us as an anticipation of depth reveals itself as another surface to scan—a marked leaf, a tattooed face, a skin, a text.

What we seek when we hunt the book is what we seek when we hunt the whale: illumination. The book and the whale are both species of knowledge. Each is a world that lives in a world, encompasses a world it also is encompassed by. When we put a book down, we feel simultaneously that we have caught its meaning and that in doing so we have lost it forever. The book and the whale dive down.

See also:
Brain
Definition

Dictionary
Idolatry
Imagination
Inspiration
Line
Nothing/ness
Tablet
Wonder
Writing

Coffin

A prophet tattooed on Queequeg's skin the entire cultural knowledge (history, mythology, geography, theology, and a theory of truth) of his tribe, and then the prophet died, never telling Queequeg the secrets his own body bore. Queequeg is a dictionary in reverse: the world a content on the cover, and blank pages within to explain. The symbols and patterns that adorn Queequeg's body cannot gain expression, for they can never fall into actual inquiry. None have a language by which to express that which is outside language's reach. Wittgenstein explores a similar impossibility: "For an answer which cannot be expressed the question too cannot be expressed. *The riddle* does not exist." The terrible tantalization of this savage arm: a star on the wrist that might point out the direction to heaven, that "starry archipelago," reveals no hint as to what it might actually mean. One may hazard a guess, but one is always wrong.

When Queequeg takes ill, when his eyes, "like circles on water" whose rings grow weaker as they expand, seem to be witnessing death's breathless nearing, he asks to make preparations:

> He added, that he shuddered at the thought of being buried in his hammock, according to the usual sea-custom, tossed like something vile to the death-devouring sharks. No: he desired a canoe like those of Nantucket, all the more congenial to him, being a whaleman, that like a whale-boat these coffin-canoes were without a keel; though that involved but uncertain steering, and much lee-way adown the dim ages.

The carpenter, pitying the poor dying man, makes the coffin-canoe to order and, once the lid is "duly planed," takes the coffin to Queequeg, who prepares for the voyage ahead by placing in the coffin his harpoon, biscuits, a flask of fresh water, and a pillow for his head. And then, more an act of will than a miracle, Queequeg recovers.

Queequeg spends hours carving his coffin-canoe "with all manner of grotesque figures and drawings; and it seemed that hereby he was striving, in his rude way, to copy parts of the twisted tattooing of his body." This carving is a careful work, carried out by one who understands that the mystery with which he's been inscribed must continue, if it contains truth, to live beyond his own living. He trusts that the nature of truth is such that his own ignorance of it diminishes naught its own essential nature. If he can't read his own body, some force in the world can, and so steer the keelless coffin home. But Queequeg, in this act of carving, accomplishes an equally strange work. He etches into the lid that, for his body contained within the coffin, serves as ceiling, as sky—carving the constellations, scratching the answers into stars. The gesture, more profound than his innate trust in the eternal nature of truth, is an act of reversal.

Queequeg's dilemma is perhaps simple. He's on the inside of himself. His body, bearing the prophet-etched mysteries, becomes radically exterior—almost the body of another. Introspection serves no end in such a quandary, for the questions that need be asked, and yet cannot be asked, are inked upon his body's surface. For Queequeg to know himself—this son of a king, and so this king himself—he must find a way to ask a question from within a book he cannot read. He is himself this book. Experience cannot help, for experience is the opposite process, moving from the world into the self to ask what the world means. Queequeg begins with the self, and the knowledge embedded in his skin is a barrier to the experience by which he might be able to explain the mysteries of the world. But by carving the figures on the lid of his coffin-canoe, by being placed within the canoe, he becomes contained by the mystery that he now merely carries. Queequeg places himself—when he dies—within the mystery that alive he but bears to others' eyes (even if the other eyes are his own), as a page bears a prayer: to be read.

↶

We read *Moby-Dick* by virtue of Queequeg's coffin:

> Round and round, then, and ever contracting towards the button-like black bubble at the axis of that slowly wheeling circle, like another Ixion I did revolve. Till, gaining that vital centre, the black bubble upward burst; and now, liberated by reason of its cunning spring, and, owing to its great buoyancy, rising with great force, the coffin life-buoy shot lengthwise from the sea, fell over, and floated by my side. Buoyed up by that coffin, for almost one whole day and night, I floated on a soft and dirge-like main.

Ishmael survives death by embracing a coffin. Inside the coffin is no body, but all knowledge—"a complete theory of the heavens and the earth, and a mystical treatise on the art of attaining truth." Ishmael doesn't read what he embraces. He does not come to truth; he does not reside in heaven or write what we read from heavenly enlightenment. He puts his arms around that which he too does not understand. The coffin that is this knowledge. The library and the mausoleum are one. The dictionary sings a dirge. We survive not merely by reading (no fact will ever add a single breath into the lungs of the drowning man), but by putting our arms around that which we'd learn. So we hover over infinite depths, waiting for rescue, the knowledge that saves us not in us but funereally buoyant in our arms.

See also:

Death
Dictionary
Experience

Faith
Friendship
Hieroglyph
Reading (Epistemology)
Savage
Spermaceti
Starry Archipelagoes
Tablet
Tattoo
Truth

CORDELIA

Charles Olson, reading the marginalia and notes scrawled on the flyleaf of the last volume of Melville's edition of Shakespeare, notes the deep influence, the inspirational ferment, of *King Lear*. Olson sees in Melville's reading the germ whose blossom unfolds in *Moby-Dick*'s darkness. A first draft of the novel, Olson says, contained no Captain Ahab. And then Melville read *King Lear* and went back to the pages already composed. Doubtless, Ahab and Lear share a boundless pride and, from that pride, a similar language—words charged electrically but darkly, the building charge of the black cloud tearing itself apart in its own massing current, whose limits can be revealed only by the lightning that, as it strikes its havoc down, lights the form that hurls it. Ahab and Lear both weather the storm they are and suffer. Both are madly humbled.

King Lear, though, offers a wider influence than Ahab so pointedly embodies. Throughout both *King Lear* and *Moby-Dick* truth discloses its difficulties. Ahab: "Truth hath no confines." Ishmael (as author): "Glimpses do ye seem to see of that mortally intolerable truth." And shortly thereafter: "In landlessness alone resides the highest truth, shoreless, indefinite as God." And Melville, writing a letter to Hawthorne, thanking him for reading and understanding his novel: "Truth is ever incoherent." No claim seems to be made on truth save the inability to make any claim at all—unless one considers one's mortality a claim; death seems to tolerate truth. Truth, and the language in which truth must be expressed (if one dares to speak of truth at all), lies deep within *King Lear* as well, and deepest in Cordelia's heart:

> *Cor.* Unhappy that I am, I cannot heave
> My heart into my mouth. I love your majesty
> According to my bond; no more nor less.

Lear. How, how, Cordelia! Mend your speech a little,
Lest you may mar your fortunes.
  Cor. Good my lord,
You have begot me, bred me, lov'd me. I
Return those duties back as are right fit,
Obey you, love you, and most honor you.
Why have my sisters husbands, if they say
They love you all? Haply, when I shall wed,
That lord whose hand must take my plight shall carry
Half my love with him, half my care and duty.
Sure I shall never marry like my sisters
To love my father all.
  Lear. But goes thy heart with this?
  Cor. Ay, my good lord.
  Lear. So young, and so untender?
  Cor. So young, my lord, and true.
  Lear. Let it be so. Thy truth then be thy dower . . .

That dowry—composed of truth and naught else—is the "Nothing [that] will come of nothing."

Lear repeats the awful sentence in a drastically different context. His fool riddles, "Can you make no use of nothing, nuncle?" And Lear answers, "Why, no, boy; nothing can be made out of nothing." There is, in the fool's wise goading, more than an attempt to prick the king's conscience. The difference in the two phrasings—"nothing will" versus "nothing can"—comes to strange meaning. The latter implies use and materiality, speaks to the abject futility of being without resource—the very condition to which Lear nominally condemned Cordelia, but also the condition he is soon to suffer. The former gains urgency at a deeper level than a concern with use or uselessness. Lear doesn't (as he thinks he is doing) merely curse Cordelia by excising her from his affection and so her share of his kingdom; he positively bestows upon her an inheritance of nothing. He opens lack; he gives, into the ordered nature of the worded world, a chaos that undoes all order. His "nothing will come of nothing"—that nothing that exists in deep contrast to the something that is or used to be—becomes the storm's rage on the open heath, and his madness occurs in encounter with the storm.

When Lear first spoke, when he cut from his heart his most beloved daughter, his word was still a king's word. When Lear spoke to Cordelia, put upon her his uttered command of nothing, he did so in a world in which his word equaled action. Lear spoke law—not simply law in a legislative sense, but the ordering force by which his kingdom existed. He spoke with the mythic power of a king's creative word. When Lear abdicates his throne to Goneril and Regan, he does so not by dividing his land between them but by granting them the power of his speech, his word. Lear is a king with an impotent tongue; his eldest daughters speak with the virile power he abandoned, but with no truth to guide that power. What Cordelia understands about her sisters, what she sees when she sees them with "washed eyes," is that the two women's language conceals their nature. In Regan and Goneril, language and truth do not coincide. Worse, language's power is to conceal truth, to hide intention, and to do so by convincing another that deceit is deceit's opposite. One listens to their words of love as one drinks a glass of poisoned wine, nurtured by that which kills. A word is both poison and antidote.

Cordelia, though, speaks no antidote. The danger she sees is too great to risk words. She understands what is at stake, and so she bites her tongue and keeps her heart in her heart's place. Cordelia sees that the king is dividing his world, and in the deepest sense, the king's world is the only world that exists (when she leaves, she enters a new world entire). The words her father wants to hear are the same words that will lay claim to the world he's abandoning. This world is not only the world that can be divided in parts on a map. It is, as Heidegger suggests, a world beneath the world: "The *world worlds,* and is more fully in being than the tangible and perceptible realm in which we believe ourselves to be at home." This home beneath the perceptible realm seems not only the storm-struck world into which the maddened Lear steps, it is also the world in which truth unconceals itself. When the world has been misspoken, the lower world emerges into, and undoes, the material stability of the upper one. The finite and the infinite collide in a "primal strife." Because she is infused with truth, with virtue that houses truth and transforms it into action, Cordelia will not speak falsely. She understands the depth of what is at stake more deeply than does her father. Her sisters speak the "truth" Lear wants to hear; Cordelia speaks the truth no one can hear, for she will not risk pulling the truth into form, into word.

Ahab knows as much of Cordelia as he knows of Lear. He, too, is involved in the work of bringing up from unfathomable reality a creature whose being exists simultaneously in both worlds: the tangible and the unimaginable. The whale breathes our air, breaching the surface of the deep world to do so, and then dives back down past sight, past mind. Starbuck and the Pequod's crew may hunt the whales as Goneril and Regan pursue their father's lands. Cordelia knows, as Ahab knows, that one must attend to the "little lower layer" where the world continues its ongoing creation. Cordelia is silent in order to protect that world, to keep it open. Her greatest gift is the nothingness her father unwittingly granted her. Ahab—in his woundedness—has also been given a "Nothing that will." But he is not Cordelia. Ahab also knows the deep world. He wants to merge with it, or to destroy it.

See also:

Child
Death
Expression
Fool
Infinite / Indefinite
Jonah
Lightning

Nothing/ness
Omen
Saying / Said
Storm
Truth
Wound

CORPUSANTS

Flames that do not burn top the three mastheads as the typhoon tosses the ship. Stubb looks up and begs for mercy. Question him and he'll say they grant mercy and luck, a hull so full of oil it saturates the masts and makes candles of them—but when the corpusants reappear, he begs for mercy again. Starbuck sees them as warning: Turn back. To travel east, the horizon the sun breaches to make of dark hours a day, is to die. Ahab looks up and commands all to do likewise: "Look up at it; mark it well; the white flame but lights the way to the White Whale!"

The white whale, of course, contains in himself a source of light. To strike a match to the oil from Moby Dick's head would cast a light that reveals a mortal glare. To see is not to die, but one sees the living world via death's light—at least when one sees, or reads, or looks in the face of those one loves by the light of the whale. As such, the heatless flame that burns atop the masts not only signals the direction toward Moby Dick, but the corpusants also participate in the deep mystery the white whale mystifyingly represents. The flames evoke in Ahab both the promise of killing the white whale and the more difficult meaning his vengeful chase uncovers. To stare up at the paradoxical flame—burning but not burning—is to see by the light of his own pursuit.

When Ahab addresses the flames—three flames that triple while he speaks and rise into the stormy sky, increasing their pallid light—he speaks to his purpose. He speaks two monologues, and as thunder is the sonic echo of the lightning strike so Ahab's second speech respeaks his first. The lightning strikes: "I now know thee, thou clear spirit, and I now know that thy right worship is defiance." Then, "I own thy speechless, placeless power; but to the last gasp of my earthquake life will dispute its unconditional, unintegral mastery in me." The thunder reiterates the points: "I own thy speechless, placeless power, said I not so?" And finally:

"Leap! leap up, and lick the sky! I leap with thee; I burn with thee; would fain be welded with thee; defyingly I worship thee!" Between the furious strike and the thunder that follows, Ahab demands recognition of his bodily separation from the flame he chases, and then he untangles the difference and is himself flame speaking to flame.

The flame erupts from darkness, with no apparent source—a bodiless light, expressing only its own illumination as it burns. The corpusant says nothing of the world; its flame cannot burn even the wood on which it lights. Rather, the corpusant seems a glare from another world, inexplicable within the laws of this one, wherein fire burns on fuel and harms the hand that would touch it. Even the sun harms us as it consumes itself. But not these flames to which Ahab speaks.

Ahab initially knows he is different. His strength is that he is Ahab: "In the midst of the personified impersonal, a personality stands here." And Ahab sees the corpusants as the appearance of the "speechless, placeless power" that lurks behind the wall, behind the mask, behind the white whale. Just as the oil that ignites to flame lurks behind the wall of the whale's skull, so some other world exists behind the flame on which this otherworldy flame burns and, burning, claims as real. What he revels in, what this sourceless light reveals, is the strength embedded in Ahab as Ahab, in his material existence, his lineage, his having been begotten: "Thou knowest not how came ye, hence callest thyself unbegotten; certainly knowest not thy beginning, hence call thyself unbegun. I know that of me, which thou knowest not of thyself, oh, thou omnipotent." Ahab's body that envelops his inner life—be it called soul, spirit, mind, or all three entwined—marks him indelibly as himself, as his own. He exists and so he can pursue that whose existence is in question. His very mortality gives him access—his being body, his being blood—to the unsourced, eternal world that taunts us with its infinite power, but which, lacking muscle, missing sinew and tendon, only haunts the world it creates. Whereas the corpusants are lights that "leapest out of darkness," Ahab is "darkness leaping out of light, leaping out of thee!"

Ahab is darkness because he is a body, and because he is a body he blocks light, casts shadow. Or, as a word leaps darkly from the blank page that makes it legible, so Ahab defines himself as Ahab, darkly existing against the light by whose power he exists. The crux is the location of both crisis and identification. Ahab recognizes himself as himself; he self-defines. He glories in the genealogy that roots him in his existence. But he also sees that, in tracing his lineage back to its earliest root (a root as mythical as it is historical) to Adam, he brings himself to the same horrible questions he asks of these flames: How did I come to be? The answer is as deadly as the question. Ahab's genealogy, and so the lineage of all, taps down into the same "speechless, placeless power" from which the corpusants arrive. There lurks some world within the world, one in which no speaking names, one in which no point places. The definite falters when the limit breaks.

Ahab's "defiant worship" is to recognize that unspeakable world and speak of it, to recognize that placeless world and still draw a line on a chart to sail towards it. Ahab hates the impossibility he reveres. It is his holy blasphemy.

See also:

Adam
Ahab
Death
Definition
Faith
Idolatry
Lightning
Reading (Doubloon)
Storm
Vengeance

Cosmogony

Pursuit

As the Pequod sails in its harborless hunt into Java seas, and so through the inestimable riches of the Spicy Isles, a "continuous chain of whale-jets" moving forward in a vast crescent—as in the sweep of one of the Milky Way's arms—is spotted from the cross mast. Stunsails are set, and the Pequod surges forward in pursuit. But Tashtego sees in their wake another species of white-spouts, spouts that "constantly hovered, without finally disappearing." Ahab looks back through his eyeglass and sees his ship pursued by pirates. Ahab paces the deck, "in his forward turn beholding the monsters he chased, and in the after one the bloodthirsty pirates chasing *him*."

The Pequod here occupies a curious position, one akin to a problem Wittgenstein poses. Wittgenstein presents a series of dots

●　●　●　●　　●　　　●　　　●　　　　●

and asks the reader to identify the dot with which the new pattern commences. The difficulty arises through a peculiar confusion. The final dot of the first series cannot be deciphered from the dot that begins the second. The fifth dot above exists in two separate patterns simultaneously—its life is a double life. The Pequod here suffers a similar sort of doubleness, not of pattern but of pursuit. The ship is both hunter and hunted and, as such, identifies simultaneously with the whales she hunts and the pirates hunting her. She is bloodthirsty after profit, and of worth that makes her bloodily pursued. The Pequod gains on the whales at the same rate the pirates gain on her, and the success of flight (which here is also that of survival) is thoroughly entwined with the failure of the chase. What the whalers want speeds past their reach as their speed finally leaves astern those who want them. Abject failure and complete success occur in the same instant. Opposites do not reconcile, but coexist. The Pequod is the site of this crisis.

As in Wittgenstein's example, the single dot of the Pequod does not—in this moment, in this pursued pursuit—contain its own discrete meaning. The Pequod is as a word in a sentence, or a sentence in a book—belonging to all that came before it and subject to that sense-in-pursuit, and at the same time clamoring after the yet-to-be-spoken in which it desires to make a context, to make a claim. As does a word the world it names, the Pequod pursues that which it wants to capture and, in capturing, bring into sense, into meaning, into profit. Indeed, its own meaning is incumbent on succeeding in its purpose.

What is a whale ship that catches no whales? What is a word that references no world? An empty vessel armed with dark lines attached to sharp points, pushed forward by wind in a page. At the same time, the Pequod is that world escaping word, speeding past the reach of those who would capture it. Its sense outruns reference at the exact time that to which it would refer outspeeds its barbed pursuit.

ORBIT

When the Pequod finally outdistances the Malays, the whales "gally," slow down, quit their flight (perhaps from excessive fright), and begin "in all directions expanding in vast irregular circles." The image evokes the cosmos that forms after chaos—the rings that assemble around some center whose gravitational power creates the spiraling system that protects it. What before was a pursuit charted in lines (of desire, of flight) has suddenly rewritten itself into a system that mirrors universal order. Trespass and threat have become creative repetition, circles (of whales as of stars) enclosing other circles until the center, from which all creation occurs, is formed.

The men aboard the Pequod lower the whale boats and continue their hunt. But the gally doesn't break up, the system doesn't fall into disorder and back into flight, but continues revolving. The ability of the boats, and of the men aboard them, to enter into the ringed orbits of the whales is a result of the continuing echo, or residue, or resonance, of the confusion the Pequod just experienced. For the men in the boats are still simultaneously hunter and hunted, pursuer and pursued. The whalers can pierce into the cosmogony the whales in their fear (or in their sudden lack of fear) are repeating, because the men exist as whales as much as whalers. The whalers have lost their distinct semiotic existence. As they encounter whales, and as they wound them, the system does not fall apart. The rings continue to orbit around a center. The wounds seem strangely, inexplicably self-inflicted.

The boat that Ishmael and Queequeg are in—Starbuck's boat—traverses the cosmos and enters the center. Within the space created by the wide and turning circles of the other whales, a vast and still lake has formed, the water clear to great depth. Within this innermost fold are the cows and calves of the whale pod, the mothers and children of the whole outringing constellations that encircle them. At the center is the source. In this center, becharmed or bespelled, the smaller whales swim up to the boat, so close as to let Queequeg pat their foreheads. It is here, in this center, that the sublime occurs:

> But far beneath this wondrous world upon the surface, another
> and still stranger world met our eyes as we gazed over the side.
> For, suspended in those watery vaults, floated the forms of the
> nursing mothers of the whales, and those that by their enormous
> girth seemed shortly to become mothers. The lake, as I have
> hinted, was to a considerable depth exceedingly transparent; and
> as human infants while suckling will calmly and fixedly gaze
> away from the breast, as if leading two different lives at the time;
> and while yet drawing mortal nourishment, be still spiritually
> feasting upon some unearthly reminiscence;—even so did the
> young of these whales seem looking up towards us, but not at us,
> as if we were but a bit of Gulf-weed in their new-born sight.

These men, these whalers, who have themselves just suffered the confusion of a contradictory though simultaneous life, now witness, by virtue of bearing their own confusion, a parallel though deeper confusion. In the center of this whale galaxy, in the stillness occupying the place of the sun in our own ringed system, they find the newborn whales suckling, still bearing the residue of the infinite life from which they were just pulled into form, still bearing witness to the creative force of which they are themselves the primary example. Form as yet unaware of having been formed. The men see this because they are part of the same mystery—not observers merely, but observing participants.

Queequeg, looking down, fears someone has cast a harpoon into a baby whale born some few hours ago—his fins still wrinkled from the womb. What Queequeg sees is not a hempen line but an umbilical cord, "buoyantly rising and spiraling" toward the surface. "Not seldom in the rapid vicissitudes of the chase, this natural line, with the maternal end loose, becomes entangled with the hempen one, so that the cub is thereby trapped." The sorrow in the image shocks. The umbilical cord is that livid rope which reared a creature from a cell, a cell from nothingness; the harpoon line pulls up by its body the creature the first cord formed. Matter turned material, and material a profit. And beneath the nursing whales the men see whales mating, as if every depth revealed a deeper ontological layer.

Ishmael seems especially attentive to, and sympathetic with, the mystery he witnesses. The evidence of creation, and the process by which creation occurs. The living material pulled from a chaotic nothing, the mortal definite that emerges from the timeless infinite, from the dark vast.

DISORDER

The cosmos returns to chaos. The whalers destroy it, though indirectly. One of the whales stabbed by a harpoon, who in pain outswam the length of line, in his turmoil and turning to remove the iron barb loosened the blade but entangled himself in the rope. As he swam among the orbits of his kind, in frenzy trying to free himself from the line that threatened to drown him, the blade tossed murderously among the others, cruelly wounding them and renewing the urgent flight. The end bespeaks the beginning. For just as the pirate-chased Pequod suffers the same crisis as the whales it hunts, and so becomes strangely indecipherable from a whale, so the chased whales are strangely indecipherable from the whalers. Predator merges with prey. Doubleness infects all reference, merging the twain into one that is never fully one nor two, which wounds with the same confusion it suffers. The whalers are not merely implicated in the horror of their pursuit; in pursuing, they risk becoming the prey they hunt, and in wounding wound also themselves. Such is the deeper nature of what Ishmael calls our "universal cannibalism." When we wound anything, we wound ourselves. Such is the result of suffering confusion.

See also:
Chaos
Child
Crisis
Death
Duplicates
Profit
Reading (Doubloon)
Repetition
Starry Archipelagoes
Truth
Wound
Writing

CRISIS

A gyroscope maintains precarious balance within the meaning of *crisis*: a balance between life and death. At crisis a disease turns irreversibly mortal, or the patient continues to breathe. A pregnant woman reaches crisis when her labor begins. The crisis of being-in-crisis deepens easier notions of danger. Crisis is a realm, if we are to speak of it as a location, in which light cannot be separated from darkness, in which the haze through which one sees is equally light and dark, where one could claim "it's night," and another claim "it's day," and both be speaking truly. Crisis doesn't offer a means of decision between extremes because it erases the difference between those extremes, hazes the boundary by which choice is possible.

To choose life in the midst of crisis is also to choose death, but not to be reconciled to that inevitable confusion. One wants life, wants to live, but crisis denies such desire's efficacy. Or one wants to die and suffers the same impossibility. The crisis will decide itself, unless one skilled in the maieutic arts intervenes: the midwife's wisdom, Socrates' questions. Not our own will guides us from crisis—crisis empties our will of power. But another's voice can cast to us a question, and our answer, perhaps, rescues us. In crisis, we respond. We respond with the great benefit of having suffered confusion, of having lost definition, of finding life and death imploded into a single confusing star whose light shines darkness, or dims brilliance, and so forces us to see in paradox. There is no more poignant moment than when we are faced with the absolute inability to decipher between life and death, when we are lost completely, when the eye cannot claim light as light nor dark as dark, when the heart's first pulse speaks *life* and the next pulse says *death,* and someone asks the sufferer a question and so elicits from the answerless the piercing beam of an answer. We grasp upward toward an answer to a descending question as a drowning man reaches upward to grasp the rescuer's hand.

~⌀

Crisis makes a literal, though nonfigurative, sense of T.S. Eliot's lines in "Little Gidding": "What we call the beginning is often the end / And to make an end is to make a beginning. / The end is where we start from." We know before we ever open the book that *Moby-Dick* ends in crisis. Its first sentence, "Call me Ishmael," is haunted by the residue of the fated conclusion the book witnesses and, in witnessing, continues to pursue. Here is a man, a narrator and author both, who has forsaken his given name for an allegorical one of his own choosing: Abraham's first son, born to the handmaiden Hagar, whose rights of primogeniture end null and void. Our narrator opens his tale (if we can reduce the narrative and non-narrative complexity to its fundamental vein for a moment) by claiming for himself the great absence of covenant lost. Such loss makes of *Moby-Dick* a realm of crisis. I do not mean the crisis the tale tells, the tragedy of the action being narrated. I mean the crisis that the story must be told. Crisis forces language into the same doubleness into which crisis casts a life, a doubleness not of life and death but of interior and exterior. The word in the mind and the word on the page exist simultaneously but oppositely. The former word promises the comfort of self-recognition, and the latter threatens the same self with interpretation by another. Crisis translates form into other form, though the difference may be imperceptible.

Ishmael's self-selected name is chosen out of the crisis that impels him to tell his tale, to write his story. His chosen name unfolds a terrifying reality: the world's entire promise has been broken, and what was to be our possession—the bounty of the fields, the fecund goodness of the earth—is but a blank page waiting for words to claim from crisis another world in which to dwell. Ishmael recounts an action occurring on a ship, but in recounting, in the act of memory uttered, he does a far more profound and desperate work. Ishmael considers the difficulty of Ahab's life and

death—the mad, defiantly devout pursuit to exact revenge on the crea-
ture that mortally wounded him before—and rescues himself by think-
ing on his captain. We enter into *Moby-Dick,* when we do so patiently,
understanding that the comic wryness of the first paragraph masks an
admission of the narrator's suicidal impulse. We witness quick crisis. The
book to come is as much the story of Ishmael's not killing himself as it
is the story of the death of Ahab and his crew. Ishmael had to survive
himself before he could survive the destruction of the Pequod.

See also:

Chaos
Child
Coffin
Death
Etymology
Paradox
Plato
Reciprocity
You / Thou

DEATH

Ahab is a man with "a crucifixion in his face." He confronts those whalers looking up at him on the quarterdeck with a gaze that peers out through death's visage. Ahab stares at his crew, and his eyes are impenetrable, revealing nothing of the life of the mind that circulates electrically behind them. His crew does not see in Ahab's eyes his deep seated, vulnerable, naked self. His eyes are not an entrance into the mystery of his inner life but a barrier denying access. Ahab has a cross in his eyes: a contradiction and a sacrifice.

Ahab stares at his crew from the impenetrability of death. This death does not predict the future, though one could easily claim a foreshadowing in that gaze which reveals the tragedy to come. This death in Ahab's face predicts nothing at all. Death ends life: a barrier through which all, though each alone, must pass, and none passing through death end anywhere we know. Ahab's gaze is not time's façade, nor the opposite of time. He gazes through a suffering that opens onto eternity (or so we assume)—not the comfort of heaven or the horror of hell, but that of which none know or can know. To Ahab's face the philosopher has no answer, and the theologian offers a guess.

Ludwig Wittgenstein makes a simple yet radical and related claim in the *Tractatus Logico-Philosophicus*:

> Death is not an event of life. Death is not lived through.
> If by eternity is understood not endless temporal duration but timelessness, then he lives eternally who lives in the present.
> Our life is endless in the way that our visual field is without limit.

Ahab's gaze takes in not only the whole crew assembled below him, but also the ocean out to the horizon. Likewise, the crew looks up at him, and then to the sky. Our vision ends at a horizon that seems to mark the edge of the world, but marks only the end of our vision of the world— our experience of it. The world goes on, but what do we know of it?

Death is such a horizon: one does not live through it. No words describe it. No answers solve its riddle, for death is not a riddle but a mystery. Unlike the living horizon that retreats at every step taken toward it, death is a horizon we cross. Our own self is the coin we put into Charon's hand: our face in relief on one side, and the other side blank. Such is Ahab's crucified gaze. He confronts us with death unanswerable. And in that most fundamental of human moments, one person looking into the face of another—that look from which spring ethics and metaphysics, the gaze that between two humans holds the possibility that both exist—Ahab gives us proof that being human abuts a limit. Ahab's gaze seems to claim that there is more to know that we cannot know. Death does not deny life, it ends it.

See also:

Coffin
Dictionary
Fate
Hero
Orpheus
Plato
Time
Wound
Writing

DEFINITION

To classify the things of the world, one needs a language. Such a language orders, makes possible classification, gives to the discerning mind the basic elements of its judgments. If one's world is the ocean, then define what lives in water. If one is Ishmael, then define whales.

By his own survey's account, no book has yet accomplished an adequate definition of the whale. Most were written without the author ever having seen a whale, and those of slightly greater accuracy were written by men who came across whales washed ashore, already dead. Only one book was written by a "real professional harpooner and whaleman," but this Captain Scoresby wrote of the right whale, or green whale, and so offers little help in defining the leviathan Ishmael places before us: the sperm whale. Implied in Ishmael's critique of the plenteous books of little "real knowledge" is an argument that experience must precede definition. Language in this cetological, pseudoscientific, philoso-philological world is secondary to the work of whaling. Or, more to the point, it should be. The trouble is that one does not learn one's language in the process of new experience. Ishmael knows what a "whale" is before he knows what a Whale is. Expression occurs before experience and, in an irresponsible mind, shapes the nature of experience before the event has been lived. We are all to some degree necessarily irresponsible: we recognize before we know. We see through the lens of a definition that preexists the moment we're living in the world.

Ishmael, our philologist-whaler, understands this etymological dilemma. He has, as he says, "swam through libraries and sailed through oceans." The awful trick of definition requires the impossible work of erasing the terms by which one speaks of the world in order to experience the world directly, and so to define anew, and speak of it again. To do so, if anyone can do so (will oneself to aphasia and by some Möbius turn on silence's surface end up fluent), requires one to create a "classification of the constituents of a chaos." Chaos here is both silence and frenzy—the possibility to speak in parallel of the whale's possibility to give light, the process before the worded illumination.

The paradox of this philologist-whaler's work is that one has for a hook another definition. At best, a definition does not encompass the object it names, but brings what it names up to light. Ishmael offers a simple rule: "a whale is *a spouting fish with a horizontal tail*." As a side note, a whale also breathes air in lungs and has, like us, a heart rebounding with warm blood. Definition as verification, or, more wondrously, definition as the process of language searching itself for error. What does one do with the whale brought up on its wordy-hook? Catch and release and let the beast dive back into the unfathomable region that makes its name a question, or kill it and see what it is you "know."

See also:

Accuracy
Chaos
Classification
Death
Dictionary
Imagination
Inspiration
Phrenology
Quest / Question
Reading (Epistemology)
Soot
Writing

Description

Ishmael is a writer who doubts the precision of words but goes to great lengths to be precise. The skin of the whale cannot be defined because the skin of the whale is indeterminate, but Ishmael describes every nuance of his confusion. He abandons his cetological dictionary because the living whale never comes fully to light, and so resists definition. He is obsessed with the difficult failures of interpretation, even as his most valiant effort is interpretive. He writes chapters entitled "Of the Monstrous Pictures of Whales," "Of the Less Erroneous Pictures of Whales, and the True Pictures of Whaling Scenes," and "Of Whales in Paint; In Teeth; In Wood; In Sheet-Iron; In Stone; In Mountains; In Stars." The horror of whiteness is its whiteness.

Language's failure masks its success. We assume the work of language is to bring to light that of which one tries to speak. We think we want to be understood, that we want to understand—and language is the basic capacity by which such clarity occurs. We continue to think—it seems impossible not to—in mimetic terms. Language describes as it refers. But the description falls short of transparence. The reference has always existed within the same doubtful scrutiny to which it's now subjected. We speak it even as we know it fails. We can do so because even in its failure, language is useful. We may never speak our meaning fully (not even to ourselves), but we speak it into shape enough for our meaning to be recognized.

The assumption underlying our words is simple: that we speak in order to show meaning. *Moby-Dick* threatens such inherited notions of language's purpose, language's possibility of meaning. A word, like a whale, dives down. It sounds. The descriptive capacity we profit by when we speak may be but an accidental quality of language's darker, depth-ridden, actual activity. The ocean's surface responds to wind and weather blowing upon it, but we cannot know the calm of the whole. The surface ripples, and we who float on it are endangered by the gale. But the wave top is the least part of the whole, as when we speak what we seem to say is a lesser quantity than the full work language accomplishes, plunging down and echoing back to some bedrock source to which we have no access, though our language does. Description distracts us from language's work much as the ocean's surface distracts us from its depth. We occupy our minds with what we see when we speak of what we see, but language's work may not be illuminating. It might blind us with a momentary light in which world and word seem to relate, but the light is lightning-like, and only deepens the darkness in which it continues to compose its unspeakable work, once the first flash is done.

See also:

Accuracy
Death
Lightning
Reading (Epistemology)
Skin
Truth
Whiteness

DICTIONARY

Ishmael writes a whaler's dictionary. Expand the gesture past its cetological limits and the dictionary promises a repository for every word by which the world has been described. A dictionary is a sum-knowledge, made up of the minute components by which any epistemology may be built. But a dictionary is not without limit. A page is but a map that offers words to reveal the world. Each word claims a stake in that world, which is not circumscribed by geography, but opens—as the world is of the solar system, and the sun of our galaxy, and our galaxy of a galactic cluster, and that cluster of thousands of galaxies a mere mote in the universe that spills past our speaking it—into possibility, an approach toward truth. A stone is true differently than a thought is true, though both are of the world.

For the dictionary to be accurate to that which is, it would need to be as infinite as the world it attempts to articulate. But words, countless as they may seem, are of a definite number, capable of combining in an indefinite but limited number of ways, some of which permutations make sense, others of which do not, and all of which can only describe the world as such. Language is a human construction, and speaks the world's limit as it speaks the world. The means to express all possible experience are bound and placed between covers. One reads to the horizon of the margin, then turns the page.

The truer meaning of a dictionary cannot be found within the myriad definitions it offers as its use. Rather, a dictionary comes into greater meaning when it's kept closed and one senses what language may be powerless to illuminate—though to open the book and speak may indeed give us a glimpse of what it is we want to say.

Wittgenstein claims that such a sense of the world as a limited, defined whole is mystical, the transcendent feeling:

The sense of the world must lie outside the world. . . .

The feeling of the world as a limited whole is the mystical feeling. . . .

There is indeed the inexpressible. This *shows* itself; it is the mystical.

Ishmael's dictionary gives us such a notion of the limited world. The dictionary closed on a table reverses its use for definition and comes into meaning not by containing it, but by being contained. A dictionary exists within the world it defines, is itself defined, a condition that undermines the authority it seems to claim. A dictionary is a light inside a limit; a dictionary is a funereal business. The tomb engraved with gilt angel, the globe on the sepulcher. The life inside it—those thousands of words—explains itself when it means to explain the world. To speak, to write, to use language ends in the discovery of a limit. That limit divides the utterable from the unspeakable, within which what exists *shows* itself, and will not bend to be spoken, to be defined. The whale is a "dumb brute." Its silence is otherworldly. A whale shows itself, if the whaler is lucky, as the whaler watches. Before the whale breaks the surface of the sea, the sea seems to the whaler infinite in every direction. The sea-surface is a page whose reach ends in the ringed horizon. Here is a world. Awe contains within it a reverse: the urge to cease wonder and start knowledge. We look up a word to help us explain. The names use other names to name themselves. Tautology of definition. Inside the dictionary there is no outside. But when the dictionary closes, "there is indeed the inexpressible." We touch it when we close the book.

See also:

Coffin
Death
Definition
Knowledge

Paradox
Profit
Reading (Epistemology)
Writing

Doubloon

A Meditation on a Coin

Ahab holds a bright coin up to the sun. The coin is gold, glints in the light—at a certain angle in Ahab's hand it reflects light like the full moon. This coin, this sixteen-dollar piece, will be the reward for the man who spots Moby Dick and "sings out!"

The whale will rise to take a breath, vulnerable to eye and lance. Seeing the whale inspire, the man on the masthead draws in his breath and exhales his song. He sings and earns a coin. His inspiration is not his song; his song sings at inspiration.

⁀

Ahab nails the coin to the mast. The coin is a little sun suspended in the ship's middle. The whalers walk in circles around it, each in orbit of the little sun. All have agreed to hunt the white whale that is their captain's pursued object. The coin is promised to the one who sees Moby Dick first. The coin is a weight, and has a pull. The crew is a planetary system lorded over by a man who promises to give them the sun in whose gravitational pull they orbit. He gives them a center, and he promises the center will not hold. He promises that each man can be, could be, the center of his own system. Ahab promises them the sun in their pocket.

⁀

Gravity aboard the Pequod is a force of desire. Desire is a point outside the man desiring, a gravitational point around which a man circles. As the men orbit around the center mast, the ship moves forward in a straight line. The coin nailed to the mast casts forth a golden line that keeps the Pequod's aim true. Men orbit around a point of desire, but desire points itself forward. As Ahab is madness maddened, so in the sea-world desire itself is desirous. A distance is covered by linking desire to desire; desire also opens distance. Desire nears and then, as a magnet pushes away a magnet of same polarity, desire pushes away. A line on a map charts desire. A line is a means of approach and a means of flight. The means of gaining proximity, of gaining purchase, are also the means of repulsion and loss. Flip sides of the same coin.

〜

The distance between desire and the desired is a distance of exchange. The coin is a medium of exchange. Seeing the whale earns you sixteen dollars, the sum that is the sun. To see the whale is to begin the process of exchange. What is the white whale worth? Whoever first sees the white whale begins a chase that is economic. *Purchase*'s etymology is to seek, to pursue in order to obtain. What does one purchase when one pursues Moby Dick? What is the nature of Ahab's currency exchange?

〜

A purchase promises a transmigration of meaning. One substance is exchanged for another we believe of equal value. To see the white whale is worth either sixteen dollars or the sun. We purchase blankness with light. We pursue the horror of whiteness with the purchase of witness. We want to catch—as Ahab wants to catch—the white whale at the point of exchange. The commodities are high risk: spiritual terrors and mortal dangers. Their names are the white whale's attributes: omniscience, omnipresence, omnipotence, and immortality. We want to see what in the world they might become. A coin buys us into the market.

See also:

Cosmogony
Hunger
Profit
Prophet
Reading (Doubloon)

DUPLICATES

Trusting to one's own genius, as Emerson commends, is no easy task. One feels as if one must have the ground beneath one's feet, solid though imperceptibly rising to Parnassian heights, where the thinness of the air invigorates the blood. Genius must speak with the conviction of truth. But truth is colder than the heights from which it is revealed: impenetrable, inalterable, stable as the mountain on the mainland. One forgets that a mountain is memorial to the unimaginable upheaval that thrust it skyward. Genius is not the granite that endures the world; genius is the molten turbulence, that threat inside the fault, which reminds us a stone is not a source of fiery inspiration but a result. I have no granite thoughts. A different genius is required. A genius, as Simone Weil defines it, which is nothing other than "the supernatural virtue of humility in the domain of thought."

Melville, of course, gives us the needed image in all its humble audacity: the whaling ship. As Ishmael, whimsically pedantic, describes it:

> Every one knows what a multitude of things—beds, saucepans, knives and forks, shovels and tongs, napkins, nut-crackers, and what not, are indispensable to the business of housekeeping. Just so with whaling, which necessitates a three-years' housekeeping upon the wide ocean, far from all grocers, costermongers, doctors, bakers, and bankers. And though this also holds true of merchant vessels, yet not by any means to the same extent as with whalemen. For besides the great length of the whaling voyage, the numerous articles peculiar to the prosecution of the fishery, and the impossibility of replacing them at the remote harbors usually frequented, it must be remembered, that of all ships, whaling vessels are the most exposed to accidents of all kinds,

and especially to the destruction and loss of the very things upon which the success of the voyage most depends. Hence, the spare boats, spare spars, and spare lines and harpoons, and spare everything, almost, but a spare Captain and duplicate ship.

What could be more "supernaturally humble" than a single ship, necessities stocked in duplicate, facing innumerable threats upon the indefinite ocean? To my mind, the least of these dangers are the injuries endemic to the whaler's profession: terrible storm and terrible calm, severed limbs, stove-in boats, drowning. The simplest image horrifies: a ship on the boundless ocean, a punctuation mark (a pip) on a blank, marginless page.

To sense deeply the nature of this ingenious self-reliance, we must press upon the notion of boundlessness. We might begin by noting that this paradoxical phrase—*to press upon boundlessness*—is itself an effort of utmost futility. What, in the scope of infinity, is a "three-years' voyage"? When on Christmas Day—a day, by no mere coincidence, on which God condensed infinitude into human form—the whaling ship Pequod sets out on the opposite task, casting its own definite form out into indefinite expanse. A voyage begins on a certain day (one can mark it on a calendar), and from a certain location (one can circle it on a map). One can chart the lines that mark the voyage across the globe: time, speed, and place. But certain days have secret lives that time cannot describe. Christmas occurs annually, but each repetition undoes the temporal progress of the day to day, year to year, and returns us always to the same inalterable day. Ahab's ship exists in two worlds, is anchorless between them. In such a voyage there is neither gain nor motion, and no time passes. It is the only defined form in a world that mocks such definition. Its only resource is itself. We find ourselves in strange waters: far from shores, from bays, from ports, from any sense of land at all, save the ocean that at times becomes the rolling expanse of America's prairies, until, just as quickly, the deep regains its depth. The ocean indefinite in breadth as it is in depth, the sky an ocean above it. And our humble safety, our inspired form, our guiding genius, is a ship filled with *duplicates*.

A word is a kind of duplicate. A word stands in for the object it represents. We trust the word to convey enough sense to adequately refer to the world it attempts to describe. Such duplicates are the only means of resource contained within a ship upon an ocean that, to revisit Weil, seems as infinite as thought. We'll say our words again and again, until we believe the reference is not arbitrary but demonstrative of a connective principle. Upon the sea, we must see what it is we have to say—to do so is to stay afloat.

The voyage aboard the Pequod shares language's repetitive crisis. Ahab's mad chase re-utters the whaling trip on which he suffered his mortal wound. Ahab's urge toward revenge, his "defiant faith," rests on a voyage that occurs before our book begins. What Ahab senses, and what we suspect in our speaking, is that the repetitions serve as a strange map back to an original utterance, when world and word were linked. Such is the crisis of genius. For deep within the notion of genius is the sense of absolutely unique expression that reveals to us the nature of the world. But genius has at its disposal only language—not the ontological *logos* that carries within its verbal confines some guiding numen that equates the word with the object the word names: an indwelling, informing presence. We speak in duplicates—ad infinitum, ad nauseum—whose relation to the world might be no more than the nymph's relation to the cicada, an empty shell that describes nothing of the winged creature that springs from it. On ship, we have no resource but that which we brought with us—words that are things, but not the things they describe: a form, a definition that in being spoken undoes its own form to approach another, a harpoon with the rope lining out from the blade's honed point, a nib in a pen.

A book is just such a vessel. We must rescue it by its own means—I mean, we must read it. Launch hundreds of pages into the boundless thought through which it must voyage, with no means to travel but its own store of duplicates. All we have is the text. The act of reading is an act of duplication: unlocking the image from word and so seeing in replica what the author saw. One might turn to another text to explain this text in front of us; one might think that critical reference anchors, but it does not. A book meets another book as a ship meets a ship upon the sea—by good fortune, by good intent, but only a gam.

A gam, though, might be enough. Here letters are exchanged. Communication occurs. Knowledge is shared—of news from home, of whaling grounds, of where the hunt next should go, if the white whale has been seen. A gam: it must be enough.

See also:

Cosmogony
Dictionary
Letter
Paradox
Reading (Doubloon)
Repetition
Time
Truth
Writing

ETCHING

Ishmael's library, home upon shore, contains many volumes in which the title page and end page are marked so:

> As for the bookbinder's whale winding like a vine-stalk round the stock of a descending anchor—as stamped and gilded on the backs and title-pages of many books both old and new—that is a very picturesque but purely fabulous creature, imitated, I take it, from the like figures on antique vases. Though universally de-nominated a dolphin, I nevertheless call this bookbinder's fish an attempt at a whale; because it was so intended when the device was first introduced. It was introduced by an old Italian pub-lisher somewhere about the 15th century, during the Revival of Learning; and in those days, and even down to a comparatively late period, dolphins were popularly supposed to be a species of Leviathan.

At the opening of the first page, and on many a last page, an error is stamped, and the indentation of this error filled with gold. We begin and end a book in error and mistake. The bookbinder's whale serves not as linguistic information (it might be unfair to claim the bookbinder's whale as any sort of information at all). It is decoration—an embossed ornament. The book-binder's whale is also the emblem that inaugurates the eye to the knowledge about to follow; it is also the cipher that closes knowledge when the experience of reading is done. On one page, the anchor rises with a dolphin curled around its chain, and with it both the promise of voyage and life pulled out of watery abyss. On the last page, returning what has been seen back into the ocean in which it lives—now dropping anchor, the voyage done. Between raising and lowering anchor, a voyage has been run, a book has been read. Is your hold full? How many barrels have ye? Are ye safe and wealthy in the spicy isles? Have ye come home? What cargo do ye bear?

～

An etching is the effort to mark significance by removing material. To write "whale," carve it out of the wood, burn it out of the metal, and write *e-l-a-h-w*. Then fill the wound with ink and press a page upon it. The world reverses when the page off the press is lifted and makes sense. We recognize it until we see in it error. "Whale" spelled *wale* or *wail*, or the tail of a serpent on the sperm.

Etching is the art that understands that the only procedure by which to reach knowledge is to suffer the opposite. Like the whalers on board the Pequod, we must cross the line. We must pick up an awl, not a pen. We must write on stone, not paper, to suffer what the world suffers: reversal.

Such knowledge is suspect, but how else can knowledge be? The book proceeds by betrayal. As Ishmael, our author, says, "I myself am a savage, owning no allegiance but to the King of Cannibals; and ready at any moment to rebel against him." So a page relates to a page: obedient to the meaning the previous page established, and ready at any moment to grow savage.

Two Grave Concerns

Exodus 20:4

> You shall not make for yourself a graven image, or any likeness
> of anything that is in heaven above, or that is in the earth be-
> neath, or that is in the water under the earth. . . .

Letter to Nathaniel Hawthorne, November 17 [?] 1851

I have written a wicked book, and feel as spotless as the lamb.

↩

The world is nothing on Nothing etched. Creation first happens negatively.

↩

Lear: "Nothing will come of nothing."

↩

Queequeg: an etched labyrinth of a man.

↩

The skin of Leviathan is "obliquely crossed and re-crossed with numberless straight marks in thick array, something like those in the finest Italian line engravings."

See also:
Accuracy
Cordelia
Inscribe
Line
Silence
Skin
Tattoo
Tzimtzum
Wound
Writing

ETYMOLOGY

Moby-Dick opens in crisis as deep as the crisis in which it ends. I do not mean the crisis of Ishmael's name: that crisis of identity and misidentity can only be understood in hindsight, the result of what the *me*—of "Call me Ishmael"—has witnessed and survived. The crisis I'm referring to occurs in the prefatory material with which *Moby-Dick* begins before it begins. We meet two strange characters, a "late consumptive usher to a grammar school," who supplies us with an etymology, and a "sub-sub-librarian," who offers us a set of extracts. Both characters seem caught in the shady afterlife—not of heaven, but of the infinite library that seems both the edge of, and edged by, eternity (container and contained at once).

We must allow ourselves to feel the deep strangeness of the gesture. The Usher cares for tomes by wiping away the collected dust with a handkerchief "mockingly embellished" with all the flags of the world. The nature of the mockery is central. For it's not simply that the nations which thought themselves eternal have died away, nor merely that the books written have outlived the cultures that wrote them, but that the book is as mortal as we are. To be brought into form, be it a cell in a womb or a word on a page, is to be subject to that return to formlessness known as death. The dead tend to the dead.

This Usher gives us three etymologies, the first of which, from Hackluyt, asserts that if one is to speak the word *whale* without the *h* one pronounces it in such a way that the word cannot be true. Of course, the intrigue of such a statement is enhanced by the fact that the *h* is silent. What kind of word are we dealing with when mispronouncing silence is to speak falsely? The Usher ends his etymology by listing all the names for "whale" in a variety of cultures. He begins with Hebrew and ends with Erromangoan. This list is not as simple a gesture as it seems. Not only do we confront the linguistic, post-Babel reality that no single word refers doubtlessly to any object or creature, but also the very notion of truth as introduced in the Usher's first quote is brought into terrible question.

The complexity of the list doesn't end by simply roughing the surface by which language functions as a truth-value. To begin with Hebrew and to end in Erromangoan is to create a timeline of linguistic discovery. In the metaphoric space of this library, this shelved world after the lived world, the primary language was Hebrew. It is the original language, out of which all creation was written; it's worth noting that in midrashic tales of the creation, Hebrew is understood as a written force previous to its being a spoken one. Erromangoan, whose name for the whale is "PEHEE-NUEE-NUEE," is an oral language, whose word for whale is recorded by transliterating the sounds of the native language. Not only does this list of whale-words proceed from language as a written vehicle to language as a spoken vehicle, and so moves from the timeless to that which can only exist in time, the entire etymology progresses forward through time. We begin with the most ancient of cultures and end with this most recently discovered. In a radical sense, we have, pivoting on the axis of a single word, the whole history of the world. The word and the word spoken. *Whale* and "whale."

Such is preface.

See also:

Aleph
Child
Coffin
Crisis
Death
Definition
Dictionary
Experience
Letter

Saying / Said
Silence
Truth
Tzimtzum
Wonder

Experience

Ishmael sets out whaling to experience the "wonder world." One can ascribe, perhaps safely, that the first time all green whalers ship is for a similar reason: to experience. That experience manifests in different ways, some more useful than others. A man learns to be a whaler, rises within the rigid hierarchies of the whalery, and may, by experience, ascend to captain. Or one has no such aims (as Ishmael doesn't), and wants to not merely see but participate in the dangers of the world. One wants to broaden one's horizon.

Ishmael claims such a desire to Peleg on the day he signs himself aboard the Pequod. Peleg asks, "But what takes thee a-whaling? I want to know that before I think of shipping ye." And Ishmael answers, "Well, sir, I want to see what whaling is. I want to see the world."

Peleg has two responses. The first bears a poignant mystery: "Want to see what whaling is, eh? Have ye clapped eye on Captain Ahab?" And the second answer is broad mystery. He bids Ishmael to look over the weather bow and tell him what he sees. "Not much, nothing but water."

Peleg's answers are haunting and foreboding. He implies—and it's telling that he cannot speak directly but offers only gestures, insinuations, hints—that the last thing one signs up for aboard a whale-ship, especially one captained by Ahab, is experience. He forces Ishmael to see that the ocean is infinite to its horizon, and as you near that horizon, it retreats.

The horizon's dimensions are subjective. Ishmael will see only as he sees: a single point staring out into incommensurable distances. It is only in reversing the order of Peleg's answers that we may gain a sense of what he means when he asks if Ishmael has "clapped eye" on Ahab. The initial and easier understanding is that Ahab is an example of the experience

Ishmael is naïvely pursuing. But that interpretation changes when seen through the lens of the breadthless, depthless ocean. Peleg seems to warn that Ahab is not a man of experience, and that his damage is the result of that which occurs outside experience. That is Ahab's horror.

The difficulty is in understanding what, if not experience, Ahab and Ishmael and the crew entire live through when they are on the ocean aboard a ship hunting whales. More to the point, what is their life when they are chasing not whales but a single whale: Moby Dick. Martin Buber, in *I and Thou*, helps clarify the mystery:

> Those who experience do not participate in the world. For the experience is "in them" and not between them and the world.
>
> The world does not participate in experience. It allows itself to be experienced, but it is not concerned, for it contributes nothing, and nothing happens to it.

When one is in the world, when one is participating with one's existence in the existence of the whole, it is not an "experience." It is, as Buber claims, a relation. That relation does not fragment along experiential lines, the simple grammar of pursuit: subject chasing object.

Moby-Dick is for us the archetypal book of pursuit—but we understand the nature of this pursuit in the shallowest of terms. We think as Starbuck thinks if we read *Moby-Dick* as a man seeking to catch and kill a whale. Our mistake then, as is Starbuck's mistake throughout, is in thinking in experiential rather than relational terms. The world of relation, unlike the world of experience, fuses together all subjectivity and objectivity, cleaves binaries and so destroys them, while the work of experience undoes that unity. Bulkington's silence at the Spouter-Inn and, far more significantly, his silent presence aboard the Pequod throughout the novel, are not the residue of his experience but the ongoing relation with the infinite realm of the ocean. Experience speaks; a word is the end of relation, a fall into a baser, though inevitable, pursuit. Subject-verb-object are the shackles experience places on our life.

When the crew agrees to join the hunt for Moby Dick, they give up their claim to experience. Such is the lower layer of Starbuck's horror. For Ahab initiates them into his relational pursuit of an object with which he is coterminous. To chase the whale madly is also to chase his own mad self. Madness maddened. Stubb's wise dream of the whale dressed up as, and defending, Ahab is but one hint among many that Ahab and his object of obsession are a single, chimerical one. Ahab infuses his crew with his purpose, making of many wills a single will, making of many a one that chases a one that is a many. For the white whale is a deep and troubling paradox. It dwells in the infinite ocean Peleg forced Ishmael to see before he signed away his name.

The infinite is the realm of relation, and that which exists in it also widens infinitely. The ocean is the location of infinite possibility. The white whale exists in it as infinite particularity. Ahab chases that which is impossible and yet real: the single creature whose unspeakable name is All.

See also:

Ambergris

Death

Expression

Freedom

I / *I* / "I"

Letter

Magnet

Ocean

Pyramid

Reciprocity

Silence

Time

Truth

Wound

EXPRESSION

When we open a book, the face of the page confronts our face. The face of the page both masks and reveals the author who wrote the words we are reading. The author himself wears the mask of narrator, who utters the author's words for him. In *Moby-Dick,* the narrator himself wears a mask, so that Ishmael masks a nameless narrator who masks the author. All three mouths speak at once. When Ishmael says "I," he means himself as Ishmael, he means himself as the hidden-I who has abandoned his proper name to speak through an allegorical one, and he means— to an almost indecipherable degree—Melville himself, whose experience on the sea provides the source-experience from which the tale, in part, leaps. Such is the face facing our face. Such is the face that speaks to us. As readers, we are the Other implied by the unspoken "You" with which *Moby-Dick* commences: "Call me Ishmael."

The book begins and ends in silence. The first word spoken ends silence by piercing into it, not as one pierces a page with a pin but as one pierces a vacuum: with a single word void is no longer void, silence no longer silence. Void and silence become the groundless space in which the world in words occurs. The book is a world spoken to me by another. For me, this other wears the mask called Ishmael. For Ishmael, I am the You he cannot know exists.

Language occurs in expression. As Levinas writes, language donates and opens to the Other the means of consideration and interpretation. The I that speaks gives to the Other what previously existed within the speaking self. In expression, the speaking-I breaks open what "I thought, I felt, I knew," and puts words in front of the questioning Other, who does not accept them as definition but as a world open to consideration, to interpretation, to inquiry. "Language," Levinas writes, "does not belong among the relations that could appear through the structures of formal logic; it is contact across a distance, relation with the non-touchable, across a void."

One speaks out of a desire to communicate the world within oneself. Desire disrupts the silence that denies a shared world. Desire is that force within us by which we learn to betray the boundary of our selves, that border guarded by the sentinel "I." Desire finds those words that cross the limit between private thought and public communication. Expression is desire's work. That work is the trespass in which I betray myself. The I that speaks and the I that thinks are, potentially, quite different versions of "me." The I that speaks puts forth—into the void that desire alone makes habitable—a world I no longer possess. For as Levinas explains, "The generality of the word institutes the common world." This common world provides the tools for a book that hovers between a speaking-I and a listening-Other. The expressed world is not a logic but a question, a consideration; the expressed world creates the grounds from which meaning may finally occur. Levinas puts it nicely:

Language does not exteriorize a representation preexisting in me: it puts in common a world hitherto mine. Language *effectuates* the entry of things into a new ether in which they receive a name and become concepts. It is a first action over and above labor, an action without action, even though speech involves the effort of labor, even though, as incarnate thought, it inserts us into the world, with the risks and hazards of all action. At each instant it exceeds this labor by the generosity of the offer it forthwith makes of this very labor. The analyses of language that tend to present it as one meaningful action among others fail to recognize this *offering* of the world, this offering of contents which answers to the face of the Other or which questions him, and first opens the perspective of the meaningful.

The spoken world—the world of the book—is generous in that it opens possibility rather than reducing it. The questioning force that acts upon the common world between the speaking-I and the Other creates meaning by doubting the meaning of the world that arrives, seemingly, already defined.

The expressive work that put forth this world both reveals and conceals the I who spoke it. "In undertaking what I willed," writes Levinas, "I realized so many things I did not will." The work of expression—which we call the world—cannot be reduced to the intention of a single speaker. In cleaving asunder the self to speak a world, one also opens that world spoken to chance, to unintentional meaning, to rupture. The work of the world is never total.

The expressed world begins as an interior reality that, spoken, risks becoming universal. The author is the hermit walking out from his home, holding in his mouth the treasure he's hoarded, and knowing, as he opens his mouth, that the first word will glisten as it becomes other than his own. He reveals himself as he reveals his world—not completely. He listens, too, to himself as he speaks—an observer to his own life, confounded even as he confesses. And then he either retreats or holds his ground. Should he risk the latter, he sees, if he is lucky, how the world expressed becomes the tangled conduit of consideration, the world-knot that, between two minds, is never undone but pulled tighter.

See also:

Chaos
Etymology
I / I / "I"
Jonah
Letter
Saying / Said
Surplus
Vengeance
Void
Writing
You / Thou

EYES

The great sperm whale's lashless eyes are as small as a young colt's. Odder than their miniscule size—though Ishmael rightly points out that power of the eye has nothing to do with powers of vision—is their placement:

> In a word, the position of the whale's eyes corresponds to that of a man's ears; and you may fancy, for yourself, how it would fare with you, did you sideways survey objects through your ears. You would find that you could only command some thirty degrees of vision in advance of the straight side-line of sight; and about thirty more behind it. Moreover, while in most other animals that I can now think of, the eyes are so planted as imperceptibly to blend their visual power, so as to produce one picture and not two to the brain; the peculiar position of the whale's eyes, effectually divided as they are by many cubic feet of solid head, which towers between them like a great mountain separating two lakes in valleys; this, of course, must wholly separate the impressions which each independent organ imparts.

The whale sees two worlds, one on either side. The whale's mind contains two worlds—and when the whale thinks, if we can speak of the whale thinking, he processes twice the perceptual information as a human, whose senses combine the vision of two eyes into a singular scope. But the placement of its eyes also means that when the whale swims forward—placidly or in rage, in pursuit or in flight—he swims into blankness unlit by vision. Nor does the whale have binocular vision: depth cannot be gauged by sight, but only by the increasing pressure upon the whale's body as it dives.

For humans, the world is before us; we open our eyes and see the world in which we dwell. A whale opens its eyes and sees two worlds, and dwells in neither. A whale dwells in blindness. When Ishmael claims that the sperm whale is "a Platonian," he infers a philosophical reality from a biological fact. The sperm whale, unlike we who hunt him, disregards the appearance of the world, the image, the sensory stuff that convinces us of its reality. Plato claims that the world we see is but a shadow of the world that is. The actual world cannot be seen or sensed. Thought provides access to it, but only when the soul recollects for the mind the thoughts that compose its activity. To a Platonist—and Ishmael, in his reveries atop the cross-mast, clearly asserts his Platonic leanings—the whale lives in a world possessed of greater reality than our own. That world of greater reality exists, paradoxically, within our own. The sperm whale lives in a world that disguises itself in appearance.

Ahab has glimpsed such a world "behind the wall" drawn near him. Ishmael has seen the whale hurl its mass toward a ship it could not see, and destroy all aboard her. He saw the whale return the Pequod and her crew to the unseen depths in which it lives. Ishmael saw them descend back into the invisible real. He saw it with his own eyes. And Ahab fled with the white whale into the whale's nothingness.

See also:

Brain
Duplicates
Nothing/ness
Plato
Reciprocity
Scroll
Skin
Spectacles
Spermaceti
Whiteness

FAITH

The world is a whaling ship "on its passage out, and not a voyage complete, and the pulpit is its prow." So Ishmael thinks, watching as Father Mapple, the "pilot-prophet" who was once a whaler himself, climbs up the rope ladder that leads to his pulpit. Mapple delivers his sermon from a pulpit made to resemble a ship; he reads from a bible resting on a pedestal "fashioned after a ship's fiddle-headed beak." Behind him hangs a large painting of "a gallant ship beating against a terrible storm off a lee coast of black rocks and snowy breakers." After he climbs up the rope ladder, Father Mapple pulls it up after him. What Ishmael senses, and so we sense, is that what could seem mere theatrics has "some sober reason," and must "symbolize something unseen."

The symbolism of such a chapel—the church as beacon of safety among the rough seas of life—seems obvious. What is unseen, in part, is the ocean on which the pulpit floats. Surrounding the pulpit's "panelled front . . . in the likeness of a ship's bluff bows" are granite tablets bearing the names of sailors and ships lost at sea. The grave ocean buoys the pulpit. Each man listening to the sermon listens as one shipwrecked, sitting in a pew as a sailor might hold on to a plank of wood in order to stay afloat. The ship arrives as salvation.

The power in Mapple's spiritual vision, though, lies in the suggestion that faith is no sturdy salvation. The pulpit that is the prow of the world is buffeted and almost broken by the same furious ocean, subject to the same fatal dangers, as the names carved into granite stones that symbolize the ocean beyond the chapel's walls. The exercise of faith shows that the ship is still whole, neither blown against the breakers nor lost in the depths of the sea. Faith is not the continent, except when one sees that the continent itself is but a grassy boat.

Father Mapple's chapel is a place in which metaphor manifests itself as reality. As the great Puritan preachers before him, he works to remove from his parishioners' eyes the habit of thought that allows them to continue in sin. Our safety is no more than plank nailed to plank. The image recalls Jonathan Edwards' sermon "Sinners in the Hands of an Angry God," in which he brings us to understand that even our sense of standing upon solid ground is but an illusion born of our sinful, mistaken assumptions—a startling vision that is closely related to Mapple's symbolic effort. Edwards sees that our spiritual and physical realities share certain laws: "Your wickedness makes you as it were heavy as lead, and to tend downwards with great weight and pressure towards hell; and if God should let you go, you would immediately sink and swiftly descend and plunge into the bottomless gulf. . . ." Or, as Simone Weil would put it some two hundred years later: "All the *natural* movements of the soul are controlled by laws analagous to those of physical gravity." We mistake, Edwards says, the vertigo of our free fall—spiritually and bodily, for in this thinking the body and the soul share the same crisis—because we are held up as "a spider's web" holds up a falling rock. We do not sense our fall, for we think we have landed on solid earth. Yet what is the earth but a rock falling into the sun? And the sun but a star falling into the singular absence of a star? And the universe but an entity rotating within a blankness into which it also expands infinitely? A spiritual leader, a man like Mapple who is a whaler and a religious guide, senses, and is subject to, the gravitational push down to the ocean's depths—the ocean in which, if the metaphor holds, his parishioners are drowning as he speaks.

Before Mapple begins his sermon on Jonah, he kneels "in the pulpit's bows" and offers "a prayer so deeply devout that he seemed kneeling and praying at the bottom of the sea." Such is the impossible difficulty genuine faith demands. As Mapple soon says, "all the things that God would have us do are hard for us to do." That difficulty, as this "pilot-prophet" puts it before us, is to pray in two locations at once—from the prow of the ship rolling on the ocean's surface and from the still, silent, dark depths of the ocean. Mapple's actions, the manifestation of his faith, suggest that when we send our prayers heavenward from surface to sky, we mistake the abysmal depths our faith must first cross. When we pray we must kneel on the ocean's bed and look upward toward that heaven that is but the limit of the water in which we've already drowned. Then there is the sky to cross, and then infinity. Our faith exists, if faith can be said to "exist," as a plumb line extending from the surface to our bottom-most life. Faith does not measure height but sounds down into depths. A prayer is but a vibration along faith's taut plumb line, so that the self on the surface knows when the self in depth is kneeling down to speak upward, and so returns voice to the vibration. There is no heaven for us but the deep.

See also:

Coffin
Expression
Idolatry
Jonah
Paradox
Prophet
Starry Archipelagoes
Tablet
Truth

FATE

Yojo, the wooden god, divulges to Queequeg that Ishmael must choose the ship upon which both will sail. It is the idol's belief that Ishmael will "infallibly light upon" the whale ship that, though seemingly decided upon by chance, has been preordained for their adventure. Ishmael acquiesces to fate. He chooses to believe in the plausibility of Yojo's power and proceeds to the harbor to make a choice that he understands as having already been made for him. The trick of the fated eye is in attempting to see without the mistaken belief that what we see offers us a choice. The fated person who has not—as Oedipus did—had his fate revealed to him attempts to choose by removing the deliberate analysis after which choice is usually made. One looks for a sign, a resonance. The fated man looks for the choice that is choosing him.

Ishmael submits to Yojo's command but, unlike Queequeg, seems unconnected to the god's revelatory power. He goes to the harbor hoping fate will unveil the proper ship to sign aboard. But no such sign comes. He sees three ships from which to choose: the Devil-Dam, the Tit-bit, and the Pequod. Failing some intuitive recognition, Ishmael considers the origins of their names and, knowing the etymology of the word *Pequod*—"the name of a celebrated tribe of Massachusetts Indians, now extinct as the ancient Medes"—decides upon Ahab's fated ship. Fate has chained him to fate.

Fate denies choice but does not remove its onus. The belief that he cannot choose wrongly has no bearing on the need to decide. Ishmael must proceed through a deliberation with no promise that the process will reveal the best end. Fate denies the ability to choose either wrongly or rightly—in a fated world, even the wrong choice is the correct one. Ishmael finds himself in the terrible position of exercising the powers of his consciousness while knowing that he cannot determine the outcome. He is a consciousness removed from culpability, and yet he feels in his heart's depth the awful responsibility of the choice he is both making and unable to make. His mind mimics the experience he is soon to live: the peripatetic mind wandering through a series of loosely connected thoughts aboard a ship sailing in a direction he cannot choose to change or control. The fated life is a ship life. One walks on deck and below deck, one climbs the rigging to the crow's nest, one proceeds from bow to stern, but that individual motion is negated by the motion of the whole. Each sailor could walk in a different direction aboard the Pequod, but the only motion that counts is the vector Ahab has charted—just as we go about our daily lives, forgetful of the fact that as we wander from block to block, the earth spins on its axis as it circles the sun.

Fate, too, is an underground, underwater work. It forges connections the rational mind cannot see, nor rationalize when shown. The wooden god Yojo leads to Captain Ahab's ship. Ahab's namesake, as Ishmael all too well knows, is that most hated of Judaic kings, who placed Ba'al's idols in the Temple. The idol leads to the idolater—a fated circuit that mimics language when language feels fated, the inevitable link of the word with what the word means, the object of worship with the worshipper, as if prayer were but a fated language, found already formed on the tongue that prays.

See also:

Ahab
Freedom
Idolatry
Loomings
Omen
Pequod
Quest / Question
Reading (Epistemology)
Repetition
Totem
Vengeance

FEAR

Starbuck will let no man "in my boat who is not afraid of a whale." He knows he and the men he leads live by profiting from a mortal business. The whale may kill them; they may kill the whale. In such treacherous work, "an utterly fearless man is a far more dangerous comrade than a coward." Starbuck's "careful" approach to a murderous activity makes him excellent at garnering its profit, as well as making him a figure of strange (though unspoken) derision among the other mates. His courage does not negate or oppose his fear, nor does he expect it to do so for others. His courage leaps from his fear, hones his motions, rationalizes his approach to the furious engagement with the whale enraged in the squall of the hunt. He does not stop his fear nor want others to disown theirs. He casts his fear first and expects his courage to follow.

This forward thrust of fear into the dangerous work of whaling is a rational activity. Fear thinks ahead of action. Fear deliberates. Fear brings to light the specific danger faced in any given whale hunt and prescribes to courage the measured action to be taken. Starbuck's is a courage that occurs within the space fear opens. He can, in his bravery, withstand the "ordinary irrational horrors of the world." In fear, he can rationalize the "ordinary irrational" and, more generally, act in the face of those ordinary horrors. But Starbuck cannot withstand "those more terrific, because more spiritual terrors," which Ahab guides the Pequod to confront. Such spiritual terrors deny action as an activity that can rescue from fear the fearful man. His fear makes Starbuck a superstitious man, a reader of signs he cannot understand—for the deep world's dangers reveal themselves in impractical ways. Ahab, too, frightens him.

~

Abraham, in midrash and Talmud, represents *chesed*—the loving-kindness whose nature is infinite. Abraham presents in his very being a love the world cannot contain. And because the world, finite as it is, cannot contain this love, it cannot affect the world, light the world, or come to any use in it.

When God commands Abraham to take his second-born son, Isaac (Ishmael's half brother), to Mount Moriah to be sacrificed, God intends to do more than test Abraham's love and faith. When they set off to Moriah, Isaac is not a boy but a middle-aged man. And when Isaac asks who will provide the sacrificial animal, he understands that he is himself this animal. The purpose of the trip is not hidden from Isaac's eyes. It is said that Isaac questions his father to elicit from Abraham the unbearable, infinite strength of his love for the son he is about to kill in the name of the God he also loves. It seems, impossibly enough, Abraham is being asked to divide his love—a force whose nature is indivisible.

When Isaac is bound upon the sacrificial stone, fearing that he might flinch at the sight or touch of the knife's blade and so make unholy the holy sacrifice, he asks, "Father, bind me tighter." Abraham's loving nature opposes any notion of boundary, of binding, of limit. Isaac's final request forces Abraham to go against his own nature—not merely at the level of personality but at the level of his universal and spiritual significance.

It is said Isaac survived because the angels' tears melted Abraham's blade; the same tears fell in Isaac's eyes. The world he saw ever afterward appeared as if behind a thin shroud, or a mourning veil. When he stood and looked upon the rock, he thought he saw his own ashes. Isaac is Fear.

When one prays, as in the Torah, to God in "Love and Fear," one does so in the names of Abraham and Isaac. The story beneath the story, the "little lower layer," has little to do with the plot that so horrifies. The story we're told has little to do with a father sacrificing his son—it is a story of how love occurs actively in a world whose nature previously denied its effectiveness. Isaac's fear houses Abraham's love—limits it and so brings it into the world. Fear is the finite limit in which love can occur, can be ours, can add its light to the world. The story of Isaac's sacrifice is the story of the cost of bringing love to bear on the matter of the world.

ꝰ

Starbuck is a surprising choice for Ahab's first mate. Ahab knows Starbuck's nature. But Ahab also knows that his pursuit—a desire to chase the white whale that has nothing to do with the practical profitability of his business—cannot be accomplished by himself. He needs a crew, yes. But more, Ahab needs a first mate who can harness the nature of his infinite chase. Starbuck's fear houses Ahab's force. Ahab, all too obviously, is no Abraham. He seems a man of infinite power if not a man of infinite love, though he still seems capable of love—the memory of his wife and child, his love for Pip. Ahab's infinite force is his hate. Starbuck actualizes that hate, and he does so by his fear as he fears it.

See also:

Aleph
Child
Definition
Experience
Hunger
Omen
Profit
Tzimtzum

FLAME

The sun lights but the surface of the world, and when the sun sets, the world returns to darkness. At noon, the shadowless pinnacle of the day's most intense light, most of the world remains hidden in impenetrable night. The sunlight pierces but a few fathoms into the ocean, and light becomes extinct though life does not. In the depths of the ocean, the whale cannot spark a match to light his way, and need not. He swims forward in the darkness.

When the men aboard the Pequod process the whale by burning its blubber in the try-pots, they do so by feeding the fire that boils the skin into oil with scraps and "fritters" of the skin itself. "The whale supplies his own fuel and burns by his own light." The sun, too, burns upon the sun—until the star devours itself into nothingness. Then life and light are done.

When Ishmael watches by the light of the burning whale, the red, hellish light reveals those around it differently than does the light of the sun. Ishmael watches from the dark as the fire in the try-pots pushes back the edge of darkness: "Wrapped, for that interval, in darkness myself, I but the better saw the redness, the madness, the ghastliness of others." Ishmael falls to sleep in the outer darkness aboard the Pequod—"this fire-ship on the sea"—his back against the jawbone tiller to keep the ship on course. His infernal vision reechoes in his head. In his sleep, subject to witness the same hellish revelations as when awake, he unconsciously turns around, and awakes to find himself turned astern, fleeing from the absolute darkness. He feels as if he's "rushing from all havens astern," as if safety were in that place that remains undisclosed to vision, un-interrupted by light.

To know is to know in a certain light. The sun reveals a man differently than does the light of a whale. A friend by the former is a savage by the latter—lit by the flame that, self-sprung and self-devouring, exemplifies the "universal cannibalism" it reveals. Daylight will again bring familiarity. The harbor of a friend's face, the calm bay in the eyes. But such light is equally a surface revelation. The dark depths remain unlit.

See also:

Chaos
Corpusants
Expression
Eyes
Hands
Lightning
Mincer
Savage
Skin
Soot
Spectacles

FOOL

Out in the raging storm on the heath, Lear's fool speaks a king's truth. The fool does not offer comfort, but rather a riddling honesty that Lear recognizes as accurate. The fool speaks words to Lear others would say and, for saying, be hanged. In part, this power comes from the fool's ability to recognize when another person, regardless of grandeur or stature, is the butt of the universal joke. The fool sees in Lear a fool, and it is the fool alone who understands the linguistic nature of Lear's abdication. When Lear spoke-in-half his kingdom and marked on the map the division, he also removed himself from his oracular authority. Lear's voice before was Law—not merely a legislative authority, but a cosmos kept in order by *logos*. The word as coherent universal order decays into a token authority when wielded by Goneril or Regan. Word has become word. The gesture of authority remains the same, sounds the same, but the oracular word of the king that orders the world of which he speaks has become a mere text, a repetition in signs of a power that bears no coining. (Note, after Act I, Scene I, how often writing, letters, and handwriting both further and complicate the drama, and which characters are involved in such "legibility." Note how Goneril, hearing her husband proffer an opinion she dislikes, says, "No more; the text is foolish." Note how Albany would like to choke her by stuffing a letter in her mouth until she asphyxiates.)

Only the fool can speak within the vacuum of the king's language. The fool can do so because his language approaches truth not by creating it but by uncovering it. The fool speaks in riddles, the very opposite of the king's proclamation, whose word is law. (It is also worth noting, especially in *King Lear,* that the fool and the king are equally adept in punning, but it is only after Lear grows mad that he too speaks in riddles.) A riddle speaks in hidden ways—a language whose sense occurs beneath its reference. The king speaks a direct line to meaning; the king's word is simultaneous with meaning, his word is the sonic embodiment of law. The fool rhymes, disguises, and puns. He directs by misdirection, he obscures the end of any given sentence by creating obstacles to meaning.

In order to understand the fool, one must think and discover, as one does with a sphinx's question, for oneself. The fool makes one responsible for one's own interpretation. The king expects you simply to obey. The king's word is undermined by a language indistinguishable from his own, a language that replicates a power it cannot possess. The fool subverts that powerless language that wears the mask of authority by locating meaning beneath reference, by speaking one thing only in order to mean something else. Is it any wonder that Lear ends in mimicking the language of the mime?

⟿

Ahab, initially, has no fool. Ishmael and Ahab, for all we know, never speak. To Ahab, Ishmael is but one of the crew. Stubb is a fool, but of a different order. Stubb doesn't speak to Ahab so as to show his captain what Ahab does not see or cannot admit without a foolish intervention. When Stubb first speaks to Ahab, to ask him to soften the rap of his bone-leg against the deck with a "globe of tow," he is told: "Down, dog, and kennel!" Not only is the phrase reminiscent of Lear's fool's "Truth's a dog must to kennel," but it also reveals Stubb's inadequacy as Ahab's foolish pair. For the king and the fool are as intimate to one another as the flip sides of a coin. The fool is the king in reverse, and his ability to speak to the authority above him derives from his suffering the same crisis. The fool and Lear share a linguistic reality. Ahab has no fool until Pip falls into the ocean. And then Pip holds on to Ahab's heartstrings.

See also:

Ambergris
Cordelia

Friendship
Joke
Prophet
Pyramid
Reading (Doubloon)
Truth

FOSSIL

Hunting an old, sick whale weakened by some sort of stomach ailment, which farts as it swims and has lost a fin and its eyes, Flask spots a "strangely discolored bunch or protuberance, the size of a bushel, low down on the flank." Flask lances it, causing "more then sufferable anguish," and the whale dies. The crew begins its carcass-work:

> It so chanced that almost upon first cutting into him with the
> spade, the entire length of a corroded harpoon was found
> imbedded in his flesh, on the lower part of the bunch before
> described . . . But still more curious was the fact of a lance-head
> of stone being found in him, not far from the buried iron, the
> flesh perfectly firm about it.

In the whale's lately living flesh is found a Stone Age weapon. Most scholars say, so Ishmael informs us, that a sperm whale lives for one hundred years. In the watery world in which the whale lives, untouched by Noah's flood, a whale, it seems, can survive eternally. Some do. Some that lived through the destruction of the world will live through such destruction again. Ishmael knows it: "I am horror-struck at this antemosaic, unsourced existence of the unspeakable terrors of the whale, which, having been before all time, must need exist after all humane ages are over."

Ishmael's horror (not a word he uses lightly) is manifold, and it has little to do with the ever-pressing fact of the whale's mortal threat to him. The whale is by its own nature a horror. A creature sprung from no source, it horrifies in part because it cannot be explained, as if its impossible girth refused lineage from the world in which it lives. But the horror isn't only this ontological obscurity that seems to deny nature even as it overwhelms nature. The whale, too, is "antemosaic," a word that, like the whale, denies and doubles its own history, albeit an etymological one. First, born before Moses' laws, and so not subject to the ethical limits of the Ten Commandments. When the whale murders, it is not murder. Second, not part of the pattern of the whole. One way to imagine any given life against the too-wide scope of the whole world is to see oneself as a single tile in a mosaic that stretches toward every horizon, and so ends in being the world. The whale is before such a picture. The whale is not a piece of the puzzle.

See also:

Breath (Thought)
Eyes
Justice
Leg (Ghost)
Skin
Time
Vishnoo
Whale (Ghost)

Freedom

After magnetically convincing the crew to join his chase of the white whale, after rebutting Starbuck's accusation of blasphemy, Ahab gazes out at the setting sun and thinks:

> Come, Ahab's compliments to ye; come and see if you can swerve me. Swerve me? ye cannot swerve me, else ye swerve yourselves! man has ye there. Swerve me? The path to my fixed purpose is laid with iron rails, whereon my soul is grooved to run. Over unsounded gorges, through the rifled hearts of mountains, under torrents' beds, unerringly I rush! Naught's an obstacle, naught's an angle to the iron way!

The image Ahab uses to express his unerring purpose yokes together the qualities that make him such an impossible enigma. He is a man whose soul is manifest. The immortal in him—the eternal, the intangible and shapeless, the incommensurable—has become his most elemental reality while losing none of its spiritual potency. Ahab's soul and body have merged into one indecipherable entity, a consequence of the nature of his wound and a reflection of the creature that wounded him. His soul grooved to run on iron rails seems initially to speak toward fate, but the oddity of the image confirms the soul's frictionless freedom.

Ahab remains free even as he is impelled inevitably forward, subject to a destiny he is not limited by but chooses and participates in. Much of what horrifies and haunts in Ahab also intrigues and impresses: he is a man in whom fate and freedom unite. Martin Buber speaks of such a paradoxical unity and its importance:

Fate and freedom are promised to each other. Fate is encountered only by him that actualizes freedom. That I discovered the deed that intends me, that, this movement of my freedom, reveals the mystery to me . . . [T]his free human being encounters fate as the counter-image of his freedom. It is not his limit but his completion; freedom and fate embrace each other to form meaning; and given meaning, fate—with its eyes, hitherto severe, suddenly full of light—looks like grace itself.

While it does seem a stretch to claim that finding the white whale again will bring Ahab into the countenance of grace—toothed though this grace may be—he may find himself in the face of that which acts like grace, though oppositely. Not a grace that descends with kindness and love but a grace with malice in it, a grace that rises from the deep lees of the world.

This embrace of freedom with fate constitutes, in Buber's formulation, meaning. It is this quality that distinguishes Ahab's pursuit of Moby Dick from the punitive Fate of the ancient world—the fate that breaks one. Ahab's pursuit feels destined, of destiny, and as such is related to destination, to arrival, to encounter or reencounter. However one may imagine the rails upon which his soul runs, one might say as Buber does:

It is not a path of progress and development. It is a descent through the spirals of the spiritual underworld but could also be called an ascent to the innermost, subtlest, most intricate turn that knows no Beyond and even less any Backward but only the unheard of return—the breakthrough. Shall we have to follow this path all the way to the end, to the test of the final darkness? But where there is danger what saves grows, too.

Ahab pursues the white whale to strike through the white whale—to "breakthrough." His soul, which is to say his self, chooses out of its freedom the pursuit that is its fate. This fate is not the flight toward nihilism, though it may be the pursuit of nothing. That final nothing may be the darkness that fuses beginnings to ends, that destroys even as it saves, that undoes the most basic polarity of human existence and returns us to the primeval unity in which death cannot be distinguished from life. As Buber suggests, Ahab is not in his quest seeking a "new territory" beyond or behind the world in which he dwells. Ahab seeks return. He pursues the white whale back to the Season-on-the-Line where, two years previous, he suffered the wound that opened him to freedom, and so opened him to fate.

See also:
Cordelia
Fate
Loomings
Magnet
Nothing/ness
Prophet
Reciprocity
Vengeance
Wound

FRIENDSHIP

Friendship reveals itself in proximity and then survives all distance, even unto death. Friendship unfolds within:

> I began to be sensible of strange feelings. I felt a melting in me.
> No more my splintered heart and maddened hand were turned
> against the wolfish world. This soothing savage had redeemed it.

Ishmael's first realization of the unfolding of friendship resonates erotically. To find a "melting in me" recalls Sapphic descriptions of the erotic moment. Yet Eros—in Sapphic terms, in sexual terms—does not heal the torn heart, but splinters it afresh: love moves through the heart as a too-strong wind moves through a pine tree. What Ishmael finds in Queequeg, and what Queequeg finds in Ishmael, speaks to an intermixing of their most intimate selves. They find in each other the help to their individual, inexpressible, subjective harm. The nature of the help is recognition: the world has stove the hulls of both men in, and done so with a remarkably similar damage.

Ishmael was a schoolteacher who had grown suicidal. One can assume, given the extremity of the anguish (masked, almost always, behind his comic denial of such pain), that Ishmael is on deep levels unhappy, unfulfilled. Books, it seems, are no longer ballast. Filling mind with facts is a hollowness. He is a man in the midst of crisis, whose solution to not ending his life by a trigger pull is to choose the longer living hardship of life on sea, in hopes that the hardship will grant him access to adventure, romance, the whole life-promise of the "wonder-world." Meeting Queequeg is the first fruit of Ishmael's choice. He fears his exotic roommate, but in feeling fear, he feels alive.

Queequeg is a royal man, a prince, who left his island home to learn about Christianity and in doing so sullied himself, so that he cannot return. Knowledge has failed both men. One reads but finds no comfort in words. The other is illiterate, and though he bears upon his body a prophet-inked tattoo, he cannot decipher the symbols. The answers themselves are answerless, the questions questionless.

As in Aristophanes' speech in *The Symposium*, each man finds in the other his missing half. The first cut, delivered by Zeus to curb the power of the erotically whole, spheric creatures, creates in each half the sexual desire for the other, but the sexual itself is merely a mask for the unity being sought in the sexual act. The sexual attempts to heal a harm it can only exacerbate—desire sated leading only to the same desire. In this light, Ishmael and Queequeg's friendship is more intimate than sex. The healing of their friendship comes in the intimate nearing that almost solders the ragged harm of each into the whole being that— like husband and wife—they together form. Montaigne describes such a friendship:

There is, beyond all reasoning, and beyond all that I can specifically say, some inexplicable power of destiny that brought about our union. We were looking for each other before we met . . . I believe this was brought about by some decree of Heaven. We embraced one another by name. And at our first meeting, which happened by chance at a great feast in the city, we found ourselves so captivated, so familiar, so bound to one another, that from that time nothing was closer to either than each was to the other . . . Such a friendship has no model but itself, and can only be compared to itself. It was not one special consideration, nor two, nor three, nor four, nor a thousand; it was some mysterious quintessence of all this mixture which possessed itself of my will, and led it to plunge and lose itself in his; which possessed itself of his whole will, and led it, with a similar hunger and like impulse, to plunge and lose itself in mine. I may say truly *lose,* for it left us nothing that was our own, nothing that was either his or mine.

Queequeg recognizes the nature of their intimacy more directly, more innately, than does Ishmael. Queequeg realizes that between true friends, destined friends, no division is real:

> After supper, and another social chat and smoke, we went to our room together. He made me a present of his embalmed head; took out his enormous tobacco wallet, and groping under the tobacco, drew out some thirty dollars in silver; then spreading them on the table, and mechanically dividing them into two equal portions, pushed one of them towards me, and said it was mine.

The material division only hints at the deeper equality of inner sharing. What friends hold in common is the world. Aristotle writes:

> [W]henever we perceive we are aware that we perceive and whenever we think we are aware that we think, and if being aware that we are perceiving or thinking is being aware that we *are* (since our *being* is perceiving or thinking), and being aware that we are alive is something pleasant in itself (since life is a good thing by nature, and it is pleasant to be aware of the good that is present in oneself), and if being alive is choiceworthy, and especially (since people are pleased by being additionally aware of something that is good in itself), and if a serious person is the same way towards a friend as he is toward himself (since the friend is another self), then just as one's own *being* is choiceworthy for each person, so too, or very nearly so, is that of a friend.

A friend shares in "a friend's awareness that he *is.*" Friendship confirms existence—and in the most generous of ways. Against harm's haunting insistence that any given self is the world unto himself—that all that is real is judged so by the mind perceiving the real, to the horrific point that even the self thinking the world is but the idea of the self thinking the world—friendship says, "he is and I am and it is." Friendship answers skepticism with a peculiar and intimate faith: my friend is as real as me. The stakes of the world are the world. It is dangerous because it is real. One must find a friend to sail with upon the ocean. Only friends can face the awful risk that is living, and the awful wonder. One looks at his friend with the world in his eye. It is not "mine." The friend knows the world is always and ever, irretrievably, maddeningly, lovingly, longingly "ours."

See also:

Crisis
Expression
Fear
Hands
Other
Reading (Epistemology)
Savage
Tattoo
Time

GROIN

Home in Nantucket, presumably with wife and child, now physically recovered from the White Whale's wound, Ahab is found "one night lying prone upon the ground, and insensible; by some unknown, and seemingly inexplicable, unimaginable casualty, his ivory limb having been so violently displaced, that it had stake-wise smitten, and all but pierced his groin." As *Moby-Dick* opens, as the Pequod sails away on Christmas Day, Ahab is recovering from this very wound. The humiliation of such a wound, the indignity of it, troubles less than the inexplicable fact of its symbolic meaning. The wound strikes through the point of generation, and for a man such as Ahab, the wound is deepest beyond the pierced flesh. The nature of the affliction seems to deny Ahab's ability to procreate, to be fecund, to be in this world himself a maker of that which due to his potency now exists. The denial is not of fatherhood, for Ahab is a father. It is of the ability to create a world within a world already created. It is a godlike power in Ahab that is so mockingly cut, to create out of oneself that which is not oneself. One can almost hear the universe laugh at the joke.

But a laugh and a sob sound alike. Ahab learns from his wounds; his injury gives him his philosophy. Happiness and wholeness may illuminate a life, but they may also mask and blind.

> For, thought Ahab, while even the highest earthly felicities have a certain unsignifying pettiness lurking in them, but, at bottom, all heart-woes, a mystic significance, and, in some men, an arch-angelic grandeur; so do their diligent tracings-out not belie the obvious deduction. To trail the genealogies of these high mortal miseries, carries us at last among the sourceless primogenitures of the gods; so that in the face of all the glad, hay-making suns, and soft-cymbaling, round harvest-moons, we must needs give

in to this: that the gods themselves are not for ever glad. The in-effaceable, sad birth-mark in the brow of man, is but the stamp of sorrow in the signers.

The wound opens access, through the pain and suffering (neither of which is simply physical in nature but most harrowing when least bodily, as if the aching nerve but echoes a more difficult harm) it inflicts, to thoughts that bring the sufferer closer to the mystery that is the world and the world's wound. The wound opens one to the world. Suffering does not speak in sentences, if it speaks at all, but rather in questions. If one can find the Ahab-like resolve to ask anything other than "Why me?" then suffering becomes a more important kind of life than does ending that suffering. Ahab could kill himself, or he could give up. He will do nei-ther. "As touching all Ahab's deeper part, every revelation partook more of significant darkness than of explanatory light." We tend to think of light as a creative force, but to think so eases our darker suspicions—the unspeakable sense that the world is heaved up from inexpressible horror as much as it is dropped down in tangible love. The wounded man alone may mistrust the "visible world" that seems "formed in love" and see instead the "invisible spheres . . . formed in fright."

See also:

Child
Death
Description
Leg (Ghost)
Lightning
Mincer
Thought (Ahab)
Wound

Hands

When, as a young boy, Ishmael's stepmother pulled him out of the chimney up which he was trying to crawl, and sent him to bed at two o'clock in the afternoon (this punishment all the more excruciating for happening on the summer solstice), he had an unnerving experience:

> For several hours I lay there broad awake, feeling a great deal worse than I have ever done since, even from the greatest subsequent misfortunes. At last I must have fallen into a troubled nightmare of a doze; and slowly waking from it—half steeped in dreams—I opened my eyes, and the before sun-lit room was now wrapped in outer darkness. Instantly I felt a shock running through all my frame; nothing was to be seen, and nothing was to be heard; but a supernatural hand seemed placed in mine. My arm hung over the counterpane, and the nameless, unimaginable, silent form or phantom, to which the hand belonged, seemed closely seated by my bedside. For what seemed ages piled on ages, I lay there, frozen with the most awful fears, not daring to drag away my hand; yet ever thinking that if I could but stir it one single inch, the horrid spell would be broken.

A portion of the uncanny quality of Ishmael's waking experience is the sudden transposition of an inner darkness with an outer. Night arrives without dusk's preface, suddenly and inexplicably, as if the unconscious nightmares rising into young Ishmael's mind had sprung into the waking world. A boundary has collapsed which safely separates one's subjective and objective experience of self and world. The boundary that seems so thick, so impenetrable, separating self from all that is other, all that is outer, in a single midnight waking is revealed to be but an opaque isinglass membrane that a finger's strength can pierce.

Ishmael's fear, and a mystery whose grasp he still feels, pondering often upon it, marks the nature of his life's inquiry. He awoke with his hand held by what he could not hold: night's illimitable depth impossibly materialized. The terms of the subjective world have shockingly reversed: Ishmael as the object, not the agent, of contemplation. The indefinite and deep mystery of the dark world tethered to the palm of a boy, not so he can know it, but so the mystery can know him.

⌁

From the Heidelburgh Tun, which "embraces the entire length of the entire top of the head" of a sperm whale, up to five hundred gallons of spermaceti is removed. When the whale is alive, the sperm is a pure, fragrant, limpid oil. But when the oil is removed from the deep case, removed from the living property in the living whale, it coagulates into solid lumps that must be squeezed back into fluid. Ishmael is one of the whalers who puts his hands into the sperm:

> . . . as I bathed my hands among those soft, gentle globules of
> infiltrated tissues, woven almost within the hour; as they richly
> broke to my fingers, and discharged all their opulence, like fully
> ripe grapes their wine; as I snuffed up that uncontaminated
> aroma,—literally and truly, like the smell of spring violets; I de-
> clare to you, that for the time I lived as in a musky meadow;
> I forgot all about our horrible oath; in that inexpressible sperm,
> I washed my hands and heart of it. . . . I squeezed that sperm till I
> myself almost melted into it; I squeezed that sperm till a strange
> sort of insanity came over me; and I found myself unwittingly
> squeezing my co-laborers' hands in it, mistaking their hands for
> the gentle globules. Such an abounding, affectionate, friendly, lov-
> ing feeling did this avocation beget; that at last I was continually

squeezing their hands, and looking up into their eyes sentimentally; as much as to say,—Oh! my dear fellow beings, why should we longer cherish any social acerbities, or know the slightest ill-humor or envy! Come; let us squeeze hands all round; nay, let us all squeeze ourselves into each other; let us squeeze ourselves universally into the very milk and sperm of kindness.

Ishmael's experience in squeezing the sperm bears a haunted relationship to that earlier hand-holding he experienced as a child, when, awakening in the middle of the night, he felt his hand held by that of a mysterious phantom. Here, however, the uncanny disappearance of the boundary between the self and the world does not create a spell marked by paralyzing fear but instead an epiphanic trance.

This squeezing mimics the very process it produces in Ishmael. The whalers squeeze the sperm because it is becoming definite, individualized, and must maintain its unctuous state to remain of value. Doing this fluidic work is to become fluidic oneself, dissolving one's own coagulated difference into a substance that erases such difference, that immerses one and all back into an undifferentiated source in which any notion of individual self makes no sense. Whatever the material and commercial qualities that make the sperm of monetary value, its initial value is madly philosophic, threateningly religious, corybantic. It is not light, but light's source. Part of what makes the squeezing of each other's hands within the tun possible is that one cannot see what one is doing beneath the surface. It is as if when one plunges one's hands into the musky fluid the hands belong to their own mysterious activity, sending by some indefinable kindness the sensation of the nerves back to the brain, which lives an experience that seems not its own. Such is aesthetic, creative experience. What Ishmael describes in squeezing the hands of his fellow sailors parallels how a singer in a chorus describes singing—unable to distinguish her own voice from the harmonious whole. Here, "sperm" as seed, as germ (its etymological root being "to sow") gains greatest agency, greatest urgency. To put one's hands in the sperm is to return to a source in which no possibility has as yet become probability, before choice hurtles toward fate, before sequence (even the sequence of breath and heartbeat that begin a life, and ending end it) resounds into consequence.

See also:

Brain
Fear
Friendship
I / *I* / "I"
Leg (Ghost)
Nothing/ness
Other
You / Thou

HERO

The white whale dives to the ocean's bottom, a breathing denizen of the unfathomable, airless realms. Sailors aboard the Pequod claim Moby Dick delivers the devil's mail. The white whale connects surface to depth and, in his strange, alien, inexplicable intelligence, carries knowledge from one world to another. Moby Dick belongs to the depths of the chthonian world, of the underworld, of that hell older than the Christian hell, in which the Titans, as if undefeated, in darkness illuminate still dwell. Here, below the water, are those gods who swallow their children alive. Moby Dick, too, is a swallowing god. As Mircea Eliade writes, referring to Oceanic myths:

> The sea monster's belly, like the body of the chthonian Goddess,
> represents the bowels of the earth, the realm of the dead, Hell.
> In the visionary literature of the Middle Ages, Hell is frequently
> imagined in the form of a huge monster, whose prototype is
> probably the biblical Leviathan. There is, then, a series of parallel
> images: the belly of the giantess, of a Goddess, of a sea monster,
> symbolizing the chthonian womb, cosmic night, the realm of the
> dead. To enter this gigantic body alive is equivalent to descending
> into Hell, to confronting the ordeals destined for the dead. The
> initiatory meaning of this type of descent to the Underworld is
> clear—he who has been successful in such an exploit no longer
> fears death; he has conquered a kind of bodily immortality, the
> goal of all heroic initiations from the time of Gilgamesh.

The white whale not only dwells in hell, he symbolizes it. When he swims furiously upward to gain another breath, he carries a portion of hell to the surface world. Moby Dick breaches more than the surface of water when he breaks through the waves to breathe. He shatters the reality of the daylit world with a world in which light is forever a stranger, save for the light that can be thrown by flame. His is not the solar world, nor is his the lunar world. All such light stops in the depths and does not pierce to the bottom. Moby Dick's world is that hellish world Milton describes as lit by a "darkness visible." Moby Dick complicates darkness. The white whale is a creature capable of living in this hellish night darker than night, but he is also a creature who contains that element that struck by flame turns into flame. Moby Dick is a wick in the water and so promises, within the complexity of his symbolic nature, to illuminate what before was unlit.

The mythic hero descends to the underworld. This descent initiates the hero into his own nature, one capable of confronting the world beyond the daily world of commerce and duty, that world in which monsters dwell. Such monsters contain secrets, and to defeat them is to gain the secret they contained. Within the body of the monster, within the belly of Leviathan, lurks the intestinal labyrinth whose amazed complexity unfolds into the secrets by which the universe itself formed.

Ahab's fate is to become such a hero, to possess such knowledge. His initiation occurs before *Moby-Dick* begins, in that fateful first encounter with the white whale who severed and swallowed the leg of the hero who would conquer him. Ahab is the hero, incomplete. He only partially emerges from his initiatory ordeal. His leg stays within Leviathan, a fact more haunting mythologically than biologically. Ahab is caught between two worlds, between two selves: the whaling captain in the world of commerce and the hero (or shaman) in the world before time began.

We learn from the captain of the Samuel Enderby (who lost his arm to Moby Dick) that the digestive tract of the sperm whale processes solid food so slowly that Ahab's leg is likely extant in the white whale's gut. A portion of Ahab, the leg by which he bestrides the world, is lost within the secret he would learn, belongs to the realm he would conquer and, conquering, emerge unscathed, anointed as the hero his nature requires him to be. But Ahab is a partial man, and so a partial hero. He lives bodily in two worlds and cannot, as can the hero or the shaman, reconcile them into one. He cannot serve as a conduit between worlds, and his failure at managing his shamanic role as pivot between a material world and a spiritual one results in the deaths of all his crew. Ahab plunges his men toward the very danger only he is capable of rescuing them from. This failure of initiation bifurcates Ahab as much as the scar running lightning-like down his body does, divides him as evenly as his gait is divided between a leg of flesh and a leg of bone. One step is human, and one step is heroic, and the man walking upon them fails in being either extreme.

Ahab walks upon the deck chimerically: at one step he is the shaman who can conjure flame from iron, can magnetize souls, can baptize a blade in blood; at the next step, he is a man moved to tears in looking at the ocean and thinking of home. His wound's physical nature is a minor chord. The deeper wound is the rift between the mythic, chthonian world and the daily one. Ahab is both a fractional man and a man doubled. Such is the work of his wound.

See also:

Chaos
Fate
Flame
Jonah
Lightning
Magic
Magnet
Quest / Question
Reciprocity
Vengeance
Vishnoo
Wound

Hieroglyph

Ishmael describing the skin of the whale:

> Almost invariably it is all over obliquely crossed and re-crossed
> with numberless straight marks in thick array, something like
> those in the finest Italian line engravings. But these marks do not
> seem to be impressed upon the isinglass substance above men-
> tioned, but seem to be seen through it as if they were engraved
> upon the body itself. Nor is this all. In some instances, to the
> quick, observant eye those linear marks, as in a veritable engrav-
> ing, but afford the ground for far other delineations. These are
> hieroglyphical; that is, if you call those mysterious ciphers on the
> walls of pyramids hieroglyphics, then that is the proper word to
> use in the present connexion.

Beneath the lines that compose engravings—the minute scratches whose
sum total ends in a scene portrayed—are lines of another sort. Hiero-
glyphs are not, like the fine-art-etched surface of skin above it, the com-
ponents of visual information, but are a visual information in themselves.
If one can read the mystery of the hieroglyph, one finds an entire text
hidden within the symbol—a history indistinguishable from a mythol-
ogy, a religion, a metaphysics, a theory of life after death, the lineage of
kings and queens, the lives of those men and women who were gods even
as they were mortals. The body bears the text—not as explanation but
to present to the livid eye the abundant mystery, if one can but learn to
read it, if one can but happen upon some Rosetta Stone. One senses, if
one is a reader, that a word bears a mystery it always fails in explaining.
A "whale" is one such word, engraved as it is with a language beneath
language, each subsequent depth not explaining the meaning above it,

the shallower meaning it makes possible by its deeper utterance, back ad infinitum, until a first word is seen beneath the two it made possible, and beneath that first word, a blank-dread or the whale's heart, its chambers so large a man could live in a ventricle.

See also:

Chaos
Death
Definition
Etching
Pyramid Line
Scroll
Skin
Spectacles
Writing

HUNGER

Speech reflects desire because speech parallels desire. We learn to speak by asking for that which we do not have; we speak out of the same lack that evokes desire. A word is absence actualized and sent in pursuit, its desirous urgency directly correlative to the empty depths from which the word arises. The deeper the desire the more ferocious the word, until the relationship turns inverse and the words themselves increase desire, dig desire's depth deeper, and enter into the world with an expressive force that finds in no one and nothing a figure of satiety. Language as line of flight rather than line of retrieval. See Ahab. Other desires are but appetite. See Stubb.

~~

Stubb exhorts his crew to pull their oars in most curious tones:

> Start her, start her, my men! Don't hurry yourselves; take plenty of time—but start her; start her like thunder-claps, that's all . . . start her, all; but keep cool, keep cool—cucumbers is the word—easy, easy—only start her like grim death and grinning devils, and raise the buried dead perpendicular out of their graves, boys—that's all. Start her!

He speaks in oppositions, urging them to frenzy and then lulling them to ease. His method of encouragement reflects his own appetitive nature: excess and satiety. Stubb's language—as that of Ishmael and Ahab—also reflects his relation to the whale.

Stubb kills the first whale. That night, after the chase is done, Stubb has Dagoo climb overboard and cut a steak from the "small" of the whale, the area "comprising the tapering extremity of the body." Ishmael notes how the sight of the whale in its absolute massiveness kills most people's appetite, as if the sheer mass of the leviathan ridiculed hunger into nothingness. But some men crave the whale, carve it up. The taste of the whale is rich past most men's tolerance, but some men hunger after the taste of it. Stubb is such a man.

Stubb wakes the cook, Fleece (who is ninety years old by his own recollection), to ask him to prepare the whale steak. Fleece brings it to him, and Stubb commences to eat beneath the light of two sperm-oil lanterns. Stubb eats whale beneath the whale's own light. Stubb consumes with eyes as he consumes with mouth, he wants to see what he eats as he eats it. One information goes to the mind and another goes to the gullet, and both ends satisfy the same hunger. Stubb doesn't simply want to think of what he eats as he devours it. In him the acts of eating and thinking do not occur separately from one another—for him both thought and food are digestion. This link in Stubb of the mind and the gut, this bringing into conjunction of thinking and appetite, lead him to strangely Platonic reflections of which he speaks, and encourages Fleece to speak, between gorging on the overcooked whale. (All manners aside, Stubb not only speaks with his mouth full, but he speaks then most eloquently. His language is an appetitive language.) Stubb wants to eat to a sermon—but the sermon must be of his own choosing.

The sharks, as always when a whale's carcass is attached to the ship, swim in frenzy, their tails and fins knocking against the boat, tearing mouthfuls of flesh from the whale, tearing the flesh from each others' mouths, raising a hellish din. Stubb asks Fleece to ask the sharks to be quiet, to be civil as they eat:

> "Cook," cried Stubb, collaring him, "I won't have that swearing. Talk to 'em gentlemanly."
>
> Once more the sermon proceeded.
>
> "Your woraciousness, fellow-critters, I don't blame ye so much for; dat is natur, and can't be helped; but to gobern dat wicket

natur, dat is de pint. You is sharks, sartin; but if you gobern de shark in you, why den you be angel; for all angel is not'ing more dan de shark well goberned.

Stubb is satisfied with the general direction of the preaching—the metaphysical matters fill his appetite as quickly as the whale fills his mouth. Fleece's sermon parallels Father Mapple's. Both speak from the elevation of the boat above the water, and both preach to parishioners who listen from the ocean. Whereas Mapple retells Jonah's story, and in doing so speaks to the very difficulty of being commanded to utter divine words and the treachery of one's character when the messenger of those words is of questionable moral worth, Fleece preaches to the appetites of his congregation.

The thought that "shark well governed" is an angel reveals a Platonic understanding of the soul's structure: the appetitive portion of the soul must be governed by the higher order of reason. But Fleece is not exactly a Platonist, and Stubb most certainly is not a Platonist at all. Fleece, at Stubb's bidding, preaches a sermon that reveals humankind and shark-kind as kindred folk, sharing family traits. More than heart's relation to head, what matters in this shark world of ours is the size of mouth to stomach: the means of satisfying hunger. In such a world—and it is not the only possible construction of a world—the mouth spits out words so that the jaw is open for the heaped fork. The world is a use. That use ends hunger. The soul is an appetite, and aches as an empty stomach aches, and is as easily sated. It is a cycle that repeats. Faith is the line that connects mouth to anus. Here, too, the whale is a god.

See also:

Ambergris
Expression
Faith

Fear
Line
Magic
Plato
Profit
Prophet

I / *I* / "I"

Ishmael introduces himself to his readers as a me: "Call me Ishmael." The next time he refers to himself differently: "I, Ishmael, was one of that crew." The latter sentence is a curious construction. To whom else could the "I" refer that would warrant clarifying the pronoun with his name? "Ishmael" draws a line between this I and every other I, or at least attempts to forge such distinction. All say "I," but only one I says "Ishmael." The structure of the sentence confuses, perhaps even denies, such efforts at unique clarification. To say, "I, Ishmael, was one of that crew" calls attention to the failure of I and of Ishmael to refer in the fullest sense to the author narrating our book. "Ishmael" seems spoken next so as to remind the reader who this speaking-I is, or, stranger, to remind himself who he is—for we cannot forget that "Ishmael," given *Moby-Dick's* first sentence, is a self-chosen name, and that the drama of the whole book occurs within the amorphous conflict of proper noun and pronoun merging and separating into, and from, a one who never remains singular. I is a many and a one. I is one of the crew.

One way in which to read the hidden narrative told between Chapter I and Chapter XLI is to see it as the story of a me becoming an I. The grammar itself is telling: an object reversing itself into a subject. Ishmael transforms from one against whom the world, or the force that drives ferociously through the world, has struck, has afflicted and made suffer, into one who acts, who speaks, who thinks. Some wound has been healed that before had driven our narrator to the brink of suicide—or, if not healed, then he, like Ahab, has come to see more importance in his suffering than in ending it (or, unlike Ahab, has found in life's unexpected joys a brightness that limns every darkness). It is telling that Ishmael refers to himself as an I in the chapter that describes both Moby Dick's attributes and the effects on Ahab of his whale-given wound. The complete sentence, and the paragraph it begins, reveals a sort of mystery:

> I, Ishmael, was one of that crew; my shouts had gone up with the rest; my oath had been welded with theirs; and stronger I shouted, and more did I hammer and clinch my oath, because of the dread in my soul. A wild, mystical, sympathetical feeling was in me; Ahab's quenchless feud seemed mine. With greedy ears I learned the history of that murderous monster against whom I and all the others had taken our oaths of violence and revenge.

As Ishmael begins by asserting his absolute individuality, he ends by asserting a strangely porous identity, in which he hears his voice merge into others' and, worse, where his will seems to belong to another. Ishmael begins the paragraph saying "I," and ends it saying *I*. This latter *I* refuses to recognize a boundary by which its own given self maintains an exclusive separation. At a lower level, all *I* threaten the unique self with anonymity—a dwelling in the self in the world that is not egoistic in its nature, as much as this *I* speaks to an existence before ego, in which *I* was simply a region of intensity in a universal substance comprised of many such intensities. This *I* rests, as Martin Buber has it, in "the *a priori* of relation; *the innate You.*" This *I* simultaneously emerges from, and into, distinction, and then sinks back into the widening obscurity of the world the self does not experience, the unseeable world-under-the-world from which all experience must be possible.

～

This *I* participates in others as another self, a wider self, and is unable to draw back into the safety of a definite I. This subjectivity that cannot limit itself to its own mere agency reveals, as Buber has it, that "there are innumerable occasions when I is only an indispensable pronoun, only a necessary abbreviation for 'This one there who is speaking.'" As readers, Ishmael offers us continual reminders—though we can so easily forget the fact—that *Moby-Dick* occurs as a narrative with just such a notion of I. Ishmael speaks as much through the mask of I as he does through the mask of "Ishmael," both of which locate a voice without ever identifying its true nature. His actual *I* speaks from many voices—indeed, speaks for every voice. Just as Ahab's *I* magnetically sways all to his will not by convincing them of his purpose but by merging his self into theirs, so Ishmael listens in on conversations he cannot hear, gains access to private thoughts, grows seemingly and suddenly omniscient, and all while narrating as an I that exists as an *I*. It is by virtue of his *I*, an unspeakable content for it is no content, that we read *Moby-Dick*. Silent-*I* wears a mask of speaking-I.

There is another I aboard the Pequod, one who pronounces, as Buber claims, "the severed I, wallowing in the capital letter." Such a man is Starbuck; he says "I." He objectifies his own subjectivity; he makes of himself a use for him to use; he lacks the humility to suffer the pain of being or becoming a me. For Starbuck does not address himself to the world—he says "I" to the world so the world to him can be of use, of profit. He severs himself from the world as he speaks, for it is only in such severance that he can grasp it, work it, kill it, and turn it into "light."

See also:

Death
Experience
Fear
Hands
Repetition
Savage
Silence
Surplus
Wound
You / Thou

Iconoclasm

Abraham's father, Terah, earned his living by making idols. As sons often were apprentice to the skills of the father, it seems likely that Abraham, or Abram as he then was known, also carved idols. Abram and Captain Ahab share this link. I don't mean to claim Ahab as an Abrahamic figure—nothing could be further from the truth. As much as Abraham is a figure of overflowing loving-kindness, we could claim Ahab as a figure of overflowing anger-hate. If we hold them in relation—not the kind of relation which claims the other as a definitive and opposite endpoint, but rather the kind of relation that holds both Abraham and Captain Ahab in thick dialectical space, the space of living consideration—we can profit by seeing the light one throws upon the other.

Light is one aspect of the essential question. According to midrash, Abram looked up at the sun and thought the sun a god, and looked at the idols in his father's shop and thought them gods, and reached a critical realization that both could not be gods. So Abram destroyed the idols. This destruction of gods, and the sudden breach in polytheistic faith that spurred the action, was the first shattering motion toward a monotheistic religion. Faith found in a hammer. We must imagine, though. We must see the results of the destruction. The stone dust in the air. The sudden vacuum of sound, that silence when the last shard has dropped that seems a greater sonic violence than the sound of violence itself. The explosion of each given god: the unity of the stone broken back into a chaos of fragments. We find within that fragmentation the unavoidable symbol of what the iconoclasm has done: destroyed a means by which one lived and understood that living. The nourishment of life destroyed, not by the nourisher but by the nourished. The sun just a circle of heat in the sky.

Then God's voice came to Abram: "Go from your country and your kindred and your father's house to the land that I will show you." God does not tell Abram where that land is, does not name it. It will be revealed when it will be revealed. As such, this wandering from home, this most absolute of departures, the full and inevitable residue of having destroyed the idols, is not a question of distance, nor a question of time. Rather, it is the necessity, as Avivah Gottlieb Zornberg eloquently points out in *The Beginning of Desire,* of wandering through *tehiya,* or wasteland—not a condition of land at all but the condition of finding no location that is home, because one has no location. This being without marker, without place, without word, this waiting to be told when one is where one is, breaches the boundary line between exterior world and interior self. One cannot break the idol without also breaking the self.

See also:

Ahab
Aleph
Bet
Fear
Idolatry
Letter
Tzimtzum

IDOLATRY

Ahab bears a name whose mythic significance exerts a force on the individual personality—a force of interpretation, of penetration, of fate. Captain Ahab exists within the shadow of King Ahab, that most reviled of Judaic kings, who defiles the Temple with idols. Ahab is a man against whom prophecy is spoken, and I mean so doubly: Elijah foreseeing Ahab's blood being licked up by dogs in his own ill-gotten garden; Gabriel foreseeing the destruction of Ahab's boat by Moby Dick's tail. (Gabriel, in this case, the self-proclaimed incarnation of the eponymous archangel who claims Moby Dick as the embodiment of the Shaker God and prophesies against those who presume to hunt him, repeats, though oppositely, Ahab's nominal crisis.) The point is not to say these prophecies are one, but rather to show in what way they overlap, and, in overlapping, turn paradoxical—for it's only in paradox that we can gain insight into Ahab's relationship with the whale god he chases.

The deepest level of conflict occurs here as deicide. Gabriel claims the white whale as God incarnate; Ahab would kill that very whale, that very God. But the issues of holiness and faith here take a Möbius turn—the surface that looks like faith may be the worst of blasphemies, and the hate toward that same God the deepest faithful conviction. It is here that Ahab's namesake comes to bear. Not only do we have a prophet speaking to a man who kills prophets, but we also have this most infamous of idolaters desiring to kill the creature that the prophet claims as the embodiment of God. Who better than a worshipper of idols—even if the worship occurs only in the inheritance posited in a name one has not chosen for oneself—to destroy the idol?

Idolatry is a false economy: infinity captured in a graven stone. The blasphemy of the idolater arises not from the mere act of representing that which cannot be represented but in the act of defining the infinite in a particular form, a god hung in the Temple. Certainly, creating a graven image, an idol of the infinite, does not harm the infinite itself. The damage occurs in the way a definition removes from living relation our openness to what it is we wish to represent. A formal ambition removes us from source, and we turn to mimetic art in hollow compensation for severing the relation with that infinite source whose nature refuses both image and definition. Accuracy is only a question in the fallen world. Only one who has defiled such mystery (the Essence-behind-the-Veil, as in the Temple) with definition can know how to destroy definition in order to approach mystery again. Captain Ahab turns the cursedness of his name into gift.

It is within such light that Ahab's most famous of speeches needs to be seen again:

> Hark ye yet again,—the little lower layer. All visible objects, man, are but as pasteboard masks. But in each event—in the living act, the undoubted deed—there, some unknown but still reasoning thing puts forth the mouldings of its features from behind the unreasoning mask. If man will strike, strike through the mask! How can prisoner reach outside except by thrusting through the wall? To me, the white whale is that wall, shoved near to me. Sometimes I think there's naught beyond. But 'tis enough. He tasks me; he heaps me; I see in him outrageous strength, with an inscrutable malice sinewing it. That inscrutable thing is chiefly what I hate; and be the white whale agent, or be the white whale principal, I will wreak that hate upon him. Talk not to me of blasphemy, man; I'd strike the sun if it insulted me. . . . *Truth hath no confines.* [Ital. mine]

No more fervent, more violent, nor more beautiful voicing could be given to the nature of iconoclasm. Ahab here, more than anywhere else—and with a sanity that frightens, with a mystical logic that stuns—casts a light in his words that reveals his purpose. What Ahab seeks in the white whale is no ordinary vengeance. He seeks to take revenge, and by taking revenge come again into proximity of the inscrutable mystery that informs the depths—and I do not mean the depths of the ocean (for the ocean is, in this mentality, as is the sun, but a mask as well) but the depths of being, that fecund nothingness out of which appearance emerges and becomes the world.

The idolater is not fooled by the image. He has the strength of the man who can honestly say, "I am a liar." We should note, too, Ahab's comment about the sun. For within the crippling audacity of the statement—and it is in such statements that we make the mistake of seeing Ahab as a monomaniac rather than a holy fool not content with being the fool—that we can understand why Ahab must pursue the white whale and nothing else. It is because the white whale struck him, dismasted him, bestowed on him a crippling wound. One effect of such wound is destruction of the self-idol. Will-to-truth, will-to-power exert no agency against that creature that turns to face its pursuer and in so turning undoes that self in pursuit. The paradox of the destruction of the idol is that the iconoclastic gesture contains a concealed urge to damage the self who wants to accomplish the destruction. To destroy a god is to destroy a conception of the world that explained the world, that made the world livable. The self is shattered when the god is shattered—the wound is simultaneous. The world itself is not what is lost, but a manner of living in the world, a manner of explaining the world to oneself. Definition gives way to shapeless possibility, a return to essence, to anonymity. If a god is an idol, so then is the man who worships that god. Both are shattered in a single stroke. Only by such shattering can a man become, as Socrates has it, "a one and a many."

Ahab, fitting like a cog into his crew, is such a many and such a one: both the broken idol and the idolater that breaks it.

See also:

Chaos
Definition
Dictionary
Etching

Iconoclasm
Paradox
Profit
Prophet
Totem
Vengeance
Wound

IMAGINATION

"The whale has no famous author," says Ishmael. One might think that *Moby-Dick* presents Ishmael's effort to fill that gap, but that would be to misjudge our narrator's basic intent. Ishmael's first attempt to become the whale's famous author, albeit abandoned, is the cetological diction-ary. One of the notable aspects to such an undertaking is that, of all liter-ary endeavors, writing a lexicon is pointedly unimaginative. A definition cannot be a fiction if a dictionary is going to be of use. A dictionary offers the basic units by which any fiction functions—the agreed-upon commu-nity of common meaning. Ishmael says of himself, "I am the architect, not the builder." Our narrator sees himself as putting down the units of a vocabulary so that we might understand an experience of which, without his dictionary, we'd have no possible knowledge—none, that is, save an imaginative one.

As a writer, Ishmael seems extraordinarily wary of the imagination's capacity for distorting the world it brings to light. One of his obsessive concerns in *Moby-Dick* is showing the inadequacies of the depiction of whales in paintings, lithographs, and writing. Hidden within the criticism lurks a vaster critique of imagination. Ishmael sees that imagination leads to error, but he also sees the graver issue, that imagination refuses to ac-knowledge the very error that elicits its activity. The cause that underlies the various representative errors in the depictions of whales is simple: what is being shown remains unknown. The catalyst for much imaginative work is, to quote Keats, the inability of an artist to remain "in uncertainties, Mysteries, doubts, without any irritable reaching after fact & reason." One use of imagination, or one sort of imagination, works by casting light upon a substance whose invisible nature swallows illumination.

The closer one comes to drawing upon experience for representative work, the fewer imaginative errors occur:

On Tower-hill, as you go down to the London docks, you may have seen a crippled beggar (or *kedger*, as the sailors say) holding a painted board before him, representing the tragic scene in which he lost his leg. There are three whales and three boats; and one of the boats (presumed to contain the missing leg in all its original integrity) is being crunched by the jaws of the foremost whale. Any time these ten years, they tell me, has that man held up that picture, and exhibited that stump to an incredulous world. But the time of his justification has now come. His three whales are as good whales as were ever published in Wapping, at any rate; and his stump as unquestionable a stump as any you will find in the western clearings.

It is telling that the actual absence of the sailor's leg speaks to the accuracy of his painted whales, as if the real made nonexistent lends credence to the invisible made visible. The missing leg speaks of experience, and here, accuracy is a measure of proximity to the actual moment of encounter, to the actual life.

But Ishmael's understanding of experience is as complicated as his notions regarding imagination. The very difficulties that mock the completion of any given definition also amaze experience. The invisible denies the eye as deeply as mystery riddles the mind. Experience does not stand in lieu of imagination. Not only does Ishmael claim "the great Leviathan is that one creature in the world which must remain unpainted to the last," he also says that "in a matter like this, subtlety appeals to subtlety, and without imagination no man can follow another into these halls." The whale is a subject that demands but denies experience, a subject that criticizes imagination even as it necessitates it.

Ishmael forces his readers to be wary when imagination operates with too vigorous an activity, when imagination substitutes itself for experience. Likewise, he warns that experience unalloyed by an imaginative depth cannot dredge up the lees of its own most difficult importance. Ishmael says, "You must be a thorough whaleman to see these sights." In part he writes his dictionary in order to allow us to speak as whalemen speak, and so bring us closer to the ability to recognize the world he's writing. More generously, in giving us a whaling language, Ishmael allows us to dismantle our active imagination's refusal to let the unknown remain unknown, and opens instead a receptive imagination. Keats makes a similar point:

> It has been an old Comparison for our urging on—the Bee hive— however it seems to me that we should rather be the flower than the Bee—for it is a false notion that more is gained by receiving than giving—no the receiver and the giver are equal in their benefits— The flower I doubt not receives a fair guerdon from the Bee—its leaves blush deeper in the next spring . . . let us not therefore go hurrying about and collecting honey-bee like, buzzing here and there impatiently from a knowledge of what is to be arrived at: but let us open our leaves like a flower and be passive and receptive—

Imagination here is a passive, a patient capacity. It need not exert itself to make a world, for it trusts the world to arrive—as the bee arrives in the flower—to feed in its resource. Reality sups on imagination.

Such an imagination does not extend vision but receives it—it puts experience to imaginative use. That use reveals overlaps in appearance, meaning, memory—as when Ishmael sees rocks merge into Leviathan butted by the waves of the wind-blown grass—and so makes possible metaphor. Such imagination sees the inherent connection between unlike things, and in revealing their similarity limns the faintest outline of the world that before seemed unapproachable, only evanescent. Experience gives us two names; imagination speaks them into one.

See also:

Accuracy
Chaos
Definition

Experience
Plato
Skin
Soot
Truth
Void

INFINITE / INDEFINITE

The alphabet and the ocean have no discernible limit, but neither extends forever. A limit hovers veil-like before us, obscuring behind it a realm, or the possibility of a realm, into which neither vision nor thought can pierce. The alphabet combines into permutations of letters, some sensible and most nonsensical, too numerous to count, too ponderous to speak, but meaning in language is not infinite. The combinations have a mathematical limit. The alphabet is a number of volumes unknown. The ocean, too, is a volume: depth, height, and width.

It feels reductive and yet is accurate to say the alphabet is Ishmael's realm in the same way that the ocean is Ahab's. Both concern themselves with a pursuit in indefinite realms. Ishmael writes his dictionary of whales, each whale escaping definition. Ahab crosses oceans to find one whale, definite in form. Both seek a blank in an abyss. Ishmael's blank is a page. One can measure a page; one can make a book by counting depth. Ahab's blank is a white whale. One can measure a whale if one can kill it. But one can only accomplish either of these tasks in a world open to such measurements. To be unable to see the limit of any given world or work is different than being in a limitless world, writing a limitless work. Martin Buber says of man in this world:

> He perceives the being that surrounds him, plain things and beings as things; he perceives what happens around him, plain processes and actions as processes, things that consist of qualities and processes that consist of moments, things recorded in terms of spatial coordinates and processes recorded in terms of temporal coordinates, things and processes that are bounded by other things and processes and capable of being measured against and compared with those others—an ordered world, a detached world.

This world, Buber says, that "is somewhat reliable." Ahab and Ishmael, and the men aboard the Pequod, do live in this semireliable world. The ship is blown forward leagues upon the sea. Page upon page builds into a book. But neither of these activities remains solely in the indefinite world of experience, the world in which a horizon retreats but is at an apprehensible distance from the one looking. Both book and boat take part in another world, too:

> Or man encounters being and becoming as what confronts him—always only *one* being and every thing only as a being. What is there reveals itself to him in the occurrence, and what occurs there happens to him as being. Nothing else is present but this one, but this one cosmically. Measure and comparison have fled. It is up to you how much of the immeasurable becomes reality for you. . . . The world that appears to you in this way is unreliable, for it appears always new to you, and you cannot take it by its word. It lacks density, for everything in it permeates everything else. It lacks duration, for it comes even when not called and vanishes even when you cling to it. It cannot be surveyed: if you try to make it surveyable, you lose it. It comes—comes to fetch you—and if it does not reach you or encounter you it vanishes, but it comes again, transformed. It does not stand outside you, it touches your ground; and if you say "soul of my soul" you have not said too much.

It is in this latter world, where one dwells but cannot dwell permanently, that the act of whaling and the act of writing are the same work. There lurks beneath the world of experience the world that forms the possibility of experience but exists outside of it. Not what in us thinks, but what in us allows us to think, what in us makes it possible to be perceiving the world, not simply having the perception of it.

In the deepest promise of the book we sense not a transfer of knowledge from it to us but a joint seeking, a joint pursuit that propels us toward a mystery we seek to understand, a mystery of which we are also an example. The book, in its wisdom, seems soon to vanish into the world it does not speak *of* but speaks *toward*. The whale, too, lives in that deep sphere where, when it rises to take a breath, it seems the condensed form of the infinity from which it sprung. We can suspect that both—when book is closed, when whale dives down—grow diffuse, and return to the infinite world the indefinite one hints at and denies.

A book speaks and a whale breathes, and both seem in their singular activity to mask a silence, a breathlessness, to which they cannot refer but to which they both belong. Ishmael and Ahab intrigue by approaching the vertiginous experience where the indefinite world of surfaces and the infinite world of immeasurable depths collide. Actual evanescence confuses by hiding its reciprocal motion. As the indefinite horizon stretches ever further away, another motion imperceptibly advances—sometimes we dismiss it by thinking the darkness is just night. The book nears the author only as he finishes writing it. It nears him as it escapes. The whale catches Ahab, and then it dives down.

See also:

Classification
Death
Definition
Dictionary
Experience
Line
Nothing/ness
Plato
Reciprocity
Surplus
Wound
Writing
You / Thou

Inscribe

Writing, as Derrida points out in "Plato's Pharmacy," is the *pharmakon*: poison and counterpoison, venom and antivenom, simultaneously. In being spoken, a word may bear relation to the very underpinning of reality that the word attempts to reveal, to bring up from depth, to manifest. Likewise, a word in being written might obscure that relation, might merely come in the semblance of such relation—the written word might come masked, come masking the world which it presents and, in seeming to open the world to our eyes, obscure it in the most maddening of ways. Obscure it by presenting it as itself.

Writing threatens the very world it attempts to express. A defined word tries to totalize that which it refers to: the whale defined as the whale. Language promises a lexical net by which all that exists may be seen—not merely the objects of the world but also the ideas, theories, and beliefs that language objectifies. Language seems to offer us this profound comfort: what you cannot know, what you cannot experience, what you cannot recall is known, experienced, remembered in it. Language says: *I'll remember for you.*

Language seems alive—but we forget it breathes by virtue of our own lungs' breath. We forget language lives by our lending life to it, our expressive intent, our attentive reception. And we often stumble into a terrible reversal, thinking we take from language our life on loan. We substitute reading for experience when we do not read with enough actual attention to read-as-experience. That "actual attention" trusts, indeed, *believes* what it reads, not by virtue of blind faith or so-called open-mindedness, but rather by virtue of an incisive belief whose sharp edge is honed by doubt. One aspect of the *pharmakon* begs us to trust it with its own life, not to interfere, not to break the code, lest in our trespass we so disrupt the world conveyed that we damage it.

Do you, dear reader, want to find a whale? Open a book (says the book).

↝

Plato's critique of Sophistic speech-writing springs from such concerns. The term "speech-writing" fully encompasses the nature of the difficulty. A Sophist writes a speech, arguing as true whatever point he is paid to argue. Who pays for the speech delivers it himself, reciting from memory, reading from page, as if he were himself the author of these words another wrote at his request. Such sophistic activity betrays a basic trust we have when we listen to another person express his or her beliefs: that the words we hear originate in the deep privacy of that speaker's life. The promise in speaking as oneself is that one speaks from oneself. Language breaks the secret of the self. The Sophist, the speech-writer, betrays expression. He gives to another words that aren't his own, and in doing so, lets another speak from within a life that doesn't exist.

The problem is deeper, though, than such speech-writing implies. Every word is written before we write it, every word spoken before we speak it. We who speak and write pretend we control a medium more ancient than us, simply because the words are on our tongue, in our hand. We act as if our primary linguistic existence is as the interpreter and not the interpreted. We think we express our perception in the very words that bring us to our perception, speak of experience in the vehicle of understanding that experience. We think we speak from solid ground—the solid ground of our own lives. But as we speak, a continent becomes a boat, a sentence a plank, and all is afloat.

Socrates relates to Phaedrus this Egyptian myth: Theuth, an old god who invented arithmetic, geometry, astronomy, and dice, also discovered writing. He took writing to Thamus, king of all of Egypt, professing it as a means of giving wisdom and memory to all who used it. Thamus replied:

> In fact this discovery of yours will create forgetfulness in the souls
> of those who learn it, because they will not use their memories;

trusting to writing, their memories will be stimulated from the outside, by external written characters, and they will not remember by themselves, within themselves. And so what you have discovered is not a prescription for memory, but for being reminded. As for wisdom, it is the reputation, not the reality, that you have to offer to those who learn from you; they will have heard many things and yet received no teaching; they will appear to be omniscient and will generally know nothing; they will be tiresome company, having acquired not wisdom, but the show of wisdom.

The difficulty of writing is in its refusal to be located. Language exists in trespass. It moves from the utmost interiority to the utmost exteriority, and for it to function most deeply must enter into the other who is listening or reading. At no point can language be pointed to, at no point can one say, "There it is." To touch a word on a page is to touch nothing at all—a pressure that but ripples the water's surface. The word on the page acts merely as a delay between the author of the word, pulling expression from inchoate thought, and the reader, pulling the word from the page into her own thinking. If there is any counter to the just suspicions of Thamus, and, likewise, of Socrates, it's in thinking that language-as-written momentarily stills an expression that is necessarily in flux, never objectified (though capable of objectification), not defining world but carrying world forth, bearing it, transporting it, making it available to be revealed. And how is it revealed? It's inscribed:

> . . . and whoever thinks that even the best of writings are nothing but a device for reminding those who know of what they know, and that only in principles of justice and goodness and nobility taught and communicated orally for the sake of instruction and inscribed on the soul, which is the true way of writing, is there clearness and perfection and seriousness, and that such principles should be deemed a man's as it were legitimate offspring . . .

To inscribe on the soul seems an impossible paradox. How write, how inscribe, on that which by its nature has no objective existence? The only answer that suffices is that language, the honestly expressed word (spoken or written), transforms as it transitions from the self speaking to the self listening. That this space between self and other is itself alive, not equating self with other, but rather opening a space in which interior and exterior of each given subject is open to language—language which by its nature trespasses through all such boundaries. A word is cast into another as a harpoon is cast into the whale, but when the word is spoken vividly, livingly, lovingly, the honed edge pierces by a wound more profound than physical, and rather than piercing the heart into which it enters instead inscribes upon it a word, and instead of bursting the vessel deepens the bass thrum of its pulsing with wisdom gained, reddens the blood that is your own. Such inscribed entrance is teaching.

See also:

Definition
Etching
Expression
Letter
Reading (Epistemology)
Reciprocity
Tattoo
Tzimtzum
Void
Wound

INSPIRATION

A whale, like a human, has a heart. Its heart is so large a grown man can curl into one chamber and sleep. He would not be cold as he slept, for the whale is warm blooded. The heart pulses and the blood surges through the whole beast. The blood moves through the veins in the whale's lungs and transports oxygen to the muscles. So works our body. The whale's blubber keeps it warm at the ocean's greatest depths. It sounds down until it begins to run out of breath. Then, at depth, the whale pivots, swims upward, and breaches the surface to take a breath. The whale emerges from unfathomable depths to take another breath. Men see her, men take a breath, and then they "sing out!"

See also:

Brain
Breath (Thought)
Classification
Definition
Line
Orpheus

JAWBONE

Ahab chases the whale whose scythelike jaw cleaved his leg and dismasted him. This vengeful pursuit occurs aboard the whaling ship Pequod, a ship most curiously fitted out: "Scorning a turnstile wheel at her reverend helm, she sported there a tiller; and that tiller was in one mass, curiously carved from the long narrow lower jaw of her hereditary foe." The tiller connects to the Pequod's rudder; unlike a wheel that turns the ship in the direction the wheel is spun, a tiller pulled left moves the ship starboard, and pulled right moves the ship to port. The Pequod navigates via an opposition borne out in the strange, almost haunting, symbolism by which the boat maneuvers. A captain who lost his leg to a whale's jaw steers by the very weapon that created the wound.

What guides the Pequod is not merely the endless rage that pours out from Ahab in his woundedness but also the material element that gives direction to that rage, the same element that is, if not the rage's source, then that which opened Ahab's rage into an uncontrollable torrent. The jawbone controls the torrent. It turns Ahab's madness into a vectored, purposeful pursuit. There is a dark and magical thinking present in the tiller, as if Ahab understands that the only way one can pursue the cause of one's damage is by using the cause itself as the means of recovery—as if the wounded man could, by holding the knife that cut him, find again the hand that first held it.

ک

Ahab's leg is carved from a sperm whale's jawbone. Ahab stands upon it and takes observations of the sun. He mutely reckons "the latitude on the smooth, medallion-shaped tablet, reserved for that daily purpose on the upper part of his ivory leg."

Location written on the bone that marks the wound.

See also:

Groin
Pequod
Reciprocity
Savage
Totem
Wound

JOKE

Ishmael, in the chapter after which he describes his first lowering after a whale—a lowering in which the whale was not only lost but the whale boat flooded, lost in the night, and was crushed by the Pequod as it searched for them, almost killing the men before saving them—writes an unexpected judgment:

> There are certain queer times and occasions in this strange mixed affair we call life when a man takes this whole universe for a vast practical joke, though the wit thereof he but dimly discerns, and more than suspects the joke is at nobody's expense but his own. . . . That odd sort of wayward mood I am speaking of, comes over a man only in some time of extreme tribulation; it comes in the very midst of his earnestness, so that what just before might have seemed to him a thing most momentous, now seems but a part of the general joke.

In part, the comedy of the first lowering is that all survived it, and if one can speak of the larger comedy of *Moby-Dick,* it occurs darkly within the Pequod's sole survivor. *Moby-Dick* does open, for its first twenty-one chapters, comically. The book seems structured as an hourglass with the bottom half twice as large as the top. The comic upper half is mined by a thin line of sand that, sifting down through the crisis of the thin neck, becomes tragedy in the lower half. Such is the work of gravity—the cosmic force of comedy and tragedy both. Ishmael's judgment recognizes that he's in the hands of a force—as is the grain of sand—that he cannot control. He recognizes the joke only after he's been revealed as the dupe. Comedy, too, is fate. But unlike the recognition that accompanies tragedy, comic recognition realizes one's lack of importance. No Thebes will fall or be saved. No kingdom is concern. Comic recognition witnesses the tragedy it survives—and the survival becomes the importance.

~

Ishmael's judgment also concerns language. Throughout *Moby-Dick* Ishmael tells puns, most eye-rollingly awful. He speaks a whaling language where it doesn't belong—"With anxious grapnels I had sounded my pocket, and only brought up a few pieces of silver"—and amuses himself, or hopes to amuse us, with the dissonance. Elsewhere he riffs on "blubbering," and the punning list goes on. Ishmael is highly aware of the ways in which certain words are double-faced, meaning one thing while saying another. This nature of language feels sexual, dark, surprising— but rather than lead toward the lecher's double entendre, Ishmael's jokes highlight confusion, doubleness, the frustrated laugh of not being able to say what one means without also saying what one doesn't mean. Ishmael revels in the meaning that occurs in surplus of intention, but, before heading out aboard the Pequod on Christmas Day, his puns only mark and mask his own intelligence. He is a joker who doesn't get the joke. Witness his difficulty with the Spouter-Inn's keeper in getting information about his soon-to-be bedmate:

> "Can't sell his head? What sort of a bamboozingly story is this you are telling me?" getting into a towering rage. "Do you pretend to say, landlord, that this harpooner is actually engaged this blessed Saturday night, or rather Sunday morning, in peddling his head around this town?"
>
> "That's precisely it," said the landlord, "and I told him he couldn't sell it here, the market's overstocked."
>
> "With what?" shouted I.
>
> "With heads to be sure; ain't there too many heads in the world?"
>
> "I tell you what it is, landlord," said I, quite calmly, "you'd better stop spinning that yarn to me—I'm not green."

"May be not," taking out a stick and whittling a toothpick, "but I rayther guess you'll be done *brown* if that ere harpooner hears you a' slanderin' his head."

"I'll break it for him," said I, now flying into a passion again at this unaccountable farrago of the landlord's.

"It's broke a'ready," said he.

"Broke," said I—"*broke,* do you mean?"

"Sartain, and that's the very reason he can't sell it, I guess."

Ishmael's rage, and his retreat to the high tones of the teacherly life he's leaving ashore, as if to browbeat the landlord into plain speaking, results from his inability to get the joke. Ishmael tells puns to reflect his intelligence—but intelligence is of limited worth if it cannot see the world in its doubling and tripling multiplicity of meanings. This simultaneous complexity of meaning—no architecture nor hierarchy in the comic, as in the tragic, world holds—is for kings or fools to know or see. Ahab is such a king. He knows the "little lower layer." Ishmael, sadly, is no fool.

See also:

Ambergris
Cordelia
Fool
Friendship
Prophet
Reading (Doubloon)

JONAH

Jonah rode in the bowels of the whale that swallowed him, as Father Mapple reminds those listening to his sermon, and not in the whale's mouth. To ride in the mouth of the whale connotes a privileged protection within the very locus of oracular power—the God-inspired, God-sent speaker who rides upon Leviathan's tongue. To enter into that mouth only to be swallowed reverses the symbolism. The mouth here does not express but ingests. Jonah journeys to the bottom of the ocean in a whale's stomach because he fled God's command. God's command was to go to Nineveh—and speak.

Mapple's sermon on Jonah extends to greater length than the biblical story itself does. His details fascinate, deepen, reveal something of the man sermonizing. Jonah, aboard the ship on which he's fleeing to Tarshish, lodges himself in the close-aired stateroom he's appointed, and watches the lamp hanging down remain perfectly still while the cabin reels in the wave-tossed boat. "The lamp alarms and frightens Jonah." What Thomas Hooker says of the sinner seems equally to apply to Jonah: "He that hates the lantern for the light's sake, he hates the light much more." Jonah sees in the lamp's perfect stillness the command that likewise hangs perfectly still above him: to go to Nineveh and tell the city to mend its ways lest it be destroyed. No jostling of the world changes the necessity or nature of the divinely illuminating word.

Mapple, with extraordinary narrative vividness, retells the story to the point of Jonah's letting himself be cast overboard, so as to save the ship and the men aboard it, and being swallowed by the whale. Then Mapple pauses: "There now came a lull in his look, as he silently turned over the leaves of the Book once more; and, at last, standing motionless, with closed eyes, for the moment, seemed communing with God and himself." When he speaks, he startles:

> Shipmates, God has laid but one hand upon you; both his hands press upon me. I have read ye by what murky light may be mine the lesson that Jonah teaches to all sinners; and therefore to ye, and still more to me, for I am a greater sinner than ye. And now how gladly would I come down from this mast-head and sit on the hatches there where you sit, and listen as you listen, while some one of you reads *me* that other and more awful lesson which Jonah teaches to *me,* as a pilot of the living God.

The lesson, perhaps, is less evocative than the crisis out of which Mapple speaks—the same crisis he finds within Jonah. The nature of the prophet is to speak. The prophet must speak not his own words but the words that have been given him to say. In the prophet, "self" and "expression" are terms that do not in any normal sense coincide. The prophet does not speak as himself, but through himself. He is a body that contains a voice. His life and experience are a secondary quality to the primary importance of the words that he carries. To not speak, to flee such difficult expression, is to swallow words whose infinite nature threatens to destroy the finite body that contains them. One cannot digest a word, but one can lodge it in the mind and ruminate silently upon it. One can carry in oneself divine proclamation and, in refusing speech, make of one's mind the paradoxical container that can hold in finite space that infinite power which threatens to destroy it. Indeed, the promise of Jonah's words is to "proclaim judgment" upon the wickedness of Nineveh. What is wicked, God destroys; a word may preface awful power.

Mapple ends his sermon on Jonah before Jonah's own tale ends. Mapple seems to signal to his parishioners, among whom (thanks to Ishmael's ears) we must count ourselves, that the moral buried within Jonah is that one must always do the difficult task of speaking words none want to speak. Someone must speak judgment, even in this world, in which "the judge himself is dragged to the bar."

～

Jonah does eventually proclaim against Nineveh—but Nineveh repents. "This displeased Jonah greatly, and he was grieved." Jonah leaves and finds a place east of the city to watch and see what will become of Nineveh. The biblical story continues:

> The Lord God provided a ricinus plant, which grew up over Jonah, to provide shade for his head and save him from discomfort. Jonah was very happy about the plant. But the next day at dawn God provided a worm, which attacked the plant so that it withered. And when the sun rose, God provided a sultry east wind; the sun beat down on Jonah's head, and he became faint. He begged for death, saying, "I would rather die than live." Then God said to Jonah, "Are you so deeply grieved about the plant?" "Yes," he replied, "so deeply that I want to die."
>
> Then the Lord said: "You cared about the plant, which you did not work for and which you did not grow, which appeared overnight and perished overnight. And should not I care about Nineveh, that great city, in which there are more than a hundred and twenty thousand persons who do not yet know their right hand from their left, and many beasts as well!"

There seems to be a darker truth in Jonah, before which Mapple stops. Jonah wants the destruction he prophesies to occur as destruction, and when it does not, he is so grieved he wants to die. His reluctance to speak springs from a different source than his horror at the judgment he will himself announce. His horror arrives from a kind of self-disclosure—not in his abhorrence of what he must say, but in his desire to speak God's judgment. He flees not so much from God (for one understands the impossible paradox of hiding from the omnipresent) as from his own dark self—the self that cannot accept the desire for the judgment's destructive end. Jonah does not flee from the weight of his responsibility to speak so much as from the awful recognition of his desire to speak and so perform. His prayer in the bowels of the whale, his prayer from ocean's bottom, proves as much acceptance of divine responsibility as it does of darkest self-acceptance.

When Jonah finally does speak, and the words he's given work to cause repentance rather than destruction, the self-reckoning he suffered within the belly of the whale comes to naught. He is left with himself in the awful glare of the sun, self-knowing but powerless. He spoke words that were not his own as if they were his own, as if a God-given expression were a self-expression. His voice spoke a voice not his own—though the work of finding words, the choices of diction and syntax, were Jonah's. Such is the maddening complexity of Jonah's relationship to language, and the worm-eaten root of his anguish. His identity becomes infused with a language he must speak but whose power does not, and cannot, belong to him.

See also:

Expression
Faith
Fool
Hero
Justice
Paradox
Prophet
Tongue
Vengeance
Void

JUSTICE

In Lima, Peru, some time after the fateful end of the Pequod but before putting pen to page to tell its story, Ishmael tells a group of men another tale about Moby Dick. The story he tells concerns the courageous lakesman Steelkilt and the bitter, insecure, and base first mate Radney, and "is in substance and its great items" true. Needlessly harassing Steelkilt to perform a menial task after the exhausting work of manning the pumps, and doing so in order to humiliate him, Steelkilt delivers Radney a blow that breaks his jaw, blood gushing from his mouth as from a stricken whale. The captain avoids Steelkilt's outright mutiny, and convinces him, and the men seemingly loyal to him, to enter of their own will the dark hold. Two of those men betray Steelkilt. When he falls asleep the men bind and gag him and call out to the captain. The captain takes no pity on those two men who turned against Steelkilt. Instead, he has all three men hung from the mizzen rigging, and flogs the two turncoats he hung on either side of Steelkilt. Those two men occupy the positions of the thieves so often depicted in Christ's crucifixion. The captain flogs them until they cannot cry out at the lashes, their heads hanging to the side. The captain prepares to strike Steelkilt, who warns him aloud, "If you flog me, I murder you." And then, lowering his voice, he whispers something to the captain, at which the captain steps back, aghast, and does not lift his hand against the mutineer. Radney, face bandaged from Steelkilt's blow, takes the rope and lashes the hanging man. And Steelkilt begins plotting his revenge.

Steelkilt plans on knocking Radney overboard as the mate dozes on his night watch. He has woven a net to hold an iron ball and, when he sees Radney close his eyes while sitting on the bulwark and leaning against the gunwale of the boat, he will swing it around, stove in the mate's head, and cast him into the ocean, that "grave always ready dug."

The instant before Steelkilt, (in order to gain revenge redeem his honor) would kill Radney and so become a murderer (and sully his honor irreversibly), he hears from the masthead the cry of "Whale!" It was as if, Ishmael says, "heaven itself seemed to step in" to intervene. That whale is Moby Dick. They lower the boats, Steelkilt sitting directly behind Radney as the strict hierarchy (animosity no matter) of the whalery requires. Moby Dick turns toward Radney's boat, and, in "a blinding foam that blent two whitenesses together," strikes the boat, knocks Radney (but no other man) out, takes him in his mouth, and dives down. Steelkilt cuts the rope attaching the boat to Moby Dick, and the whale escapes, breaching once more, as if to show the remnants of Radney's red shirt caught in his ivory teeth.

～

Ishmael says: "Gentlemen, a strange fatality pervades the whole career of these events, as if verily mapped out before the world itself was charted." Embedded in such a notion of fatedness is a dark definition of justice. Ishmael sees, and so wants us to see, that Moby Dick's intelligence is darkly guided by bloody justice. We have upon the ocean a whale cloaked in whiteness who accomplishes the work of the Furies and the Fates both.

This justice is not legislative, does not enforce nor avenge a merely human order expressed in merely human laws. This justice extends to the depths of the world; it seeks no simple balance. This is no eye for an eye, nor tooth for a tooth. *Lex talionis* is kinder in its cruelty, for it equates each with each. Here a lashing springs back as death. Justice magnifies, not evens.

Moby Dick—if we believe Ishmael's claim of truth for the story—swims as emissary of a justice decreed by a force none see, but who attends to the world and sentences those who trespass with the harshest of reprisals. Or, more haunting, Moby Dick accomplishes this work himself. In his whiteness he embodies darkest justice—a rightness that has no claim in reason, the ferocious justice of the world's foundation, the dark fate before a story has been told.

See also:

Brain
Fate
Freedom
Letter
Loomings
Other
Surplus
Vengeance

KNOWLEDGE

Mystery retreats before knowledge. Mystery relocates its depth deeper into darkness when knowledge brightens into fact. Whaling as an industry and an experience—as opposed to whaling as an art, whaling as a relation—penetrates into mystery, sails into the uncharted regions of the globe, brings the unseen into knowledge, makes a mark on a map. Ishmael himself makes such bold claims:

> If American and European men-of-war now peacefully ride in
> once savage harbors, let them fire salutes to the honor and the
> glory of the whale-ship, which originally showed them the way,
> and first interpreted between them and the savages. They may
> celebrate as they will the heroes of Exploring Expeditions, your
> Cookes, your Krusensterns; but I say that scores of anonymous
> Captains have sailed out of Nantucket, that were as great, and
> greater than your Cooke and Krusenstern. For in their succorless
> empty-handedness, they, in the heathenish sharked waters, and
> by the beaches of unrecorded, javelin islands, battled with virgin
> wonders and terrors that Cooke with all his marines and muskets
> would not willingly have dared.

Whaling as an industry discovered new territory, laid it open to business, made an enterprise, intrepid as it may be, of the previously unknown.

Whaling's business was light. The islands charted on the maps were read beneath the light of a sperm whale's oil—and so the Bible, and so the poem, and so the book of philosophy. Such light lights the facts, lights what we know of the world, the information that's at hand—knowledge. Martin Buber defines, and despairs of, such knowing:

Knowledge: as he beholds what confronts him, its being is disclosed to the knower. What he beheld as present he will have to comprehend as an object, compare with objects, assign a place in an order of objects, and describe and analyze objectively; only as an It can it be absorbed into the store of knowledge. . . . But knowledge can also be pursued by stating: "so that is how matters stand; that is the name of the thing; that is how it is constituted; that is where it belongs." What has become an It is then taken as an It, experienced and used as an It, employed along with other things for the project of finding one's way in the world, and eventually for the project of "conquering" the world.

The business of whaling is knowledge, and a close reading of "The Advocate" reveals an uncanny parallel between the varying consequences of the American whaling industry—discovery, interpretation, the "liberation" of savage lands—and the objectifying work of knowledge. Knowledge uses relation to seek an end; that end is knowledge itself. To speak from Buber's terminology, knowledge severs relation as the basic connection between an I and a you. Knowledge changes you into it. Knowledge finds fact and turns fact into its tool.

Ahab throws away his tools as he chases the white whale: the quadrant, the log on the line. He wants to pursue, not to know where he's going. Pursuit is a relational activity knowledge may sever. Ahab is no intellect, no scholar on waves, though his intellect is overpowering. He seeks the white whale to gain entrance into that mystery which knowledge by its very nature shuts as undiscoverable. "[T]o the purely spiritual, the intellectual but stand in a sort of corporeal relation." Ahab sees that the mind makes use of facts in the same way the body makes use of an object. An idea is a handle that seems attached to a mystery, but pull upon it and one finds in one's hand a knife or a hammer or a pen. Ahab lets his ideas go. He drops them into the deep.

See also:

Leg (Ghost)

When Ahab drops with too much force from the Samuel Enderby's blubber hook back to the hard planks of his own whale boat, he receives "a half-splintering shock." Ahab fears the ivory leg unsound and asks the carpenter to make him a new one. The carpenter's remarkable utility—he pulls achy teeth, pierces ears, concocts balms—is matched only by his "unintelligence." The carpenter finds the world, and the people in the world, as a material to be worked on, a sort of soulless yet animate wood. His mind, which could have developed inquiringly, "must have early oozed along into the muscles of his fingers." The world is what you grasp—don't ask questions, just fix it. Ahab is a "queer man" to the carpenter, for Ahab is a different man. Ahab alarms him:

Well, then, will it speak thoroughly well for thy work, if, when I come to mount this leg thou makest, I shall nevertheless feel another leg in the same identical place with it; that is, carpenter, my old lost leg; the flesh and blood one, I mean. Canst thou not drive that old Adam away?

Truly, sir, I begin to understand somewhat now. Yes, I have heard something curious on that score, sir; how that a dismasted man never entirely loses the feeling of his old spar, but it will be still pricking him at times. May I humbly ask if it be really so, sir?

It is, man. Look, put that live leg here in the place where mine once was; so, now, here is only one distinct leg to the eye, yet two to the soul. Where thou feelest tingling life; there, exactly there, there to a hair, do I. Is't a riddle?

I should humbly call it a poser, sir.

Hist, then. How dost thou know that some entire, living thinking thing may not be invisibly and uninterpenetratingly standing

precisely where thou now standest; aye, and standing there in
thy spite?

Ahab confirms the rumor that the lost limb still aches, still livingly tingles,
as if it had never been swept from him. Ahab seems to take perverse
pleasure in forcing the materialist carpenter to recognize that reality is
merely convenient when it appears as matter, but that a darker reality
lays as deeply valid a claim to the nature of the world. Ahab doesn't see
the sensation of the ghost leg as a peculiarly cruel trick of the mind, a
lamentable exertion of the psyche that cannot comprehend its own dev-
astation. Ahab sees that the thought of the leg once existent materially
still exists insensibly, and so asserts to the bewildered carpenter that real-
ity also reveals itself nontangibly, and that much of reality does not "re-
veal itself" at all. Another being may be standing "uninterpenetratingly"
where any one of us now stands. Ahab's wound grants him recognition
of the world that no eyes can perceive, no hand grasp. It is not simply
that the severed leg aches as if it were still attached. The fact that a leg
that does not exist still acts upon the nerve affirms the invisible as its own
substantial reality. The gift of damage posits as real the intangible world.
Suffering is its own epistemology.

See also:

Adam
Breath (Thought)
Groin
Hands
Plato
Thought (Ahab)
Truth
Whale (Ghost)

LETTER

When two ships chance upon one another in the midst of the ocean's expanse, they near each other, and, once close enough to speak across the water that separates them, information is exchanged: a gam. Letters, often years in the delivery, are brought up, moldy with age, from the hold and thumbed through. If one should bear the name of a crew member of the other ship, then the mail is delivered—news from home so old it's no longer new, written to a man (husband, father, brother or son) who may no longer be living to receive it (and if alive, no longer the same man).

It so happens that Ahab recalls there is a letter for an officer of the Jeroboam and asks Starbuck to retrieve it. Starbuck returns with a letter "sorely tumbled, damp, and covered with a dull, spotted green mould," a letter of which "Death himself might well have been the post-boy." Starbuck cannot make out the scrawl, but Ahab can. The letter is addressed to Mr. Harry Macey, the very mate that attacked Moby Dick against Gabriel's admonitions, and who by Moby Dick was killed. The letter is put into the split end of a cutting-spade pole, and so delivered across the ocean that separates the two ships. Gabriel, however, refuses to accept the letter. He takes a knife, stabs it through the page, and hurls it back to the Pequod, where it lands at Ahab's feet. Then, at Gabriel's shout, the men take to the oars, and the boat shoots away.

There are curious parallels between the nature of whaling and the nature of the letter. A whale must be cut to become of profit. An envelope must be pierced for its content to be read. Both incisions result in illumination: the former of the very light by which the letter can be read, the latter of the happenings at home. Both are contents caught by a line attached to a nib—a spear at the end of twelve hundred feet of tarred hemp held in a tun in the whaling boat's bow, the pen that dips into the liquid coils of the ink in the ink pot. To mark a page is to wound with sense. In wounding a whale one casts into it a spear that bears the cipher of the man who cast it. The whale is wounded simultaneously by blade and by word.

What profit comes of this wound relates directly to the nature of the I who cast the line into the You. Stubb wounds a whale and eats a steak carved from that whale's tail; his profit is but a temporary satiety to a merely appetitive desire. Ahab stabs a whale and profits nothing. His profit, to be more blunt, is this nothing. The cipher of his name on his harpoon is the attempt to possess that which he wounds, to own it, to speak it, to draw it up above the wave's depths and say, finally, what it is he has hunted. Only Ahab can do this work: the wounded man who seeks to wound. His weapon is his cipher, his initial: an *A* sharpened at the point.

See also:

Death
Expression
Inscribe
Line
Reading (Doubloon)
Reading (Epistemology)
Reading (Water)
Wound
Writing
You / Thou

LIGHTNING

Leaping downward from the dark cloud through the night to ocean or to earth, lightning illuminates as it destroys. Such suddenness of light remains an afterglow in the eye, an echo in the vision that, against the fading fluorescent purple of the strike, makes the surrounding darkness darker. But in that bolt-struck moment, one sees—one sees that one saw. Lightning does not reveal the world it strikes. Lightning strikes the eye with light, and so reminds of its own activity. Lightning reminds us that we see.

When Ahab finally emerges from his quarters, as the Pequod leaves behind its northern climes, his crew sees him for the first time. A certain damage is Ahab's by repute. Peleg warned Ishmael that Ahab stands on one leg his own and one borrowed from a whale's ivory jawbone. But it is not the missing leg that strikes Ishmael as representative of Ahab's damage so much as it is his countenance itself.

> He looked like a man cut away from the stake, when the fire has
> overrunningly wasted all the limbs without consuming them,
> or taking away one particle from their compacted aged robust-
> ness. . . . Threading its way out from among his grey hairs, and
> continuing right down one side of his tawny scorched face and
> neck, till it disappeared in his clothing, you saw a slender rod-
> like mark, lividly whitish. It resembled that perpendicular seam
> sometimes made in the straight, lofty trunk of a great tree, when
> the upper lightning tearingly darts down it, and without wrench-
> ing a single twig, peels and grooves out the bark from top to
> bottom, ere running off into the soil, leaving the tree still greenly
> alive, but branded. Whether that mark was born with him, or

whether it was the scar left by some desperate wound, no one could certainly say.

This scar, gained "not in the fury of any mortal fray, but in an elemental strife," marks the wound from behind which Ahab stares out at his crew and the world. The wound from which this scar emerges is not part of Ishmael's narrative. Ahab was struck before the white whale struck him. This first wound, of which this scar is the only mention (a mark, notably, which some consider Ahab's birthmark), occurred not as a result of any "mortal fray"—be it with a whale or be it with another man—but rather from contact with the world. Ahab has been struck by lightning.

The scar that runs down his body from head to toe is the crooked, burnt line of the bolt coursing through him to the ground. Through Ahab, the power of the storm surged. He stood between heaven and earth and suffered the electric communication by which the upper sphere speaks to the lower. We cannot claim with any certainty Ahab—with the idolater king his namesake—as a prophet, but there exists no meager significance in Ahab as a figure that (willingly or unwillingly) mediates between different worlds. One doesn't suffer heaven's lowering strike to earth without likewise being afflicted by the power of that passage. Ahab is conduit and witness to powers that have almost destroyed him. He has suffered a strike from above him, and he has suffered a strike from below. Ahab is the pivot between the depths and the heights, and he bears upon his body the scars that tell of both. There is a holiness about him that merges into horror. He sees as a man who has seen that which belongs to no mortal eyes to know. He looks out from behind the lightning's beam. The scar is lightning white at his brow and at his throat.

See also:

Corpusants
Death
Flame

Jonah
Idolatry
Omen
Prophet
Storm
Wound

LINE

A meditation on the line:

> The whale line is only two-thirds of an inch in thickness. At first sight, you would not think it is so strong as it really is. By experiment its one and fifty yarns will each suspend a weight of one hundred and twenty pounds; so that the whole rope will bear a strain nearly equal to three tons. In length, the common sperm whale-line measures something over two hundred fathoms. Towards the stern of the boat it is spirally coiled away in the tub, not like the worm-pipe of a still though, but so as to form one round, cheese-shaped mass of densely bedded "sheaves," or layers of concentric spiralizations, without any hollow but the "heart," or minute vertical tube formed at the axis of the cheese. As the least tangle or kink in the coiling would, in running out, infallibly take somebody's arm, leg, or entire body off, the utmost precaution is used in stowing the line in its tub. Some harpooners will consume almost an entire morning in this business, carrying the line high aloft and then reeving it downwards through a block towards the tub, so as in the act of coiling to free it from all possible wrinkles and twists.

The line is "slightly vapored" with tar, which makes it compact, glossy, and dark.

The line is loose on both ends. If a whale was struck and dove past the length of the line, and the line was attached to the boat, the boat would lunge into the depths and be destroyed.

⁓

> Before lowering the boat for the chase, the upper end of the line
> is taken aft from the tub, and passing round the loggerhead there,
> is again carried forward the entire length of the boat, resting
> crosswise upon the loom or handle of every man's oar, so that
> it jogs against his wrist in rowing; and also passing between
> the men, as they alternately sit at the opposite gunwales, to the
> leaded chocks or grooves in the extreme pointed prow of the
> boat, where a wooden pin or skewer the size of a common quill,
> prevents it from slipping out. . . . Thus the whale-line folds the
> whole boat in its complicated coils, twisting and writhing around
> it in almost every direction.

⁓

When the harpoon strikes the whale, the whale sounds. The line speeds down with the whale at a speed that will sever a whaler's limb caught in a loop, or cut his skin as with a knife should it glance against the line.

⁓

The line is kept cursive in a tub as ink is kept fluid in a pot. When the line is attached to a nib, and the nib pierces its mark, the line quickens and grows taut.

⁓

The line connects one to what one wants. The whaler wants the whale. When the line is in the whale, the whale flees. The tar-dark line allows the whaler, once the whale has spent all his energy, to bring the boat to the body. But if the whale gains furious momentum enough, it empties the tub of line and escapes into fathomless depths. By the line we know when we're attached to what we desire, and by the line we know when what we desire has escaped.

~

The line is the most basic unit of verse. A poem is a line winding from margin to margin until the poem is done. A book is composed of dark lines. A book pursues in lines the meaning it desires to understand or convey. A metaphoric stretch can claim for the poetic line the same dangers as the whale line. The reader and the whaler are in the same boat.

~

Euclid: "A *line* is breadthless length."

~

Emerson: "Every opinion reacts on him who utters it. . . . It is . . . a harpoon hurled at the whale, unwinding, as it flies, a coil of cord in the boat, and, if the harpoon is not good, or not well thrown, it will go nigh to cut the steersman in twain or to sink the boat."

~

Etymology: a linen thread.

~

Ahab to the carpenter: "Dost thou spin thy shroud out of thyself?"

~

The white whale is found upon the Season-on-the-Line.

~

The carpenter on Ahab: "He's always under the line—fiery hot, I tell ye!"

~

Every book, unlike every whale hunt, ends in silence. The line runs out and becomes blank.

~

"All men live enveloped in whale-lines."

See also:
Etching
Expression
Inscribe
Loomings
Skin
Tattoo
Writing

Loomings

Moby-Dick opens in a double equivocation. "Call me Ishmael" forces the reader to trust Ishmael even as the reader distrusts him. Above that sentence sits: LOOMINGS. The word initially connotes the brooding weight of events to come. "Loomings" give us a dark anticipation, oddly heightened by the nominal subterfuge of *Moby-Dick*'s first sentence. This foreboding feeling that nothing to follow will obey the most basic rules of sense and reference—as Ishmael commands us to call him by a self-chosen name and, in so doing, erases, or condemns to meaningless, an unheard name which is his given one—appears first in the pun hidden within "Loomings."

"Loomings" also refers to the weaver god's fateful activity. Ishmael claims for himself, and his choice to go whaling, a degree of free will and free choice he doesn't believe in. His travels oceanward are fated activity—and any philosophical stance, any explanatory reason for doing as he does, fails to explain the nature of his compulsion.

Ishmael does make a choice in going whaling. He chooses not to choose. In doing so, he gains a sensitivity to the workings of the world that few others can claim. Ishmael takes care to note that all people are impelled to gaze out at the ocean. Ishmael claims a narcissistic urge guides us all unconsciously to the sea. In the reflection of our face on water we seem to see the vast secret of our own lives. The consequence of trying to grasp this self-secret is drowning, is death.

Of course, Narcissus tried to kiss and embrace his own reflection out of a misconstrued Eros capable of loving only himself—and so Echo languished, her would-be lover's words still in her mouth. Ishmael, though, considers the ocean a meditative mirror—different than the erotic, though just as dangerous. Such a mirror does not reflect self back to self purely, but allows one to see through one's face into the depths. If we learn to see not ourselves, but through ourselves, then the pivotal mystery of the ocean discloses itself. Ishmael sees how the ocean simultaneously alludes to an infinity out of which all being arrives and an infinity into which all being dies. He sees behind his face the infinite crisis that condenses into a single point his birth and his death—but, as in Euclid's definition, it is a point that has no part. The singular moment of seeing one's face afloat on the water's surface—half-transparent, a single point, a pip on infinite expanse—marks the self as a point through which infinity is glimpsed. To say "I," for Ishmael, is both to recognize this infinite existence as well as to be unwoven by it.

↩

Looking up from one's reflection, one sees the ocean spread out across the horizon—a horizontal infinity opposed to the murkier, darker, vertical one. A ship can travel toward the horizon, chasing the evanescent line, but to travel into depths requires destruction. In looking up, as those people standing with him at the wharf look up, Ishmael sees the waves rolling in. But unlike those around him, Ishmael sees how the waves cresting mimic the shuttle emerging from beneath the weave; he sees how the wave rolling under the wave incoming is the shuttle diving beneath the warp again. Ishmael hears in the shushing waves the mortal music of the weaver god's art.

The ocean, for all who feel compelled to gaze into it, shows in each reflected face the single stitch each individual life adds into all lives, those individual fates of which the fated have no sight except themselves, except their eyes staring back into their eyes, and so promising us we exist. Such is the music of the loom: the water pushed up onto the strand, and the water drawn back to the ocean. One cannot choose against fate, as none can gain a height by which the whole weave is seen. We see ourselves, and not our position in the whole. To say we see ourselves is not quite accurate: we see from the position of being ourselves. The eye isn't included in its own vision. We may know those next to us; we may know the events on either side of the little event that is our own life, but we know little else.

The whale rising above the waves to breathe and diving below the waves to live is God's shuttle. Ishmael, like Ahab, wants to find the whale because he senses the whale is closer to the source of mystery of which he, too, is an example. What voyage is not a voyage of fate? The whale leaves a white wake behind him as he swims, a white line we follow him by. We chase a white thread in the loom, and so chase the God who pushes the swift shuttle through.

See also:

Child
Death
Fate
Fool
Infinite / Indefinite
Ocean
Omen
Quest / Question
Reciprocity

MAGIC

Ahab does not fully believe in his ability to carry out his revenge by his own power. Ahab suspects his own will is not enough to carry out his desire. The underside of his belief in his strength is a dark recognition of his mortal weakness. He suspects this weakness because the white whale who wounded Ahab and, in wounding him, granted Ahab his mystic strength, also smote him, dismissed him, and wove Ahab's power into Ahab's harm. So he smuggles on board a devilish crew that radiates occult power, dark magic. Ahab wants to secure his success against his own limits, and so he seeks a magical means. Ahab stows away Fedallah, who "might have been an authority over" the captain himself, not for help of muscle or mind but for Fedallah's Mephistophelean power.

Ahab himself works magic—magnetizing his mates with his "energy," baptizing his harpoon in savage blood. Ahab seeks a means beyond himself to avenge the loss of his leg to Moby Dick. It might be disingenuous to claim Ahab's leg as a sacrifice: he did not offer it willingly, nor did he offer it in worship. Martin Buber furthers the distinction:

> What distinguishes sacrifice and prayer from all magic? Magic
> wants to be effective without entering into any relationship
> and performs its arts in the void, while sacrifice and prayer step
> "before the countenance," into the perfection of the sacred basic
> word that signifies reciprocity. They say You and listen.

Ahab does not say "You" and listen. Nor does he work within the counter-gaze of the white whale's countenance. Ahab chases after the whale and fears, it seems, that when the white whale turns around again to face his pursuer in the squall of reencounter, his power will fail him. Ahab wants magic as a means of success, as a proof, as a guarantee that his revenge can be accomplished. Such magical desire may be his only weakness. Ahab diminishes himself. He seeks magical means to gain an end to a relation that has no end, a pursuit that covers the circumference of the globe but of which miles are but an incidental quantity, for in the ongoing, painfully living relation Ahab is immersed in with the white whale, nothing is commensurable. In Ahab's actual world, in his actual life, in the actual source of his own power that cannot be called "magical," there is no motion, no beginnings, no ends. There is only the indefinite reality that stretches into infinity—or might, or seems to. Ahab's mistake, which leads him to seek the guarantee of Fedallah's magical influence, is a misunderstanding of his place in the world. He seeks outside of himself that which he cannot see because it is nearer to him than he is to himself.

Ahab finds himself caught in the torment of being within a primordial relation he cannot control without severing. He is, as is his leg, lost in the white whale, and the unbounded hate he expresses toward Moby Dick speaks of the unbounded power of the relation. Rather than destroying in Ahab his capacity for living, for recognizing the actuality of the world and his wounded existence in the world, Moby Dick grants Ahab access to reality. What is most horrific in Ahab is not his madness, his boundless hate, but his refusal to dwell in the actuality of the world. For him all appearance is a mask he must strike through in order to find the unseen axis of the world, the face behind a face, the agency behind all action, all being. It is heroic work, but damning. As Ahab discards the comfort of his pipe on the outset of the voyage, so he has dismissed himself from every innate pleasure and beauty the world offers as its daily manna to those who attend to it. He is, as Buber would have it, "a subject that annuls the object to rise above it," and in doing so, "annuls [his] own actuality."

Ahab seeks contact in order to destroy what he grasps, believing that only by plunging through surfaces will he arrive at the force that *informs* surface, whose dark existence gives surface shape. This is not to say he seeks God, or seeks to kill God, for such a word is meaningless to Ahab. God is another surface, another description; *god* is another word. What

Ahab does not feel is the actuality of his own life, the mortal spot that, in threatening entirely, Moby Dick also opened. Ahab bears the livid wound, but will not see it so. His lack of belief in the world is a symptom of more intimate doubt—a failure to believe in the actuality of himself, the primary reality of his own being, his own capacity to say "I." "Is Ahad, Ahad?" Ahad asks.

See also:

Hero
Hunger
Imagination
Knowledge
Leg (Ghost)
Magnet
Omen
Reciprocity
Totem
Wound

MAGNET

Ahab must convince his crew to cast their power toward his mad pursuit else he has no chance to succeed in it. He does not argue his point, but he makes his case explicit. He walks upon a dead leg—that dreadful wound delivered by Moby Dick. But Ahab does not use his leg to spur sympathy in others, or speak of his pain to rationalize his aim and so explain and give grounds for his crew to join his cause. He speaks them into recognition—"that white whale must be the same that some call Moby Dick," Tashtego says—and then he exerts his force. The result of that force speaks to its nature: "my one cogged circle fits into all their various wheels, and they revolve." The image by which Ahab reflects on his crew's willingness to join him in his vengeful chase should not be mistaken for an overtly mechanical one. The force beneath the cog that drives the gear and so drives the whole intermeshed engine is the deeper concern.

Ahab's mystic aspect pulls upon the crew, and even those who might want to resist, such as Starbuck, find little power in themselves to do so. As Ahab watches the sun set after exposing his purpose to his crew, as he thinks that "[t]he path to my fixed purpose is laid with iron rails, whereon my soul is grooved to run," Starbuck simultaneously thinks about the fateful momentum. Starbuck says to himself: "I think I see his impious end; but feel that I must help him to it. Will I, nill I, the ineffable thing hast tied me to him; tows me with a cable I have no knife to cut." The question of Ahab's force, which is also the question of how his deepest nature manifests itself in the world and so on others, must reckon with the cable no knife can cut. Emerson offers help in "Nominalist and Realist":

> The genius is all. The man, it is his system: we do not try a
> solitary word or act, but his habit. The acts which you praise, I
> praise not, since they are departures from his faith, and are mere

compliances. The magnetism which arranges tribes and races in one polarity is alone to be respected; the men are steel-filings. Yet we unjustly select a particle, and say, 'O steel-filing number one! what heart-drawings I feel to thee! what prodigious virtues are these of thine! how constitutional to thee, and incommunicable.' Whilst we speak, the loadstone is withdrawn; down falls our filing in a heap with the rest, and we continue our mummery to the wretched shaving. Let us go for universals; for the magnetism, not for the needles.

Ahab's genius works magnetically. It is not the instance of his injury, the fact of his purpose that sways his crew, but the habitual force of his "demoniac . . . madness maddened" that exerts itself upon the iron filings that are the Pequod's whalers. Starbuck cannot cut the rope because the rope is a universal force and not a particular one, a magnetism and not a needle. Ahab is a mystic physicist. He knows that a magnet of great power magnetizes the metal brought near it—aligns the compass of each individual purpose to the larger force of his own. A needle spinning round in its case is one vision of a gear; the force that drives the inter-meshed cogs of the Pequod is Ahab's electromagnetic force.

Ahab accomplishes his remagnetizing in a ceremony to dedicate the crew to his revenge. All drink. Then he has his three mates cross their lances before him, and grabs them at the axis point at which all three cross, and glances into the eyes of each: "It seemed as though, by some nameless, interior volition, he would fain have shocked into them the same fiery emotion accumulated within the Leyden jar of his own magnetic life." He shocks them with his own "electric thing"—not fully, not so that each could, by being born of Ahab's force, threaten to lessen his own maddened charge—but he shocks them enough to stand them in a line whose magnetic tug pulls through them all. When Stubb ponders the event, his new purpose, he signs it over to fate and worries not a jot: "that unfailing comfort is, it's all predestined." For those iron filings caught in the larger magnet's tow, magnetism is a form of fate.

See also:

MINCER

A Writing Parable

To write, a writer needs paper and light. Paper, too, can be burned for light. Form is also fuel. The whalers are in the business of light. To make light they make oil. They burn the oil from the blanket-pieces of blubber they unscroll from the whale. The thinner the blubber is cut, the more oil extracted. The mincer is the man who cuts the blubber. The crew shouts to him as he does so, "Bible leaves! Bible leaves!" so he remains mindful of the thinness desired. To light pages he makes pages. These pages might both be holy. He dresses in black. The raiment in which he cuts the whale comes from the whale—the skin removed from the phallus of the whale being burned. He dresses in creation to destroy.

See also:

Flame
Groin
Scroll
Writing

NOTHING/NESS

The knife, the lance, the harpoon, the pen's nib, the sperm whale's and the shark's scythe-sharp tooth, do not create the wound they inflict. The wound is created by the space the cutting implement opens. The nature of the wound, and the suffering it causes, comes from the breach created within physical matter. The wound opens a space on the body through which life leaks. The wound prefigures death not simply by causing the bearer of the injury pain, and through pain, recognition of one's mortality. That one can be breached doesn't link, necessarily, to the thought that one can be broken entire. The wound opens to death in a different, more troubling manner. What wounds in the wound is Nothing.

The wound parallels on a metaphysical plane the correspondence of individual human life and the universe. Whereas the cosmic order through which nature thrives is coined by the human order, the wound relates to Nothing. This Nothing does not deny cosmos, nor does it deny the human moment of any single life—but it makes impossible the limit of that cosmos, the limit of that life. The wound that is the presence of Nothing brought into proximity with life forces the wounded to cringe toward awareness of the impossibility of grasping, recognizing, considering one's own death. Death opens out into the Nothingness it contains. Death has no horizon, unless one can call Nothing a horizon. As Levinas writes:

> The unforeseeable character of the ultimate instant is not due to an empirical ignorance, to the limited horizon of our understanding, which a greater understanding would have been able to overcome. The unforeseeable character of death is due to the fact that it does not lie within any horizon. It is not open to grasp.

We sense, and fear as we sense, that we are open to death's grasp in a way that we could never grasp conceptually. One can feel, as Ishmael felt as a child, that nothingness in the night may gain presence and take you by the hand, may come to know you, to hold you within its phantom spell—or, more terrifying because more real, that out of the Nothing death opens, the Other who "is situated in the region from which death . . . comes" arrives.

Moby Dick, to Ahab, is one such Other. The wound inflicted by the white whale unto Ahab has opened the world—for captain and so for crew—into a horizonless Nothing ringed by an equatorial line. It is out of this Nothingness, this death-opened region, this impossible-to-know realm that is always (for each and all) out of reach, that the Other arrives—untouched by the wound that touches us, perhaps the bearer of the next wound that will end us.

But there is a work to do within Nothingness. Not the work of pursuit: Ahab's vengeance that seeks to add to Nothingness a Nothingness, Ahab's desire to wound the Wound. There is also Ishmael's work—the work of expression, which is to say, the work of putting a world within the open space Nothing creates. That world posits against Nothingness actual meaning—not, perhaps, universal meaning, or universal only as accident, but meaning that occurs between an I-that-speaks and a you-that-listens. As Heidegger says of it, "The work holds open the open region of the world." That open region is also a wounded region, is also a region wound opens. But in its unaccountable, unspeakable nature, in its deathly impossibility, lurks the bright necessity of founding a world in which one can speak—and when one speaks, one speaks of life. Located within Nothing's deathly looming is the same unspeakable mystery birth shocks us with. One senses in Nothing a beginning as inexplicable as the end one suspects one is nearing. Ishmael's work, which is the work of *Moby-Dick* itself, is to hold open the Nothingness Ahab is both maddened by and pursues. The world, if we risk imagining it as such, is but a weight that holds open the facing leaves of a lengthy book whose every page is blank.

See also:
Chaos
Death
Dictionary
Expression
Hands
Inscribe
Other
Paradox
Truth
Tzimtzum
Void
Whiteness
Wonder
Wound

Ocean

For Ishmael, the ocean is "substitute for pistol and ball." When he suffers to the point of seeing as affliction's solution murder of self or other, he travels to the coast and signs himself aboard a ship. He claims he is not alone: "Posted like silent sentinels all around the town, stand thousands upon thousands of mortal men fixed in ocean reveries." And further: "Nothing will content them but the extremest limit of the land; loitering under the shady lee of yonder warehouses will not suffice. No. They must get just as nigh the water as they possibly can without falling in. And there they stand—miles of them—leagues." Ishmael claims the ocean reverberates mystically in every human. The endless water attracts us to it as a mighty magnet attracts a single iron filing, and countless others follow the invisible, inevitable path, until a further step requires a vessel or a death.

This meditation on water provides—as difficult as the half-sarcastic tone makes it to identify the seriousness of the thinking—the first philosophical depth *Moby-Dick* explores. The ocean prefigures in its symbolic complexity the difficulty of the book to follow. It is astonishing enough to equate a bullet and an ocean. Both are lethal. To hold a bullet in the palm of one's hand requires a mortal thought in the same way standing on the edge of the ocean must. The end of each is our end. But unlike a bullet, the ocean's symbolism includes origin, includes birth. A hand can form a fist around a bullet, hide it from the eye, put it in a pocket, cast it away in disgust. A hand can cup an ounce of ocean in the palm, but close your hand around it and nothing is left—save the immeasurable volume from which the drop was uselessly pulled. A bullet gives us one end; the ocean gives us beginning fused inescapably to end, origin and obliteration, and none can cipher one extreme out from the presence of the other.

One looks at the ocean in two ways. First, as Peleg responds to Ishmael's desire "to see the world" as his reason for signing for a lay on the Pequod. Peleg tells Ishmael to go and "take a peep over the weather-bow":

> Going forward and glancing over the weather bow, I perceived that the ship swinging to her anchor with the flood-tide, was now obliquely pointing towards the open ocean. The prospect was unlimited, but exceedingly monotonous and forbidding; not the slightest variety that I could see.

The ocean ends, like life and vision, at a horizon that is the fault of the curvature of eye and earth, with no proof of true end at all. The ocean seems indefinite. It presents the eye with a line that is an illusion. We linger on its shores, or live on its surfaces, but never have a means of encompassing the whole. As such, and this point is Peleg's nauseating "joke," a single drop is as endless as all. The world is the world regardless of where you stand, and experience of the indefinite realms offers nothing to vitalize the would-be philosopher's meager thoughts, for in such an ocean as the Pequod sails upon, to move anywhere is to move nowhere—the profound Nowhere—at all.

But one also moves one's eyes from the horizon and looks down: "And still deeper the meaning of that story of Narcissus, who because he could not grasp the tormenting, mild image he saw in the fountain, plunged into it and was drowned. But that same image, we ourselves see in all rivers and oceans. It is the image of the ungraspable phantom of life; and this is the key to all." Water offers to us our own reflection, but not as mirror does. We see our own face on the surface of the water, but we see through our face the depths below. The image horrifies because it links together self and the chaos from which, and into which, self dissolves. The moment of seeing one's reflection on the water pinpoints human life as a single recognizable instant pivoting precariously between two opposite oblivions: the fecund source and the blank end. We see through our own face that we are composed by possibilities wider, stranger, darker, more mysterious, than we can define by simply saying of ourselves: "I." We are composed more of what we do not know, and can never know, than we are built of *terra cognita*. To look over the weather bow, or to gaze in the pond, forces us to realize that our definition expands past the horizon of our knowledge. One grows dizzy enough to drown.

ᴗ�___

Friedrich Nietzsche, *Beyond Good and Evil*:

> . . . does one not write books precisely to conceal what one harbors? Indeed, he will doubt whether a philosopher could *possibly* have "ultimate and real" opinions, whether behind every one of his caves there is not, must not be, another deeper cave—a more comprehensive, stranger, richer world beyond the surface, an abysmally deep ground behind every ground, under every attempt to furnish "grounds." Every philosophy is a foreground philosophy—that is a hermit's judgment: "There is something arbitrary in his stopping *here* to look back and look around, in his not digging deeper *here* but laying his spade aside; there is also something suspicious about it." Every philosophy also *conceals* a philosophy; every opinion is also a hideout, every word also a mask.

When the whaler-philosopher, unlike the hermit-philosopher, lays aside his tool, it rests against no ground. It falls down with the man as he drowns.

See also:
Chaos
Death
Infinite / Indefinite
Loomings
Storm
Truth

OMEN

An Ominous Series of Events Culminating in "The Chase—First Day"

A tempest squalls up from the east, the direction in which Ahab seeks Moby Dick. The west-blowing gale would send them fleetingly homeward.

The high-rolling, storm-frenzied sea breaks through Ahab's whaleboat.

The corpusants palely burning on the mastheads.

The compass needles spinning in circles.

The storm's electric current reversing the polarity of the compass needle. East reversing into west.

The log snaps from the line. No method remains to calculate the Pequod's location. The ship is but where it is. The ship without reference.

A sea hawk, when Ahab is aloft scanning the expanded horizon for the white whale's spout, snatches Ahab's hat in its red beak and, flying afar, drops it in the ocean.

Sighting Moby Dick, earning the doubloon at his own singing out, Ahab lowers. Moby Dick catches the captain's whale boat in his mouth and bites it in two, casting Ahab into the waters. Ahab is a single point afloat, his head "like a tossed bubble which the least chance shock might burst." Then the white whale swims concentrically around him, a malicious planet nearing the soaked star it orbits.

～

The two mates, once all are saved, comment:

> Stubb saw him pause; and perhaps intending, not vainly, though,
> to evince his own unabated fortitude, and thus keep up a valiant
> place in his Captain's mind, he advanced, and eyeing the wreck

exclaimed—"The thistle the ass refused; it pricked his mouth too keenly, sir; ha! ha!"

"What soulless thing is this that laughs before a wreck? Man, man! did I not know thee brave as fearless fire (and as mechanical) I could swear thou wert a poltroon.

Groan nor laugh should be heard before a wreck."

"Aye, sir," said Starbuck drawing near, "'tis a solemn sight; an omen, and an ill one."

And Ahab rebuts his first mate:

"Omen? omen?—the dictionary! If the gods think to speak outright to man, they will honorably speak outright; not shake their heads, and give old wives' darkling hint.—Begone! Ye two are the opposite poles of one thing; Starbuck is Stubb reversed, and Stubb is Starbuck; and ye two are all mankind; and Ahab stands alone among the millions of the peopled earth, nor gods nor men his neighbors!"

~

Ahab's world is not some cipher-filled medium begging translation. What can be read reveals itself to be read. What is spoken can be heard. But Ahab's world—his ocean world, his "earthquake life"—in which he has spent but three years on land in the last forty-four, is blank, is silent. On one side of him is all humanity: men and women who either laugh at the impenetrable fact of the world or see inside fact a mystery to be translated, an omen, a hint. Such humanity cannot let the intangible, the illegible, the silent, the blank, become real, for such aspects of the world seem "to remove the thing which elemented it." The other half, the godly powers to whom our tangible world must seem but a shadow of their intangible one, say nothing. They inform form, empower power—and then withdraw.

Ahab believes, but he believes defyingly, that should the gods speak, they will speak so we can hear them. We will not need a book to translate. The world is not exegetical. We will not guess at revelation as we would at mystery. "The 'supernatural' was only the natural disclosed," Emily Dickinson says. Ahab might agree; more likely, Ahab might reverse the terms. He is not content to wait for disclosure. The chase forces the point. Patience, for Ahab, is not reverence but cowardice, or akin to cowardice. One must work to listen. To listen, one must circumnavigate for a year the whole world. One must return to a point. Such is the experiential grammar that undergirds the widest world's sense.

See also:

Corpusants
Cosmogony
Dictionary
Fate
Idolatry
Jonah
Loomings
Reading (Doubloon)
Reading (Epistemology)
Reading (Water)
Storm

Orpheus

Ahab and Orpheus share a work. Orpheus descends into the underworld's dark night to sing back to daylight his beloved Eurydice. Ahab sings no song—save when sighting the white whale he "sings out." Ahab rescues no beloved. But Ahab, too, desires descent. The nature of his work is inspired by the same lowering motion whaling enacts.

Orpheus sings and fascinates the night, in which Eurydice, as Maurice Blanchot writes, "with her closed body and sealed face," follows him. The song is the work she follows, the desired following desire back to daylight, releasing her from the nameless, "nocturnal obscurity" of her deathly living. Orpheus turns to see if she follows, wanting to see with his eyes what he accomplishes in song, and, in betraying his song, loses both Eurydice and his own life. The finite pull of the song, whose power is in its singing, is pulled under by the infinite night and silenced. Blanchot warns us not to judge this failure:

> But not to turn toward Eurydice would be no less untrue. Not
> to look would be infidelity to the measureless, imprudent force
> of his movement, which does not want Eurydice in her daytime
> truth and her everyday appeal, but wants her in her nocturnal
> obscurity, her distance, with her closed body and sealed face—
> wants to see her not when she is visible, but when she is invisible,
> and not as the intimacy of a familiar life, but as the foreignness of
> what excludes all intimacy, and wants, not to make her live, but
> to have living in her the plenitude of her death.

The Eurydice that follows Orpheus's song is not the same Eurydice he lost. Song cannot recover what was as it was; song recovers impatiently what has suffered change; song desires to disclose that change and, in bringing it to light, claim responsibility for it. Song impatiently wants to be the mystery of which it sings.

> Orpheus's error seems then to lie in the desire which moves him to see and to possess Eurydice, he whose destiny is only to sing of her. He is Orpheus only in the song: he cannot have any relation to Eurydice except within the hymn. He has life and truth only after the poem and because of it. He loses Eurydice because he desires her beyond the measured limits of the song, and he loses himself, but this desire, and Eurydice lost, and Orpheus dispersed are necessary to the song, just as the ordeal of eternal inertia is necessary to work.

The inspired moment, claims Blanchot, is not revealed in the song itself, or some futile measure back against desire's own force to guess at what caused the song to be sung—the inspired moment is when Orpheus turns around and, in turning around, betrays his own gift, betrays his love, betrays the inscrutable night and the face that stares out at him from its depths. The song no longer promises compensation for the work of singing it. For such words there is no reward, not even the reward of the having had done it, the base comfort of the perfect past tense. In turning around, in wanting more than the song being sung can by its own beauty realize, Orpheus "encloses within the song what surpasses the song." For all song, even those wordless melodies that speak more distinctly, more realistically (for in music reality seems wider than words know how to show) than any word could ever accomplish, fills itself with the content of its utterance, its own humming content, its tune.

> Orpheus's gaze is Orpheus's ultimate gift to the work. It is a gift whereby he refuses, whereby he sacrifices the work, bearing himself toward the origin according to desire's measureless movement— and whereby unknowingly he still moves toward the work, toward the origin of the work.

The moment the work fails—and this is why failure cannot be lightly renounced, why success is far greater a danger to work than dissolution—failure sets free again the uncertain origin, and those who in that uncertainty dwell, without drawing up into certain light the very content such light would kill. To be known is a lesser mortality than to be glimpsed, to be wounded by the glance, and to withdraw back into the depth of unknowingness. To accomplish this failure in work, this work that releases inspiration back to the mystery that birthed it, Blanchot says:

> Orpheus has to possess the power of art already. That is to say: one writes only if one reaches that instant which nevertheless one can only approach in the space opened by the movements of writing. To write, one has to write already. In this contradiction are situated the essence of writing, the snag in experience, and inspiration's leap.

Ahab doesn't sing; Ahab's art is whaling. Whaling is an activity at which he is remarkably skilled. Ahab doesn't write; Ahab draws lines. These lines occur on a page but refer to currents under the ocean. He knows of them from "the snag in experience" that allows him to succeed with such awful accuracy in his pursuit of the white whale. All his art works to find a single whale. As Orpheus is only Orpheus in the song, so Ahab is only Ahab in the chase. His mad efforts—his work in lines, his lined brow, his equatorial destination, his harpoon line—all lead him to a point at which none will be of use. Like Orpheus, Ahab will fail. And as Orpheus dies when Eurydice descends back to death—singer and song and she sung of all become one—so Ahab will die by the same line he casts into Moby Dick. In the line, mortality can course suddenly, irreparably backward through grammar. The object can lethally turn back upon the speaking subject, lashing him to his own pursuit.

Such, in part, is Ahab's failure, strung by the neck as Moby Dick swims away, both connected by the same line. Such is his astonishing failure. Here is a pursuit that does not end in death; Ahab's death continues in pursuit. No other failure so reveals Ahab's madness. The revenge is merely a disguise—one he puts on as intention to fool even himself—to protect the nature of his real work. The real cannot survive the revelation of its actual intent. Then desire is merely a motive and not an inspired motion. Ahab does not work to retrieve the whale from the foreignness of death, from invisibility, and lay claim to revenge by removing it from its source. Ahab chases the whale because pursuit is what he knows how to do, and that knowledge is the requirement for participating in a work that can aspire toward failure. That failure binds Ahab to the white whale, brings him to mortal intimacy with the inscrutable, nameless, unearthly thing he chases. Ahab dies in pursuit and, in death, becomes instead the pursuing.

See also:

Hero
Inspiration
Line
Wound
Writing
You / Thou

OTHER

Ludwig Wittgenstein, in the *Tractatus Logico-Philosophicus,* writes:

6.42   Hence also there can be no ethical propositions.
        Propositions cannot express anything higher.
6.421   It is clear that ethics cannot be expressed.
        Ethics is transcendental.
        (Ethics and aesthetics are one.)

That final parenthetical sentence makes a radical claim. Not only does it claim for aesthetics the same inexpressibility of ethics, but it also, if the analogy holds true to the unity it asserts, claims in aesthetics an ethical import inseparable from its more typical artistic meaning. More important than aesthetics' expressive qualities—to say or paint or imagine into appearance a world—is the twin aesthetical and ethical realm that makes such expression possible. As ethics, according to Wittgenstein, orders the world by being outside of it, so aesthetics shapes the world while being outside the world. It is this notion of transcendence—as if to sense the real we must imagine that which envelops the world, and yet imagination cannot give image, word cannot grasp, that in which the whole is held—that nulls propositional power. A sentence describes the world, and in describing, shapes how we see it. Aesthetic language teaches us to see at the same time it attempts to reveal to us what we see. Aesthetics masks the world in a revealing light. Ethics is the same structuring force, for we act within the world we see. Seeing the world is our first act. Aesthetics and ethics are not in the world, but they come to use in the world, becoming separable, folding each other into the cloud of each other's meaning, or cleaving one from the other to a barely traversable distance, or transforming into opposites. The mutability is of interest if not importance—that is, the changing shape of aesthetics and ethics as they lower into the expressible world, the propositional world, must interest those who relate to them through expressive means—but those means have no effect on the unity of ethics and aesthetics as they exist outside of the world they order.

This issue of ethics and aesthetics, of the world and what lies outside the world, is of deep concern aboard the Pequod. Beyond the mere mechanics and cruel technology of the whale ship, beyond the pursuit of profit and the vague superstitions, are two protagonists whose pursuits parallel one another but whose ends differ almost completely. Ahab chases the white whale, and his pursuit requires the participation of every single man aboard his ship. Ishmael pursues a dictionary that enlarges into a book—a book of wit, witness, collection and recollection. Ishmael in his pursuit also requires everyone to be aboard (indeed, we only know who is aboard the Pequod by virtue of his work). But Ahab and Ishmael require, and respond to, the necessary reality of the Other in vastly differing ways.

The extent to which the world becomes real to us depending on our own activity in making it real is a question that is impossible to answer. We would have to be outside our own power to witness it. But we lend from our subjective reality that nameless force which recognizes reality in another. To what we lend that reality—and to what capacity an awareness of such work makes us question the certainty of our own—reveals our ethical (and aesthetical) nature.

For Ahab, the white whale is real—and he is real in relation to it. All else is either a distraction or a means. Ahab's concern is in maintaining the relational space that keeps Moby Dick, as Martin Buber would have it, as the You to his I. Moby Dick is Ahab's Other. The world, and all those in the world, lack reality: Ahab won't lend it to them. As such, Ahab sees no ethical obligation to his crew. They exist for him below the threshold of ethical responsibility. He lends to them not the reality of being a You, of being an Other, but rather his own capacity to say "I." When Ishmael, in the chapter entitled "Moby Dick," says "I, Ishmael, was one of that crew," it gathers within it a strange importance. His pronominal relation to himself has radically altered. Ishmael has gone from an objective me-existence—"Call me Ishmael"—to a subjective I-existence. He accomplishes this reinvigoration of self, this renewed capacity to say "I," by the force of Ahab's I-saying. It is in joining Ahab's quenchless feud, a feud that Ishmael says "seemed mine," that Ishmael gains a capacity to say "I" again. Only from such I-saying can reality be posited. It is by virtue of Ishmael's ability to say "I" that we read the book he has put before us. In expressing it he lends his world—the world of the Pequod and the men aboard her—reality, and in doing so makes that same world real for us who by reading of it participate in it.

Ishmael philosophizes on his relation to the Other. He does so nowhere more poignantly than when tied to Queequeg by the "monkey-rope." The monkey-rope is tied fast at both ends—one around Ishmael aboard the Pequod, and one around Queequeg who, as his job requires, stands upon the whale as it's being stripped. It is a dangerous business, this whaling life. If Queequeg should lose his footing and plummet into the waves, honor requires that Ishmael, who should have held him up, also jump overboard; that, as if they were two men wedded into a single creature, they die together. Such is their umbilical connection—each life grants life to the other. In reverie Ishmael says:

> So strongly and metaphysically did I conceive of my situation
> then, that while earnestly watching his motions, I seemed distinctly to perceive that my own individuality was now merged in
> a joint-stock company of two: that my free will had received a
> mortal wound; and that another's mistake or misfortune might
> plunge innocent me into unmerited disaster and death. And yet
> still further pondering—while I jerked him now and then from
> between the whale and the ship, which would threaten to jam
> him—still further pondering, I say, I saw that this situation of
> mine was the precise situation of every mortal that breathes; only,
> in most cases, he, one way or other, has this Siamese connection
> with a plurality of other mortals.

Ishmael finds in Queequeg that first representative of an Other to whom he is wholly obligated, wholly responsible. He opens his eyes hereafter on the world revealed by seeing the face of the Other—and so is taught, as above he realizes his lesson, his ethical, and aesthetical, reality. Emmanuel Levinas deepens the great importance of the point:

> To approach the Other in conversation is to welcome his expres-
> sion, in which at each instant he overflows the idea a thought
> would carry away from it. It is therefore to *receive* from the Other
> beyond the capacity of the I, which means exactly: to have the
> idea of infinity. But this also means: to be taught. The relation
> with the Other, or Conversation, is a non-allergic relation, an ethi-
> cal relation; but inasmuch as it is welcomed this conversation is
> a teaching. Teaching is not reducible to maieutics; it comes from
> the exterior and brings me more than I contain. In its non-violent
> transitivity the very epiphany of the face is produced.

Ishmael, unlike his captain, sees in the face of the other the visage of the Other, whose epiphany reveals the infinite world that Ahab, in his blindness, also pursues. Ishmael learns from Queequeg that each other radiates with a reality that overflows the subjectivity of the I. He learns that every single other can also be this epiphanic Other, this face that overwhelms the I with the revelation of the infinity from which it derives, and the drive behind his mode of expression occurs within this ethical, ontological realization. There exists no better explanation for Ishmael's method as a narrator.

What we hear when we read *Moby-Dick* is not a postmodern preview of fractured point of view, whose wit chips away at subjectivity and omniscience at the same time. We hear, instead, an author who is writing a book about an event he's lived, and writing of those he lived among. He's seen them, Ishmael has—he's looked into their eyes. And the dissolution of the first-person narration that becomes more and more pronounced as the book progresses—as if Ishmael's I disperses as a spirit witnessing and eavesdropping upon the whole crew—is so because, as he nears the end of each person's life, he recognizes more widely the need to use his words to express their own reality. In doing so, he limits his. Ethics and aesthetics are one.

See also:
Death
Expression
Flame
Friendship
Hands
Reciprocity
Savage
Surplus
Time
Writing
You / Thou

Pacing

Ahab spends his sleepless nights pacing the deck. As the crew slumbers in hammocks but six inches below the planks, Ahab's jawbone leg knocks loudly above them, the motion of his thoughts entering and interrupting their dreams. He paces the same planks, almost ceaselessly:

> Did you fixedly gaze, too, upon that ribbed and dented brow; there also, you would see still stranger foot-prints—the foot-prints of his one unsleeping, ever-pacing thought.
>
> But on the occasion in question, those dents looked deeper, even as his nervous step that morning left a deeper mark. And, so full of his thought was Ahab, that at every uniform turn that he made, now at the main-mast and now at the binnacle, you could almost see that thought turn in him as he turned, and pace in him as he paced; so completely possessing him, indeed, that it all seemed the inward mould of every outer movement.

Ahab wears in the planks of the deck the same lines he wears into his brow by his pacing, restless thought. The deck is but his forehead turned horizontal, as it would be could he sleep—as are the unfurrowed brows of those trying to sleep beneath the knocking of his bone-foot. The parallelism so explicitly set up between Ahab's brow and the dents upon the deck made by his thought-obsessed pacing implies that the deck, and so the Pequod entire, are an aspect of their captain's inner nature, inner drives. As much as the crew sleeps below the deck, they also sleep within Ahab's mind, restless with his restlessness, appearing to him as signs by which he can accomplish his goals, as dreams condense into people, and the people solve the psychic crisis.

The uncanny nature of life aboard the Pequod is that the ship ceases to be simply a ship but is reflective, is emblematic, of the inner life of the man who captains her. The boat is in the brow, and the brow is the deck of the boat. Absolute interiority and absolute exteriority have lost, on the Pequod, their opposition. Separate worlds mix, contaminate one another—call each separate reality into question, not by combining into a new one but by merging one into the other, so that the force of thought exerts itself on the scarred wood of the deck, and both, though differing, are the same. The ship is also a thought of a ship. The men aboard her must reckon with the thought that guides their purpose. They live within that purpose. The purpose isn't theirs.

See also:

Breath (Thought)
Jawbone
Magnet
Pequod
Pyramid
Thought (Ahab)
Wound

PARADOX

Martin Buber sees the human "religious" situation as an "existence in the presence" that is "marked by its essential and indissoluble antinomies." These antinomies exist simultaneously in us and cannot be solved by synthesis, by relativizing, nor by constructing a model of the world in which one's freedom exists deeper in the self than the necessity that belongs to the world of surfaces and appearances. There is but one world, Buber says, and one self. That self exists in the crucible between the irreconcilable antinomies of the actual world:

> Henceforth, when man is for once overcome by the horror of alienation and the world fills him with anxiety, he looks up (right or left, as the case may be) and sees a picture. Then he sees that the I is contained in the world, and that there really is no I, and thus the world cannot harm the I, and he calms down; or he sees that the world is contained in the I, and that there really is no world, and thus the world cannot harm the I, and he calms down. And when man is overcome again by the horror of alienation and the I fills him with anxiety, he looks up and sees a picture; and whichever he sees, it does not matter, either the empty I is stuffed full of world or it is submerged in the flood of the world, and he calms down.
>
> But the moment will come, and it is near, when man, overcome by horror, looks up and in a flash sees both pictures at once. And he is seized by a deeper horror.

Such a notion of self, of I, doesn't cohere. The horror of the I is its lack of any definition. Beneath the mere solidity of the uppercase authority of the pronoun, a simple dictionary safety, a grammatical anchor in subjectivity,

I is open, without boundary, an area of intensity in which a thinking and a life occur, and to desire to solidify the I into a known quantity is to betray the indissoluble antinomies of the world. To make a known shape of one's life, to desire a solid limit, a graven boundary, is to remove oneself from the world, to make an object of it, and to retreat to the safety of being oneself an object living within an object. A thinking thing living in an object thing.

But one can seek to maintain one's place in the nexus of antinomies. Ahab is such a man. The wound offers an image of the difficulty, for the wound speaks to the leakiness of I: the opening through which the world and the self intermix and exchange potencies. The world wounds, and the wound lets in the world. The point of rupture afflicts the wounded man with reality that cannot be reconciled by notions of "here versus there," "I versus It," or "me versus world." The wound replaces opposition with conjunction, and the binary relationship between I and all else becomes dialogical, and so opens the world to expression.

Expression, too, is pursuit—as is the Pequod's quest. Expression pursues the universe it participates in. Much of the difficulty in understanding Ahab's chase after Moby Dick is in seeing that the physicality of the pursuit, the catching of wind in sails, has nothing to do with the actuality of the pursuit. Just as Peleg encourages Ishmael to realize, as he stares out toward the horizon where a squall is blowing up, that all the world can be seen from where he now stands, just as a sailor, having heard the Town-Ho's story, exclaims, "The world's one Lima," *Moby-Dick* reveals, as captained by Ahab, that the world is not a circumference to chart on a map. Such is the true nature of the whalers' superstitions about Moby Dick, his unexplainable ubiquity. Such is the explanation of Fedallah's ringing cry at midnight of sighting Moby Dick from the masthead, and the subsequent nightly sightings of the white whale's "spirit-spout." Moby Dick is ever near, just on the verge of sight, always about to turn his fearful visage back toward the ivory-toothed ship of fire chasing it.

The significance of Ahab's year-long pursuit has nothing to do with the travail of leagues and miles, of distances covered and maps charted. It speaks to no journey but rather highlights the difficulty of staying within a single place that is no place at all. Ahab's effort, and the tortuous difficulties it puts him and all his crew through, exemplifies the cost of refusing to leave the place of utmost paradox, of utmost wound. Ahab's chase exemplifies his refusal to escape difficulty. He chases the creature that introduced him to the depth of irreconcilable paradox not to end the paradox but to wound the body that bears the mystery in it, to create in the agent of mystery the same crisis of paradox, and so enter the same wound he bears.

See also:

Expression
Freedom
I / *I* / "I"
Magic
Nothing/ness
Other
Reciprocity
Savage
Wound
Writing

PEQUOD

Ahab's ship, as Ishmael knows, takes its name from "a celebrated tribe of Massachusetts Indians, now extinct as the ancient Medes." The Pequod (or Pequot, or Pequoit) were exterminated by New England's Puritan forefathers in the mid-seventeenth century. Depending on one's political leanings, Ahab's ship connotes in its name vastly different meanings. Ishmael, in coming to the sea, has abandoned his land-life—a teacher, yes, but also a hint of descending from a notable family. (Melville's grandfathers on both sides were Revolutionary War heroes, one the defender of Fort Stanwix and the other a participant in the Boston Tea Party.) When Ishmael walks down to the harbor to choose the whaling boat he and Queequeg will ship upon, he walks as a man who has radically changed the definition of his own life. He walks to the harbor under the command of the idol god Yojo, to whom he and Queequeg prayed the previous day.

There is a hidden struggle of identity within the decision Ishmael is attempting to make, and that struggle occurs on edge of the wild lands that mark the territory of the "savages" from that of civilization. Ishmael decides upon the Pequod. He supposes himself fated to do so—a belief we have no capacity to judge. We can insinuate that he decides upon the Pequod not out of any identification with the glorious past of his country's history, but rather at the recognition of the tribal name of the noble Indians destroyed. He chooses the savage history, for he is himself in the process of becoming savage. The Pequod is a crucible of oppositional nominative forces: the destroyer and the destroyed. One cannot, in any honesty, be certain to which meaning the ship's name refers. But we can be sure that the fate of the ship, and those aboard her, looms in her name.

Those who work within her, live aboard her, bear a complicated relationship to the dual versions of the same history the Pequod evokes. A whaler aboard the ship bears the burden of her history, a narrative told always by the victor. For those outside that history, it presses down upon them as a yoke presses oxen. Simultaneously, there exists an unwritten history, a wordless but equally real account of those vanquished—the silence in which the silent describe themselves. Ishmael exists, in part, within this silence—subversive to all authority, for its very wordlessness is the only true threat to "official account." Its silence denies appropriation into any authoritative account, for it refuses to engage in, to recognize, the linguistic grounds that are the victor's most lasting spoils.

The story of the Pequod's destruction is written down by Major John Mason. I quote at length in order to better gain a sense of what history Ishmael both flees and dwells in:

> Then Captain Underhill came up, who marched in the rear; and commending ourselves to God, divided our men, there being two entrances into the fort, intending to enter both at once; Captain Mason leading up to that on the north-east side, who approaching within one rod, heard a dog bark and an Indian crying "Owanux! Owanux!" which is "Englishmen! Englishmen!" We called up our forces with all expedition, gave fire upon them through the palisado; the Indians being in a dead, indeed their last sleep. Then we wheeling off fell upon the main entrance, which was blocked up with bushes about breast high, over which the captain passed, intending to make good the entrance, encouraging the rest to follow. Lieutenant Seeley endeavored to enter; but being somewhat cumbered, stepped back and pulled out the bushes and so entered, and with him about sixteen men. We had formerly concluded to destroy them by the sword and save the plunder.
>
> Whereupon Captain Mason seeing no Indians, entered a wigwam; where he was beset with many Indians, waiting all opportunities to lay hands on him, but could not prevail. At length William Heydon espying the breach in the wigwam, supposing some English might be there, entered; but in his entrance fell over

a dead Indian; but speedily recovering himself, the Indians some fled, others crept under their beds. The captain going out of the wigwam saw many Indians in the lane or street; he making towards them, they fled, were pursued to the end of the lane, where they were met by Edward Pattison, Thomas Barber, with some others; where seven of them were slain, as they said. The captain facing about, marched a slow pace up the lane he came down, perceiving himself very much out of breath; and coming to the other end near the place where he first entered, saw two soldiers standing close to the palisado with their swords pointed to the ground. The captain told them that we should never kill them after that manner. The captain also said, We must burn them; and immediately stepping into the wigwam where he had been before, brought out a fire-brand, and putting it into the mats with which they were covered, set the wigwams on fire. Lieutenant Thomas Bull and Nicholas Omsted beholding, came up; and when it was thoroughly kindled, the Indians ran as men most dreadfully amazed.

And indeed such a dreadful terror did the Almighty let fall upon their spirits, that they would fly from us and run into the very flames, where many of them perished. And when the fort was thoroughly fired, command was given, that all should fall off and surround the fort; which was readily attended by all; only one Arthur Smith being so wounded that he could not move out of the place, who was happily espied by Lieutenant bull, and by him rescued.

The fire was kindled on the north-east side to windward; which did swiftly overrun the fort, to the extreme amazement of the enemy, and great rejoicing of ourselves. Some of them climbing to the top of the palisado; others of them running into the very flames; many of them gathering to windward, lay pelting at us with their arrows; and we repaid them with our small shot. Others of the stoutest issued forth, as we did guess, to the number of forty, who perished by the sword.

Over seven hundred were killed in less than an hour; only seven escaped. They killed them in their sleep; they set their houses to flame. The ship Pequod bears in its name both the activity of mass murder and its consequence, bears both the guilt of the aggressor and the affliction of the victim. One history speaks and one refuses speech. The Pequod is a ship that speaks as it unspeaks itself; *Moby-Dick* contains, astonishingly enough, a parallel narrative impossibility. Every utterance is countered by the unutterable: both occur in a name.

See also:

Etymology
Experience
Fate
Omen
Savage
Silence
Truth

PHRENOLOGY

Phrenology believes that form need not express; form is expression. Matter reveals mind. The head is no printed page, but the phrenological reader can decipher the bumps and wrinkles into a text. That text records the physical manifestations of the thoughts occurring below the skin and skull. The head is, to the phrenologist, a topographical map to the mind's molten thought. The phrenological impulse doesn't end with the human species as its only subject. A whale too has a forehead—large as a wall. Ishmael attempts—impossible as the task may be—to "put that brow before" us, so we may "read it" if we can. Beneath the page Ishmael places the sperm whale's forehead. His imperative to us is to read as physically real the body we can only imagine through the text. The effort, if we read with visionary force, places the page of the book as a paper mask before the visage of the whale—and to put one's hand to the page and press down is to feel the brow of the beast we're reading. Behind the words on the page the page comes into its own meaning—a surface riddled with thought. We have come to expect, through long habit and long experience, that when we turn a page we'll find another, covered in the same signs. We know that beneath a page is another page we know how to read. Ishmael questions the ease of such habitual expectation, as if behind the page is the thought that precedes a word, and behind the thought the wordless possibility of the thinking. A page pasted to a forehead. Then the forehead as a page.

Of the sperm whale, Ishmael says: "In profile, you plainly perceive that horizontal, semi-crescentic depression in the forehead's middle which, in man, is Lavatar's mark of genius." An open book, viewed along its horizontal profile, shares the same mark. Both a whale's and a book's physiognomy reveal each as containing genius.

ᐧᴐ

A whale must be caught to be seen; a book must be opened.

A sperm whale's genius is mute—he does not speak it. The sperm whale's genius is "declared in his pyramidical silence."

A pyramid's silence is the silence of the tomb—the walls that surround death. Upon those walls are symbols. Each symbol is a complex of words reified into image.

A book is a worded complex. Each word is a picture made up of letters. A letter has a value in the eye and a value in the ear.

These do not speak themselves, though they show themselves if the book is open.

The open book shows its genius.

A book is a silence that speaks.

A book is a silence we speak for, because it cannot speak itself.

The sperm whale has no tongue. It swallowed a prophet to speak.

See also:

Brain
Classification
Description
Hieroglyph
Jonah
Omen
Pacing
Pyramid
Scroll
Skin

Plato

Almost from the moment a whaling ship leaves port, a whaler climbs the mast, stands upon the crosstree, and begins his lookout for a whale's spout. Such an activity, gaining height in order to expand the horizon of one's eye—as the horizon is but the outermost limit of the eye's circumference—does not belong exclusively to whalers. The first masthead climbers, so Ishmael claims, were the Egyptians, who "with the prodigious long uplifting of their legs" climbed the pyramids in order to name new stars. Not simply to name new stars, but in seeing the stars to consider those patterns by which the constellations form, and so to reflect the cosmos' tale back to the humans who live beneath them, a story they forget they first spoke themselves. Ishmael knows those starry whales the Egyptians from their pyramid mastheads first sang out the sight of:

> Thus at the North have I chased Leviathan round and round the
> Pole with the revolutions of the bright points that first defined him
> to me. And beneath the effulgent Antarctic skies I have boarded
> the Argo-Navis, and joined the chase against the starry Cetus far
> beyond the utmost stretch of Hydrus and the Flying Fish.

The whale emblazoned on the night sky swims in a dark ocean whose limits no whaler can know, but could fathom only by leaping from masthead to starry whale's back and so riding into the open realm of the universe.

Such grandiose reveries are not uncommon to the whaler watching for whales from the masthead. As Ishmael describes it, the occupation is rife with speculative reverie and philosophical pleasure. A whaler of a certain mental disposition one should be wary of:

Beware of such an one, I say; your whales must be seen before they can be killed; and this sunken-eyed young Platonist will tow you ten wakes round the world, and never make you one pint of sperm the richer.

Perched above the deck, swayed by the gentle waves, warmed by the trade winds that gently blow, the philosophical whaler ceases his diligent lookout and allows his mind to scan more ethereal realms. The sky and the ocean seem infinities that merge, and the soul watching the union feels himself to be infinite with them, the all-extending blue of ocean and sky reflective of the "bottomless soul." Such a whaler seems to stand at great height upon that philosophical masthead, Plato's Divided Line, and keeps his eye open, if he remembers to look, at the point where the material illusion ascends and widens into its immaterial reality. The whaler, unwittingly but inevitably, participates in the same transition, the reality of his soul widening past the limit of his body, hypnotized by the world he's swaying in, not judging it but merging into it so that "at last he loses his identity." The Platonic whaler ceases being an *isolato* and becomes an everything:

> [He] takes the mystic ocean at his feet for the visible image of that deep, blue, bottomless soul, pervading mankind and nature; and every strange, half-seen, gliding, beautiful thing that eludes him; every dimly-discovered, uprising fin of some undiscernible form, seems to him the embodiment of those elusive thoughts that only people the soul by continually flitting through it.

The danger here is surprising and endemic to whaling. For unlike the philosopher who from the safety of his or her armchair thinks upward into Ideal Forms, the Platonic whaler climbs upward and looks down. There is an unspoken vertigo in Ishmael's speculations: the sea he looks into becomes the sky (indeed, in its gentlest moments, which can last months, the still ocean reflects the clouds above it as if they floated in its own blue depths). Gravity, to the philosophy-addled mind of the whaler on the crosstree, feels like a force that pulls one upward into the sky above—but the sky above is actually the ocean below. And the work of the Platonic whaler is to watch as Forms return from thought into body, soul into matter, and when the finny proof arrives from under the deep ether, he must sing out his discovery. For whaling reverses the Divided Line, turning it from a theoretical ascent into a plumb line. A whale, for all we know, for all Ishmael knows, may disperse as it dives, widening out into the whole substance of the ocean, returning as a soul returns to its source. The surface of the ocean may be Lethe. The whale cannot speak of the depth from which it emerges.

The risk of the whaler caught in philosophical inquiry is a gravitational danger. He can fall. And when he falls, he does so collapsingly. Each yard he falls his lost identity solidifies back into himself. As he falls he suffers doubt—for as Ishmael knows, it is "over Descartian vortices you hover." The vortex is the doubt of the single self that exists above the abyss of all that is not self, of all that doubt can remove. When a sailor falls into the ocean, it is not his name that falls, it is not Ishmael that falls, it is always I that falls. And falling undoes the I into the depths in which the whale holds his breath and lives. I am not my own idea; I am not my own idea as I'm falling.

See also:

Babel
Hands
I / *I* / "I"
Inscribe
Inspiration
Nothing/ness
Starry Archipelagoes

PROFIT

How one hears the homonym reveals much about oneself and how one perceives the context of the world: "profit" or "prophet." The woods of the seer and the woods of the savage are also the masts and planks of the whale ship—each version has its worth.

Ahab is a man who hears "prophet," and knows most men hear "profit." Within the ambiguity, within the double meaning of the homonym, Ahab can accomplish his pursuit while allowing the crew to feel it is accomplishing its own. There is no differentiating one word from the other in the ear, and the pursuit of both looks the same. To profit and to prophet, one chases whales.

The profit-world is commensurate. It has means that reach ends; it has tools that function. One profits from experience in the profit-world. One knows how to act in order to gain the outcome one wants. In the profit-world, cash fills pocket at the end of the day's work—even if that day lasts four years, and, in those four years, you touch ground not once.

Ahab is wise to this profit-world, and knows he must seem to dwell in it, so none pierce through the homonymic confusion into his "subtle insanity." He knows the "full terror of the voyage must be kept withdrawn into the obscure background." He knows his crew will gallantly chase Moby Dick only as long as they have "food for their more common, daily appetites." So Ahab lowers after whales meaningless to his pursuit of prophet, so his crew may hunger and feel hunger sated, and so hunger meagerly again. Ahab hungers past appetite. The stomachs of his crew are lined with profit. Ahab trusts all hunger will be insatiable in the end, for in the end hunger will be infinite.

See also:

PROPHET

Ishmael and Queequeg's bosom-bond friendship is not the only curious pairing aboard the Pequod. Ahab and Pip—the "madness maddened" captain and the tambourine boy—share as deep, though different, a connection. As moving as Ishmael's confession that he and his wild harpooner stayed up, sharing the same bed through the morning's dark hours, divulging "the very bottom of their souls to each other" as married couples do, are Ahab's sentiments toward Pip: "There is that in thee, poor lad, which I feel too curing to my malady. Like cures like; and for this hunt, my malady becomes my most desired health." Ahab considers Pip "a holiness." He brings Pip to live with him in his own chambers. Ahab says: "Thou touchest my inmost centre, boy; thou art tied to me by cords woven of my heart-strings." So deep is Ahab's affection for Pip, which is to say, so deep is Ahab's identification with Pip, that the little black boy alone threatens to undo Ahab's purpose. Aristotle simply and lovingly defines a friend: "A friend is another self." If so, Ahab's seeing Pip as a likeness unto his own condition bears investigation, for to understand Pip, or to see Pip as Ahab sees Pip, gains us a privileged insight into how Ahab understands himself.

One of Stubb's men sprains a wrist, and poor Pip must take the injured man's place in the whale boat. In his second lowering, when the darted whale gave "its customary rap" to the boat's bottom directly under Pip's seat, Pip leaped, "paddle in hand," out of the boat. Worse, Pip became entangled in the whale line, and as the whale speedingly fled, "poor Pip came all foaming up to the chocks of the boat, remorselessly dragged there by the line." To save Pip's life, Stubb allows Tashtego to cut the line. The whale escapes, but the boy is rescued. Stubb warns him to hereafter "Stick to the boat, Pip, or by the Lord, I won't pick you up if you jump; mind that." Pip is good, he tries to mind. But on the next lowering he again leaps from the boat, and the boat speeds away in the chase, leaving Pip abandoned, his "ringed horizon" beginning "to expand around him miserably." The experience is harrowing, and leaves harrowing consequences:

> By the merest chance the ship itself at last rescued him; but from that hour the little negro went about the deck an idiot; such, at least, they said he was. The sea had jeeringly kept his finite body up, but drowned the infinite of his soul. Not drowned entirely, though. Rather carried down alive to wondrous depths, where strange shapes of the unwarped primal world glided to and fro before his passive eyes; and the miser-merman, Wisdom, revealed his hoarded heaps; and among the joyous, heartless, ever-juvenile eternities, Pip saw the multitudinous, God-omnipresent, coral insects, that out of the firmament of waters heaved the colossal orbs. He saw God's foot upon the treadle of the loom, and spoke it; and therefore his shipmates called him mad.

Pip thinks himself dead. He refers to himself in the third person, speaks livingly of the loss of his life, and so lets it be a lesson to all.

There remains in the strangeness of the story a helpful parallel to Isaac's sacrifice. The method of sacrifice differs greatly, of course, but the residue of the event is hauntingly similar. It is said that Isaac rose from the rock on Moriah and saw his own ashes, as if the sacrifice, though he lived, had been accomplished. Pip, too, looks back and sees himself drowned in the ocean's depthless abyss. He continues to live in witness of the evidence of his own death, and such impossible contradiction gives to Pip his madness and his holiness—both of which are in him the same point. This self-witnessing Pip manages, unwillingly as it may be, arises from his having died twice. First, he dies by the line—the very figure of attachment, be it to whale or to page. To be cut from the line is to have no resource again in attachment as a solution to the problem of the self in the world. He dies the second time by abandonment. The result of abandonment is a life-threatening expansion of boundary. The horizon out-rings itself past limit, and sky and sea lack border. The indefinite world unfolds into the infinite. This infinite abandonment infinitely wounds. Pip's soul drops out of him and merges into the ocean. As it does so, it does not lose Pip's inherent identity. His soul returns to him. He is "rescued." But he has seen underneath the world, where the unwarped threads have yet to weave the world into fate. He sees God's foot on the treadle. Pip no longer sees with his eyes, for eyes by such darkness are made blind as swiftly as by staring at the sun. Pip sees with his soul.

The nature of Pip's abandonment exposes him to the infinite source that alone can utterly threaten the world, for it alone created the world, and so exists outside it. All other damage is but another example of "the universal cannibalism." Pip, and Ahab before him, experienced a threat beyond the continuous self-harm of profit and use in which the world daily revolves. Ahab loves Pip because he sees they've suffered the same wound. No balm can heal it. No salve saves. What comforts—and threatens—is that one is not, even when abandoned, even when severed, ever alone.

Ishmael lives, and then he writes a book.

See also:

Death
Fear
Fool
Friendship
Infinite / Indefinite
Jonah
Leg (Ghost)
Line
Loomings
Plato
Profit

PYRAMID

William Blake offers two paths to wisdom: "If the fool would persist in his folly he would become wise," and, "The road of excess leads to the palace of wisdom." One could argue that both maxims, to varying degree, are explored in *Moby-Dick*. Of the latter, one might question whether Ahab's excess brought himself or any of his crew (including the sole survivor) wisdom palatial or a hovel wisdom. Of the former, we find on board a variety of fools, one of whom dreams a curious dream:

> Such a queer dream, King-Post, I never had. You know the old man's ivory leg, well I dreamed he kicked me with it; and when I tried to kick back, upon my soul, my little man, I kicked my leg right off! And then, presto! Ahab seemed a pyramid, and I, like a blazing fool, kept kicking at it. . . . While I was battering away at the pyramid, a sort of badger-haired old merman, with a hump on his back, takes me by the shoulders, and slews me round. 'What are you 'bout?' says he. Slid! man, but I was frightened. Such a phiz! But, somehow, next moment I was over the fright. 'What am I about?' says I at last. 'And what business it of yours, I should like to know, Mr. Humpback? Do *you* want a kick?' . . . Says I, on second thoughts, 'I guess I won't kick you, old fellow.' 'Wise Stubb,' said he, 'wise Stubb,' and kept muttering at it all the time, a sort of eating of his own gums like a chimney hag. Seeing he wasn't going to stop saying over his 'wise Stubb, wise Stubb,' I thought I might as well fall to kicking the pyramid again. But I had only just lifted my foot for it, when he roared out, 'Stop that kicking!' 'Halloa,' says I, 'what's the matter now, old fellow?' 'Look ye here,' says he; 'let's argue the insult. Captain Ahab kicked ye, didn't he?' 'Yes, he did,' says I—'right

here it was.' 'Very good,' says he—'he used his ivory leg, didn't he?' "Yes, he did,' says I. 'Well then,' says he, 'wise Stubb, what have you to complain of? Didn't he kick you with right good will? it wasn't a common pitch pine leg he kicked with, was it? No, you were kicked by a great man, and with a beautiful ivory leg, Stubb. It's an honor; I consider it an honor . . . that ye were kicked by old Ahab, and made a wise man of. Remember what I say; *be* kicked by him; account his kicks honors; and on no account kick back; for you can't help yourself, wise Stubb. Don't you see that pyramid?

Stubb's dream reveals his subconscious realization that Ahab and Moby Dick share such a deep connection that the pursuer and the pursued have not only transposed personal characteristics but also seem to have a strange sympathy for one another. Although it is easy, and even apt, to interpret the dream as a manifestation of Stubb's comprehension of Ahab's immovability of person and purpose, it is the "little lower layer" that reveals a more mysterious truth. For the dream to be reciprocal symbolically—for Ahab to be the white whale, and the white whale to be Ahab—we must find the overlapping point of connection that allows Stubb's dream to focus into wise revelation. When Ishmael fills in the folkloric history and superstitions that surround the whale the Pequod is chasing, he mentions a curious physical fact: the white hump is shaped like a pyramid. That Ahab, in Stubb's dream, transforms into a pyramid (versus, say, a sphinx—as later reference would allow) places the fulcrum of symbolic equivalence on the pyramid's tip.

That a pyramid serves as a tomb no doubt prefigures, to a degree, the tragic outcome to which all, save Ishmael, will succumb. But a pyramid is no normal tomb (to say the least). A pyramid is tomb for royal persons, and fitted out—as some might say a ship is fitted—with all the goods required to journey through death to life immortal. The mountainous stasis of the pyramid is actually a jib filled with celestial wind. The pyramid is a nexus between two types of dwelling: the mortal life on earth and the unknowable life that occurs after the former has ended. The pyramid belongs to neither realm but is the vehicle of passage between them. And when the pharaoh wakes—and waking here is arrival—he sees upon the inner walls of the burial chamber hieroglyphs that tell him, now that he has rejoined the gods, the story of who he was on earth. The writing is within the tomb.

What wise Stubb's dream reveals is the living symbolic connection that fuses Ahab and white whale together. Death not as end, but means. One cannot say a means to what. One can merely read the hieroglyphs to gain a sense of who and what one was and, by such memory, illuminate a reality one guessed at as one guesses at fate when alive on earth, knowing fate extends purpose past mortal confines, mortal knowledge, and mortal life.

See also:

Ambergris
Coffin
Death
Fate
Hieroglyph
Joke
Omen
Reciprocity

Quadrant

Before Ahab destroys his quadrant—the scientific yet "cabalistical" tool that allows him to calculate his position on the ocean—a far different compass shows the dilemma of direction. "The four slain whales that evening had died wide apart; one, far to windward; one less distant, to leeward; one ahead; one astern." Every direction in which the Pequod could sail is the same direction, as if in sailing east, as it does, the Pequod has already arrived at the center. The ship sails toward where it has already arrived. But the ship gathers the massive carcasses to it and proceeds to the equatorial line.

Ahab knows, or understands beneath any active knowledge, that the center denies location. The center makes of a single place an everywhere, a point that is a sphere, undoing boundaries in which such information as latitude and longitude carry meaning. In the center one sits, waits, sails forth, but never moves. Ahab sails through the center to find a line: one encounters crisis in contradiction.

Contradiction denies an instrument's ability to render profitable information. Ahab's recognition of this futility, the particular quality in which the quadrant fails, reveals him to himself:

> Thou sea-mark! thou high and mighty Pilot! thou tellest me truly where I *am*—but canst thou cast the least hint where I shall *be*? Or canst thou tell where some other thing besides me is this moment living? . . . what after all canst thou do, but tell the poor, pitiful point, where thou thyself happenest to be on this wide planet, and the hand that holds thee: no! not one jot more!

The sun, up at which Ahab gazes through the quadrant's tinted lenses, looks down and sees all. But the solar omnipotence communicates nothing to he who looks up at the sun for knowledge. Such light confirms merely that Ahab is Ahab, is gazing up, is standing right where he is standing, wanting to know what is not his to know. The quadrant confirms Ahab's subjectivity by confirming his body. In confirming his body, it painfully reifies his strength—a muscular power to carry out the mind's will, the soul whose power infuses the sinews and tendons of his strength. But in defining his singularity, it excludes Ahab from the wider world in which he conducts his pursuit. The quadrant says: strength without knowledge. And then Ahab with his strength destroys it.

See also:

Ahab
Corpusants
I / I / "I"
Knowledge
Ocean
Omen
Pacing
Reading (Doubloon)

QUEST / QUESTION

If fate's cloth seen from above is a tapestry that weaves into image the world and we who live our lives in the world, the same cloth from underneath reveals the chaos that makes possible that upper order. The human situation, more often than not, allows us access only to the world embroidered, visible, cosmic. The whale has a different life. The whale looks up and sees the raveled chaos that above the surface forms into the sensible world. Ahab—as does a drowning man when his eyes are divided in half by the water's surface and he sees the upper and the lower spheres at once—has witnessed fate doubly. Ahab belongs to neither world: not to fate as cosmic decree nor to fate as cosmic possibility. More to the point, Ahab belongs to both worlds—irreconcilable even though the opposite sides of the same cloth—simultaneously.

Ahab addresses the severed head of the first sperm whale the Pequod kills and in his speech reveals something of his purpose. He speaks to the whale out of his own doubly-fated condition:

> "Speak, thou vast and venerable head," muttered Ahab, "which, though ungarnished with a beard, yet here and there lookest hoary with mosses; speak, mighty head, and tell us the secret thing that is in thee. Of all divers, thou hast dived the deepest. That head upon which the upper sun now gleams, has moved amid this world's foundations. Where unrecorded names and navies rust, and untold hopes and anchors rot; where in her murderous hold this frigate earth is ballasted with bones of millions of the drowned, there, in that awful water-land, there was thy most familiar home. Thou hast been where bell or diver never went; hast slept by many a sailor's side, where sleepless mothers would give their lives to lay them down. . . . O head! Thou hast

seen enough to split the planets and make an infidel of Abraham, and not one syllable is thine!"

Not only does Ahab give some possible explanation to the cause of his own seeming blasphemy, having himself witnessed something of the whale's epistemological domain, but he also speaks deeply to the nature of his quest, his question. Here Ahab gives voice to the riddle of his lowest layer.

The whale lives—and by all accounts lives an intelligent, conscious (even conscientious) life—in the deepest portion of this actual world. What inflames, in part, Ahab's madness is the knowledge that the world cannot reveal itself to him as actual in the enormity of its actuality, in its actual depth. There is that which exists but which is not his to know. The world extends past human limits, the wall drawn near him that is the extent of his own life. But the whale, which breathes on lungs as we do, whose blood like ours is warm, knows this unknowable world, this lowest world that is ours only in insensate death and so is not ours at all. Ahab, our mortally wounded captain who walks on life and death, leg and bone, realizes that human life ends in time before the world ends in limit. There is that which exists which is outside our scope. Ahab's courage, his quest, is to break through that merely mortal limit and, in doing so, witness the whole (cognate to holy) world. He asks a severed head to divulge its secrets. He chases a white whale that seems to be the embodiment of the secret itself. Ahab believes the riddle has an answer.

See also:

Chaos
Death
Fate
Freedom
Hero

Orpheus
Pyramid
Silence
Tablet
Truth

READING (DOUBLOON)

The gold coin minted in Ecuador and nailed to the mainmast is, as mad-prophet Pip calls it, the ship's navel. Who first sees the white whale and gains for his pocket the doubloon undoes the center-life of the ship, this coin imprinted with symbols, which also exists as talisman for the whale Ahab and his crew chase. To spot the whale is to undo the knot that keeps internal life from leaking out into the world, the sacred spot around which blood circulates, around which men circulate, around which the body balances—the center in all its overreaching multiplicity of associations, the place of undisturbed purpose, the center that is always center, a portable Jerusalem, the bright coin that blesses the mast whose sails catch the wind and, in motion, expands the evanescent horizon to utmost circumference. The small, gold world within the sunlit world.

Many on the crew stop and gaze at the coin they are loathe to steal. They look at it and translate its pictorial symbols—"zoned by those letters you saw the likeness of three Andes' summits; from one a flame; a tower on another; on the third a crowing cock; while arching over all was a segment of the partitioned zodiac, the signs all marked with their usual cabalistics, and the keystone sun entering the equinoctial point at Libra"—into meaning. Ishmael eavesdrops on this reading and, later, when Stubb reads and hears Flask coming, Stubb hides and eavesdrops, and Ishmael listens at a further remove. The reading each character speaks, the effort at translation, occurs on a more difficult plane than a lexical reading. Rather than words, one reads symbols, whose relation to what each signifies is both thicker and more distant, more personal and more universal.

Ahab reads first:

There's something ever egotistical in mountain-tops and towers, and all other grand and lofty things; look here,—three peaks as proud as Lucifer. The firm tower, that is Ahab; the courageous, the undaunted, and victorious fowl, that, too, is Ahab; all are Ahab; and this round gold is but the image of the rounder globe, which, like a magician's glass, to each and every man in turn but mirrors back his own mysterious self. Great pains, small gains for those who ask the world to solve them; it cannot solve itself.

The temptation, given the "egotistical" translation of the symbols on the coin, is to use the passage as evidence of the monomania so easily ascribed to Ahab. But Ahab thinks at a deeper layer than the mere ego that weighs the world by a mistaken plumb line reading its own selfish depths. What Ahab sees is more frightening than himself, than his own reflection. His pride does not come back to himself as a return upon his investment in the extraordinary power of his will. Ahab sees that our efforts to read the world are always obstructed by the world's giving us back ourselves as the problem. One cannot read—a coin or a book—as anyone other than oneself.

The act of translation, of doing a work that brings meaning across an abyss, is never pure. But Ahab's critique proves deeper than simply recognizing the severe limits of subjectivity. Ahab sees in the world a mirror behind whose polished surface dark reality does its secret work. One cannot read into such darkness—and the world is this darkness. To read, oddly enough, expresses desire. To read is to trust that meaning can occur, and the act of reading is desirous of that meaning. Desire implicates the desiring self with the fact of its own hunger. When one reads, one is accused of wanting what it is one wants. Ahab doesn't want himself—himself he all too abundantly, all too tragically has. Ahab wants that which hides its power, the other side of the coin, and which, in mirrored return, gives him but another aspect of his own might.

The self-revelatory pattern continues. Starbuck reads into the coin the comfort of an easy morality and stops reading when truth threatens to undo the safety. Stubb brings an almanac to compare astrological notes, as if fate were a course in comparative literature, and the effort to understand reaches toward a comic ad infinitum of book explaining book—the universe as exegesis. Ever-hungry Flask looks at the coin and thinks of spending it. Queequeg, whose text-tattooed body is its own symbolic mystery, looks to see if a symbol on the coin matches a symbol on his thigh, in hopes, one assumes, that the coincidence can illuminate meaning.

And then Pip arrives: "I look, you look, he looks; we look, ye look, they look," a grammar repeated thrice. Ahab reads first and Pip reads last. The order cannot be seen as the bookends of the extreme of beginning and ending but as a circle brought back to the same point, the orbit of the reading complete. Pip, after his abandonment in the ocean and exposure to infinity, returns mad, speaking "God's foot on the treadle." In Pip, Ahab finds his own likeness. If reading does reveal self as self attempts to disclose world, then Ahab's reading and Pip's reading must reveal the same, or nearly the same, point. At one level, Pip does not read at all, but he reveals the grammar beneath language that makes any reading possible. As Ahab realizes a self must be a self to read, and so self limits interpretation within its own boundary, so Pip reveals that language itself is subject to its own self-limiting laws. Pip doesn't read so much as make an observation that reading itself reveals rules that it cannot help but abide by—that beneath language is an order that language itself is helpless to explain.

But Pip also prefigures Ishmael's abandonment—Ishmael who does not read the coin but reads others' readings of the coin. Beyond the grammatical conjugation of the verb "to look" lies another interpretation, harrowing as it is illuminating. For Pip also speaks intransitively. The language of the wounded man—and Ahab, Pip, and Ishmael all suffer a similar result, though bear a different kind, of woundedness—lacks the ability to transition from the subject and verb to the object. I look. I fear. I know. I doubt. I hurt. I want. The sentence can go no farther, for the only certainty is the pain of the self beginning the sentence, and the world that might come to heal or exasperate mortally the wound cannot arrive, because it has eclipsed the boundaries of objectivity. For each has glimpsed through the indefinite everything the infinite All, and of All, there is no speaking.

Ishmael begins *Moby-Dick* by putting himself forward as an object. He does not say "I am"; he says "it's me." And in saying "me," in putting the self in the sentence as the object, utters the word by which the world can be rebuilt.

See also:

Cosmogony
Crisis
Doubloon
Expression
Hieroglyph
Inscribe
Profit
Prophet
Reading (Epistemology)
Skin
Soot

Reading (Epistemology)

Queequeg is illiterate but he reads. Ishmael returns from Father Mapple's sermon to find Queequeg occupied in a sequence of events that, seemingly unrelated, correspond to each other by speaking to the same failure:

> Returning to the Spouter-Inn from the Chapel, I found Queequeg there quite alone; he having left before the benediction some time. He was sitting on a bench before the fire, With his feet on the stove hearth, and in one hand was holding close up to his face that little negro idol of his; peering hard into its face, and with a jack-knife gently whittling away at its nose, meanwhile humming to himself in his heathenish way.

Beneath the slight humor of Ishmael's tone lurks the strangeness of Queequeg's activity. He sits not in religious reflection so much as in critical occupation, emending the god. To whittle away at the idol's nose undercuts the symbolic reality to which the idol refers. The purpose of the idol, of the totem, does not rest in the wooden god's representative qualities. To think an idol needs one degree more of verisimilitude in order to represent more perfectly the god it symbolizes is to reveal a skeptical distrust of its actual meaning. Queequeg, in carving the idol to correct an impossible likeness, reveals a schism in his relationship to his own pagan faith. It is as if he knows but cannot accept that the god in his hands is but wood. His faith is a doubtful activity.

When Queequeg realizes Ishmael is in the room, he puts the god away and picks up a bible. Ishmael watches him, bemused but attentive, as Queequeg places the large book on his lap and begins "counting the pages with deliberate regularity; at every fiftieth page . . . stopping a moment, looking vacantly around him, and giving utterance to a long-drawn gurgling whistle of astonishment." Queequeg continues to count pages in batches of fifty, "as though he could not count more than fifty, and it was only by such a large number of fifties being found together, that his astonishment at the multitude of pages was excited." Queequeg approaches the bible as an object of meaning rather than an object that contains meaning. The book is but a symbol of a library god who pours his power into countless words, just as the idol is composed of the splinters and grain of wood imbued with a power beyond the material of which it is composed. Queequeg's whittling is as much an act of attempted reading as is his counting with growing astonishment the onion-thin pages of the bible—and the sorrowful revelation is that, in both interpretive acts, he is equally illiterate.

Queequeg is a character, as is Ishmael, of haunted exile. Such profound homelessness helps them to recognize one another as the "bosom friends" they become—the homoeroticism that is the surface of their "married" bliss serving merely as the pseudosexual surface of the deeper commingling of similar souls. Queequeg, we learn, is royal blood, but rather than simply ascend to his pagan throne, he desires to learn about Christianity in order, he says, to help his people "become better." Queequeg leaves his island, a home that appears on no map, tattooed by a prophet with the entire knowledge of his people but without the knowledge to read the book that is his own body, and sails off on a whaling ship in order to gain a new knowledge. His desire to learn to read another way of life, another language in which he could think, results in his inability to return home. He is exiled between a knowledge he bears and cannot grasp, and a book he can grasp but which brings him no knowledge. It feels reductive to claim he exists between a symbolic, paperless world and the world of linguistic knowledge. Certainly, he is irretrievably caught in the chasm between a symbolic world and a semantic one—but the crisis runs deeper than the mind can explain, for the crisis denies the mind its own innate powers. Queequeg is a spiritual aphasiac. He has lost his own language and is unable to learn another. If fluency unfolds as a different capacity than mere comprehension of, and communication in, a given language, and instead, language at the "little lower layer" represents all that can be known, represents every possible permutation of meaning and law which the world invariably obeys, then to be without language is not merely to be savage or illiterate, unlearned or dumb. It is not to find knowledge merely withheld but to find that knowledge as possibility is gone. If Queequeg holds the idol in one hand and the bible in the other, both are blanker than blank. Mute epistemologies echo silent over silent abyss. Queequeg is caught between two worlds, and neither is open to him. What seems in Queequeg his natural goodness, his simple ethical kindness and care, is no argument of the nobility of the savage. Instead, his character—that is, the pressure of the soul that "cannot be hidden"—is his home. Queequeg is a man only and "always equal to himself."

As Ishmael intently watches Queequeg count/read the bible, he begins "to be sensible of strange feelings." He sees Queequeg suddenly not as an exotic curiosity, but as an Other who exists as fundamentally as Ishmael himself exists; Ishmael sees him as a friend. He goes over to help Queequeg with his reading:

> We then turned over the book together, and I endeavored to explain to him the purpose of printing, and the meaning of the few pictures that were in it.

Ishmael chooses an unexpected topic given the source of the material he's trying to explain. Rather than paraphrase biblical stories, rather than gloss theological concerns, Ishmael seems to give a lecture on the history of print as media, and it seems just as likely that he is offering the same technical minutiae in relation to the pictures. Ishmael places meaning, as does Queequeg, on the material object rather than in semantics. He seems to understand, agree, or be sympathetic to the possibility that a word and a totem function similarly. A word, too, is a visible symbol. It carries a symbolic onus that exists outside of its lexical meaning. As such, it's no surprise that Ishmael agrees to perform with Queequeg his pagan rites. The word and the idol are twins.

See also:

Reading (Water)

A book is a depth that presents itself as a surface. A first page sits upon the future. A last page sits beneath its own history, a text that is a depth above it. The present tense of the open page is a surface floating between opposing depths—anticipation and memory. The boat and the book share a circumstance, as those who sail aboard a boat share a circumstance with those who hold a book. The boat rides the ocean's surface between an unknown depth and an unknowable height; the whaler and the reader are subject to the weight of both mysteries. Those riding in the boat cannot see below the surface of the wave and so must wait for a sign to emerge from the creature they hunt. They wait for a "leviathanic revelation." The reader has a text, an object that bears a language from which meaning can be gathered. The whaler has no text. The whaler hunts an object from which a profit can be gathered. Both meaning and profit occur in depths that emerge on a surface. Both meaning and profit can be lost.

Whalers who sight a whale lower boats and row after it. The whale sounds down when it senses their approach. A whale breathes as men breathe—with lungs. A whale rises to the surface to gather breath. The whalers look over the boat's edge for a sign. The ocean does not bear words as text open upon it; water dissolves ink; water mocks legibility. The whalers do not look for a word, but for breath rising faster than the whale who exhaled it. Breath bears vowels. The first letter of the Hebrew alphabet—*aleph*—is silent; it takes the sound of whatever letter it is next to. A breath is silent but all words are borne on breath. A whaler watches for the breath that pronounces the whale. It appears as a bubble that bursts as it meets its own element. On the page it would appear as lightning—not a word but the light by which a word is seen.

See also:

RECIPROCITY

The whale that cannot run out the line and escape to freedom is caught. We near the whale by virtue of that line and, in nearing it, learn how to open it to gain what illumination we seek. For a normal whaler, that illumination equals profit. But Ahab differs. He pivots on this most central of American puns; he turns *profit* into *prophet*. Not that Ahab is a prophet—though I suspect, in a different context, he could be argued as such. Ahab might refuse to say the words given to him, much as Jonah initially does, not out of an instinct toward self-preservation but out of an intuition that to speak God's words is to remove oneself from God's presence. If it's presence one is pursuing, then one learns to bite one's tongue in order not to speak, lest the first syllable create chasm.

I don't mean to imply that Ahab is a silent man. I mean to say that Ahab is a man who understands that a word, like an idol, contains a silence within it, and the word's truest meaning occurs only in relation to this silence. This relation is a relation of belief, and that Ahab is a man who hates what he believes in diminishes naught the nature of his faith. We like to think of men of such will as mad, but they are not mad. As Martin Buber writes in *I and Thou*:

> Free is the man that wills without caprice. He believes in the actual, which is to say: he believes in the real association of the real duality, I and You. He believes in destiny and also that it needs him. It does not lead him, it waits for him. He must proceed toward it without knowing where it waits for him. He must go forth with his whole being: that he knows. . . . He must sacrifice his little will, which is unfree and ruled by things and drives, to his great will that moves away from being determined to find destiny.

Men such as Ahab are possessed of a violence that is holy. It is not a spoken quality; there is no proof of it. Such will functions magnetically—an essence of the material that leaks out of the material in order to function. It is the force that seeks reconciliation with its matching and opposite force—not the body. Ahab is such a magnet—such is the nature of his control over the crew, such is the nature of his startling repair of the compass the lightning storm confused.

It is here, within the paradoxical nature of Ahab's will, a will fully directed at hunting Moby Dick, that certain mysteries can be shown. If anyone has the right to tell this story, it is not exactly Ishmael. If anyone, it should be Ahab who gets to write "I" and tell his tale. But it's not—and not simply because Ahab is towed away by the line he himself cast into Moby Dick. It is because Ahab knows that within the mysteries of the I-You relationship, to speak of it, to turn it into a tale, is to sever the inscrutable connection by which the relationship keeps alive. Here is the vast difference between our two heroes—a difference Melville, I think, puts in purposeful parallel. In Chapter XLIV—"The Chart"—Ahab is described as he charts the course by which he'll pursue and find Moby Dick:

> Then seating himself before it, you would have seen him intently study the various lines and shading which there met his eye; and with slow but steady pencil trace additional courses over spaces that before were blank. . . . While thus employed, the heavy pewter lamp suspended in chains over his head, continually rocked with the motion of the ship, and for ever threw shifting gleams and shadows of lines upon his wrinkled brow, till it almost seemed that while he himself was marking out lines and courses on the wrinkled charts, some invisible pencil was also tracing lines and courses upon the deeply marked chart of his forehead.

This reciprocity marks the nature of Ahab's relation to the white whale. Ahab is written as he writes. Ahab does not write words. He writes a steady line, a line of pursuit that is also a line of approach. Against all of blank infinity Ahab alone knows how to see inside all possibility the nature of absolute certainty. He is certain because he is not telling his story. He has no distance from which to tell it. His language is a line, not a word, a means of approach, not a lexicon.

Ahab finds the white whale exactly on that point on the line—the equator—where he was wounded. This return is not a repetition of event; this return is not repetition at all. Ahab is caught in the terrible symmetry of the universe's functioning, a mythic cycle that removes one from the center only to reaffirm the suspicion that no circumference actually exists. Ahab returns to find he's never left—to be even more blunt, he returns because he has never left. He dwells in the real beneath the world, beneath the wave, from which Being emerges in Form both to convince and to fool us, and then dives back down and is not seen again except (and in whaling this trope is literal) in inspired moments. Ahab's end is not tragedy—or if tragedy, it isn't the tragedy we think it is. The tragedy isn't Ahab's death, nor is it the crew's demise. The tragedy shows the great cost of what it means to be a man inspired. The tragedy illuminates what it is to say "You" with one's whole being and for answer receive a wound. Ahab is a man that says "You."

～

Ishmael says "me." In beautiful counterpoint to Ahab at his chart (though in a scene implied rather than shown), Ishmael sits at a desk, writing his own book: a lexicon of whales and whaling, its pages illuminated by the flame of the very creature he's studying. The whale by the whale's own light. Ishmael doesn't speak, he writes. Writing is a commodity of speech insofar as it turns speech into form. The written word is not alive except for, as in Zeno's paradox in which the flying arrow is motionless, the moment in which you read the word and, in reading it, still it, remove it from its living motion. Memory extends backward over the rest, anticipation extends over what's to come. The text is a fast fish, as is the reader—and both, like all of us, live "enveloped in whale line."

Ishmael writes; he lives in time. Unlike Ahab, Ishmael is doomed to repetition. He has a story to tell, and so he must tell it. And as with all true stories, one is alive only in the telling, only in the place in which the blank world reexerts itself on the legible one. Here is a heavenly vision: finding the first page in sequence after the very last. The book as a circle. The book as Ouroboros—its silent tail in its silent mouth. You. You, you might say. You might beg You to "Call me Ishmael," and then tell another man's story and hint that it's also your own.

See also:

Fate
Freedom
Hero
I / I / "I"
Jonah
Line
Pacing
Prophet
Quadrant
Silence
Time
You / Thou

REPETITION

Fate occurs in repetition. Ishmael knows this as he and Queequeg weave a grass mat on the day of the first whale sighting:

> There lay the fixed threads of the warp subject to but one single, ever returning, unchanging vibration, and that vibration merely enough to admit of the crosswise interblending of other threads with its own. This warp seemed necessity; and here, thought I, with my own hand I ply my own shuttle and weave my own destiny into these unalterable threads.

The image implies that the weft convinces us of free will, the design woven into fate by which a life coheres into image, but the warp is defined by hands other than our own, and the hidden order is not ours, and over it we have no decree. One might believe the shuttle in one's hands is one's life. But the wise man sees the warp repeats, each repetition indistinguishable from the next, and feels less unique, less in control. He fears he holds in his hands but the appearance of his life.

REPETITIONS DURING THE FIRST LOWERING

I.

Flask, driven almost to frenzy by the sight of white water, tore off his hat and "finally fell to rearing and plunging in the boat's stern like a crazed colt from the prairie."

Ishmael, describing his horror of whiteness, makes an extended analogy. He likens himself to a "young colt" from Vermont "far removed from all beasts of prey" that, when a "fresh buffalo robe" is shaken behind him—though he has no experience nor knowledge of the beasts of the Great Plains—with "bursting eyes" paws "the ground in phrensies of affright."

2.

During the first fray with a whale: "The whole crew were half suffocated as they were tossed helter-skelter into the white curdling cream of the squall. Squall, whale, and harpoon had all blended together; and the whale, merely grazed by the iron, escaped."

Ishmael on entering the Spouter-Inn in New Bedford finds a "portentous, black mass of something hovering in the centre of the picture over three blue, dim, perpendicular lines floating in a nameless yeast." Within the painting Ishmael sees "a sort of indefinite, half-attained, unimaginable sublimity" that takes hold of the imagination with a need to discover the painting's subject. Much study reveals "that one portentous something in the picture's midst"; it is a painting of a "Cape-Horner in a great hurricane" and "an exasperated whale" caught in the act of "impaling himself upon the three mastheads."

3.

In the midst of the squall, night coming on, and the whale escaped: "The wind increased to a howl; the waves dashed their bucklers together; the whole squall roared, forked, and crackled around us like a white fire upon the prairie, in which, unconsumed, we were burning."

Ishmael upon first seeing Ahab: "He looked like a man cut away from the stake, when the fire has overrunningly wasted all the limbs without consuming them."

〜

The ocean with its waves figures a loom. The waves are a weft. And the men on the boat live aboard a shuttle.

See also:

Fate
Freedom
Loomings
Ocean
Plato
Pyramid
Soot
Whiteness

SAVAGE

How many years pass between Ishmael's survival—orphaned of all the world—and his picking up pen to recollect the experience is unknown. A careful reader notes how often, and how inexplicably, the present tense of the narration is broken by hints of time passed—time in which another life may have occurred. When, at the Spouter-Inn, Ishmael realizes the frightful harpooner who will share his bed is covered all over with tattoos, he contextualizes by recalling the story of a white man who, after long sea-voyages, returned similarly etched. Far later, hundreds of pages deep, we realize that this "other man" was Ishmael himself, who spent years between the wreck of the Pequod and the writing of *Moby-Dick* wandering the watery world aboard other ships, and, abandoning ship, exploring the savage islands.

Ishmael's wandering implies being lost, if in no other way than a parallel to the silent lostness of Bulkington, whose experience at sea negated his ability to stay on land. Ishmael, though, is differently lost. Ishmael is not silent—or, if silent in his past, not resigned to stay silent now. The world of *Moby-Dick* exists for us because he speaks it to us. But between the speaking that becomes this book and the event the book recounts occurs another life—a life in which he loses his proper name, and the identity latched on to such given appellation, and through which he renames himself "Ishmael." The years between "then" and "now" allow, or force, or slowly illuminate the necessity of Ishmael moving from I meaning a particular name and identity, through namelessness, to this Ishmael whose I begins as a me. Ishmael spends years gathering strength for the necessary betrayal of self against self and from this betrayal speaks, expresses, creates. Ishmael's self is also his Other.

Ishmael, it seems, continues collecting his cetological information, the study of which occupies the majority of the novel he writes. As such,

Moby-Dick's narration occurs in two different strands of time, almost perfectly woven into one another. We have the timeline of all that occurred leading up to and aboard the Pequod, and we have the information that interrupts that plot—information gained after horror. *Moby-Dick* cannot burgeon into its fullest complexity, which is to say its fullest meaning, without realizing that the novel's construction bookends years of which nothing can be said, for the work of the book is to fill that silence, and to do so, it must mark its boundaries, however shifting and amorphous the shape those limits bound. Certain chapters highlight this oddity. When Ishmael tells the story of the Town-Ho to his drinking mates in Peru, one realizes that he is telling stories about Moby Dick without being able to reveal his own history with the awful whale. Ishmael is preparing himself, finding a way to speak not about a subject but about a life shattered by a singular event, a crisis that negates the ability to tell of it.

His work, though, is not only oral. He does not simply collect and recount stories about Moby Dick. Ishmael also travels to inquire more deeply about the nature of the sperm whale. He continues to seek an accuracy his subject denies, but as his inquiry lengthens through tragedy and years, he is implicated in the very information he wants to gather.

Ishmael makes a royal friend after the princely Queequeg dies. He befriends King Tranquo, who, like Montezuma, collects the marvels of the world for his enjoyment. Chief among these wonders is the skeleton of a full-grown sperm whale. The skeleton serves as a place of worship for King Tranquo's people, an eternal flame kept burning in the whale's skull, the smoke rising up through the water spout. The vertebrae of the leviathan are etched with hieroglyphs. The structure that supported the "mystic-marked" skin of the sperm whale is itself mystic-marked—as if one could tear the pages from a book to reveal the architecture that makes it a book and realize the structure is but a surface to be written upon again. There is no material body that is not a writing surface, no body that is not a book.

Ishmael realizes the point by actualizing it. Here he reveals himself as that stranger he spoke of in the Spouter-Inn:

The skeleton dimensions I shall now proceed to set down are copied verbatim from my right arm, where I had them tattooed; as in my wild wanderings at that period, there was no other secure way of preserving such valuable statistics. But as I was crowded for space, and wished the other parts of my body to remain a blank page for a poem I was then composing—at least, what untattooed parts might remain—I did not trouble myself with the odd inches; nor, indeed, should inches at all enter into a congenial admeasurement of the whale.

The act of the tattooing, and the information the ink bears, confuse into a single gesture vastly different methods of recognizing meaning in the world. Ishmael, in the continuing wake of the experience aboard the Pequod, fuses together scientific inquiry and savage symbolism. The markings upon Ishmael bear a parallel meaning to the markings upon his great friend Queequeg—both express not merely a knowledge, definable and finite, but a holy cosmology that makes possible the world it describes. The tattooing, covering almost his entire body, implicates the body in the mind's work. Ishmael, our Platonic whaler given to philosophical reverie on the crosstree, has long since fallen into the "Descartian vortices" he warned against. The result is not the further separation of body from mind, but the full collapse of one into the other. Ishmael's experience is carved into the body by which he experiences the world. This work is a savage work. Ishmael must learn to be bewildered so that his words do not diminish the wildness of the world, to write so that the writing act itself does not distance him from the very world he's attempting to near. To do this work he must also become other than he is; he must become savage. He must dwell as deeply in the world as he delves into thinking about the world. He must bear on his body the proof that to think, to write, is to exist deeper in the world, rather than to remove oneself from it.

In doing so, he suggests the book in our hands is the most unexpected object, for it isn't an object at all, or is so but accidentally. To claim

Moby-Dick's skeletal structure—surely an enterprise "in which a careful disorderliness is the true method" if there ever was one—as poetic comes as no surprise. What is surprising to think is what Ishmael himself suggests: that the poem he was "then composing" on King Tranquo's island is the book we hold in our hands, and that the parchment of the page is but an extension of the blank on his body, and the ink that makes the words is but an etching marked beneath the skin. The primitive word that pulses with the blood beneath it: the book as the body, the book as vascular, the book as savage.

See also:

Accuracy
Crisis
Experience
Friendship
Hieroglyph
I / *I* / "I"
Justice
Other
Reading (Epistemology)
Silence
Skin
Tattoo
Time
Writing

Saying / Said

Ahab paces, night after night, consumed by a thought. It would seem safe to say that thought's axis must be the white whale's proper name, Moby Dick. One might guess that the monomaniacal mind cleaves to a single word and, in a type of mental echolalia, repeats it alone, unable to move from any other word to any other thought. The living electricity of the healthy mind has been lightning-struck, and the synapses that before led thought across the wide range of human endeavor have become a fulgurite. Now thought runs through the same calcified channel and can branch out nowhere past the fused matter buried in the mind.

Ahab's first words about the white whale come as a subtle surprise. He paces on the quarterdeck before his crew, and the pacing presages the speaking. "'D'ye mark him, Flask?' whispered Stubb; 'that chick that's in him pecks the shell.'" Stubb's metaphor is more apt than he realizes. The etymological root for the word that describes a chick emerging from its shell: *disclosure*. Ahab is about to speak his mind. After holding up a "sixteen dollar piece" of gold and offering it as reward to whoever first sings out for the white whale with wrinkled brow and crooked jaw, Ahab elaborates:

> "It's a white whale, I say," resumed Ahab, as he threw down the top-maul; "a white whale. Skin your eyes for him, men; look sharp for white water; if ye see but a bubble, sing out."
>
> All this while Tashtego, Daggoo, and Queequeg had looked on with even more intense interest and surprise than the rest, and at the mention of the wrinkled brow and crooked jaw they had started as if each was separately touched by some specific recollection.

"Captain Ahab," said Tashtego, "that white whale must be the same that some call Moby Dick."

"Moby Dick?" shouted Ahab.

Ahab shouts a question, not a recognition. It is as if Tashtego's speaking the white whale's name again inaugurates Ahab into a use of language he had forgotten. The proper noun designates the name not by type—a whale recognized as a species of whales, a use of language that deeply concerns Ishmael—but by appellation. Moby Dick can only be Moby Dick, and so it is surprising, and on deeper meditation, unnerving, that Ahab should forget the name that one would assume he repeats to himself ritualistically, maniacally, obsessively. Ahab's mind, it seems, his thoughtful life which is "madness maddened," does not speak itself in language. His life is not a said life. Ahab's very body speaks his thoughts. He paces; he wears a rut in brow and a rut in wood. One assumes his thought is a linguistic activity, an effort at plotting revenge, making a plan, forming an argument. But in Ahab there is no argument, no plan, no plot. There is the ongoing saying of his wounded situation, a language that does not rise into words, that occurs before the semiotic crisis of whether or not "white whale" could ever utter itself near to the *white whale*. Ahab is in the stuff of language itself, not on the wordy shoals that threaten meaning with alternate interpretation. Ahab's mind is not the fulgurous residue of the lightning-struck mind, and the strength of his purpose is not merely a symptom of his injury—he is deeper, he has no shallows. Ahab is saying what he cannot say.

His question—"Moby Dick?"—results in realization. As Tashtego, Dagoo, and Queequeg describe the white whale known by the name Moby Dick, Ahab realizes that he must put his force into words. He sees that language is of use: a commerce equal in persuasive force to the doubloon nailed to the mainmast. He repeats the name: "it is Moby Dick ye have seen!—Moby Dick—Moby Dick!" The exuberance isn't simply his dark joy of this moment in which the crew recognizes and knows the name of the white whale Ahab plans to convince them to hunt. The exuberance arises, too, from the realization that Moby Dick's name is a catalyst to provoke in others the chemical reaction that lends Ahab's fury to them, a fraction of which becomes their own. The word—once said, once spoken—emerges from the possibilities of all meaning in which Ahab paces his time and becomes a single form, exchangeable, worldly, said.

See also:

Description
Dictionary
Doubloon
Expression
Nothing/ness
Pacing
Paradox
Profit
Reading (Doubloon)
Reciprocity
Soot
Totem

SCROLL

The whalers "cut in" to the first slain whale on a Sabbath day. They cut "a hole for insertion" of the blubber hook "just above the nearest of two side-fins," and once it is inserted, "the main body of the crew" commences to heave on the rope that winds through the intricacies of the tackle swaying from the main-topmast and ending in the hook in the whale. "More and more" the ship

> leans over to the whale, while every gasping heave of the windlass is answered by a helping heave from the billows; till at last, a swift, startling snap is heard; with a great swash the ship rolls upwards and backwards from the whale, and the triumphant tackle rises into sight dragging after it the disengaged semicircular end of the first strip of blubber.

The whale's blubber "envelopes the whale precisely as the rind does an orange," and the skin spirally strips from the whale until the carcass is bare. The image resonates beyond the biological description Ishmael, in his scientific mode, gives. The whale seems enscrolled. The scroll is its own skin. Its skin, we learn, is everywhere marked with lines as from fine Italian engravings and, below those marks, etched with hieroglyphs and other mystic signs. The whalers prepare the blubber for processing into profit by unwinding the scroll on which the whale's own text is etched. The whale will be processed into oil that, lit, casts light onto pages. The first five books of the Bible, the Pentateuch—or, in the Jewish tradition, the Torah—are a scroll. Before the blubber is put into the try-pots it is sliced as "thin as Bible-leaves." The source of one kind of light is a strange sort of literary analysis that burns the page before reading it.

See also:

Etching
Eyes
Inscribe
Mincer
Profit
Skin
Spectacles
Spermaceti
Tattoo

Silence

The sub-sub-librarian, appearing in the voluminous prefatory material, does no less ambitious work than the usher does with his *Etymology*. The sub-sub gives us a concordance of sorts, if we can turn the notion of concordance inside out. Instead of a book that lists the usage of all words by a single author, we have here the usage by all authors of a single word: *whale,* or *leviathan.* We begin with Genesis—"And God created great whales"—and end in Anonymous Ballad:

> Oh, the rare old Whale, mid storm and gale
>> In his ocean home will be
> A giant in might, where might is right,
>> And King of the boundless sea.

In between we brush against fiction, biological tracts, cetological treatises, poems, fables, captions below etchings, an entire panoply of written documents. The sub-sub's work, which at first seems like an accumulation, actually functions in a far different, far more disturbing way. The nature of the *Extracts* isn't anthology, isn't the positive recording of utterance and lexical usage to be turned to as reference. It isn't written in order to exist. Rather, the sub-sub's work functions negatively, uttering to remove speech, recording to erase reference. Just as, in modern astronomy, binocular telescopes can divide a single star's light into two beams that directed against each other cancel the same star's light (and so find a planet reflecting that star's light), the sub-sub writes down every written reference to whale/leviathan to strike the words against themselves, using language to cancel language. Whale is struck against whale; leviathan spoken cancels out leviathan. To say *all* is to provide the blank space for a new speaking. One can only reach nothing (a positive, almost

Heideggerian space) by noting every instance of language that makes nothing possible. Utter it all, and the blank page returns. We open *Moby-Dick* in echo of the tragedy to come. The silence after the Pequod has sunk with all the men aboard her, the silence out of which witnessing Ishmael speaks, is related to the silence the book struggles to create in order to begin. The blank silence of the novel's end has the written silence of its beginning clenched in its mouth: an Ouroboros (and the whale once thought a serpent), a circumference (and the whale hunted on the equator). Silence must occur before creation. "Call me Ishmael," like all first words, is spoken over the empty water, the silent page.

See also:

Aleph
Chaos
Crisis
Experience
Nothing/ness
Storm
Tablet
Tzimtzum

Skin

A creature's skin defines its outermost physical limit. Skin also marks the boundary of its broadest connection to the world. The skin is a threshold—half-philosophical and half-biological—between the external and the internal. World and mind, yes, but skin also divides an outer geography from an inner one: the hidden organic cosmos by which a creature lives and which, to some stoical minds, reflects the larger cosmos that both mirrors and threatens it. The skin is a woundable, wounded surface. The skin bears marks: scratches, scars, tattoos, ciphers. The skin is a continuous act of translation, a barrier to, and medium of, expression. A scar discloses history; a touch predicts.

"The question is, what and where is the skin of the whale?"

Blubber wraps scroll-like around a whale. "That blubber is something of the consistence of firm, close-grained beef, but tougher, more elastic and compact, and ranges from eight or ten to twelve and fifteen inches in thickness." Skin is a surface, but in the whale, the surface is a depth.

Surface to Depth

First: One can with but a finger's strength "scrape off with your hand an infinitely thin, transparent substance, somewhat resembling the thinnest shreds of isinglass, only it is almost as flexible and soft as satin." Once dried, this infinitely thin skin thickens and contracts, and "being laid upon the printed page" exerts "a magnifying influence." This skin is but "the skin of the skin."

Second: The surface below "the skin of the skin" is "almost invariably . . . all over crossed and re-crossed with numberless straight marks in thick array, something like those in the finest Italian line engravings."

Third: The quick eye delineates beneath the engraved lines "those mysterious ciphers on the walls of pyramids" called hieroglyphics.

DEPTH TO SURFACE

Undecipherable symbols beneath the finest etching lines beneath a magnifying lens: the whale's skin is a text beneath a palimpsest that magnifies its own mystery. His bulk demands to be read—Leviathan as Great Library—but offers a reader no clue as to the meaning of the text. To read we burn its page into oil, then burn the oil in a lamp above the book we're pondering.

The whale's skin begins in the infinitesimal and ends in the indefinite. The parchment torn and burned casts back light that makes legible another page. The whale is a book that cannot be read. The whale is a book beneath a book, meaningless itself but making possible meaning above it, as the bed of the ocean (which scratched upon the whale those undecipherable marks) makes possible the ocean. The ocean, like the whale's skin, is a surface and a depth.

See also:

Brain
Etching
Hieroglyph
Infinite / Indefinite
Line
Ocean

Soot

Ishmael, fishing up a few coins from his pocket, searches for modest chambers in New Bedford while waiting for the next ferry to take him to Nantucket. Wandering down darker and darker streets on a freezing December night, the northern lights and Orion beautiful but cold above him, he forsakes each inn that seems too convivial with cheer as likely to cost him too dear and walks toward the sea. This search for lodging that moves toward ever more grim accommodations parallels strangely the suicidal rationalization that brings Ishmael to abandon his teaching post to become a sailor in the first place. Ishmael acts out, almost unconsciously, the same grim, seaward compulsion of which he speaks and thinks—his actions bespeak his mind. What Ishmael experiences, and how he acts in response, reveals a simultaneous inner activity, so that the bleak (and darkly comic) search for lodging is but the outward manifestation of the same search occurring within.

Ishmael walks down "blocks of blackness" until he comes upon "a smoky light proceeding from a low, wide building, the door of which stood invitingly open." He steps in and "the first thing I did was to stumble over an ash-box in the porch." In his half-macabre and half-fatuous humor, as the ashes fly up, almost choking him, Ishmael wonders if these are the ashes of Gomorrah, and so thinking, hearing a loud voice within, pushes open an interior door to find "a hundred black faces turned round in their rows to peer" at the ash-covered man in the threshold. The "black Angel of Doom" of a preacher doesn't stop in surprise at the intrusion, but goes on in his teeth-gnashing fury, urging his parishioners on to weeping and wailing. None seem surprised at Ishmael's appearance, in part, perhaps, for being covered in dark ash he appears as black as they. Ishmael backs away, not so horrified at not belonging in the church as of the odder possibility that he does belong. He has become, suddenly, other than himself—an ash-covered change that foreshadows the deeper work of otherness upon which Ishmael will soon embark.

He goes back out into the black night and finds himself before the Spouter-Inn. Ishmael goes in, presumably ash coated still, coming dark from out the dark, and his attention is captured by

> a very large oil-painting so thoroughly besmoked, and every way
> defaced, that in the unequal cross-lights by which you viewed it,
> it was only by diligent study and a series of systematic visits to it,
> and careful inquiry of the neighbors, that you could any way ar-
> rive at an understanding of its purpose. . . . But what most puzzled
> and confounded you was a long, limber, portentous, black mass
> of something hovering in the centre of the picture over three blue,
> dim, perpendicular lines floating in a nameless yeast.

The humor in the scene is underscored by Ishmael's unexplainably ob-sessive need to interpret the painting's content. He looks at it from mul-tiple angles, nears it and steps away, attempts to find a stance from which meaning could become clear, and, failing, asks strangers what they think the painting might signify. Of equal depth, and equal curios-ity, Ishmael is himself a besooted smudge of a man—one whose inquiry into the painting's meaning is matched only by his inquiry into his own dark mysteries. What Ishmael guesses about the painting he also guesses about himself:

> —It's the Black Sea in a midnight gale.—It's the unnatural com-
> bat of the four primal elements.—It's a blasted heath.—It's a
> Hyperborean winter scene.—It's the breaking-up of the ice-bound
> stream of Time. But at last all these fancies yielded to that one
> portentous something in the picture's midst. *That* once found out,
> and all the rest were plain. But stop; does it not bear a faint resem-
> blance to a gigantic fish? even the great Leviathan himself?

Ishmael senses that to read so as to solve the mystery of what one is reading is itself to forge a meaning upon the work. Interpretation here is a "portentous" activity, disclosing the desires and fears, hopes and yearnings, of the one doing the reading as much as it reveals any accurate knowledge of that being looked at. More important than any conclusion Ishmael can come to—and the only conclusions available to him arise from solving his own sooty mystery—is facing the task such mystery forces with "unimaginable sublimity" upon him. His inability to find a definite reading of the painting has everything to do with his inability to define himself. A mystery reads a mystery—both coated by the residue of wood burnt to give heat and light, whose warmth and illumination now gone bear only the evidence of flame having spent itself on life's behalf, and whose work is now to recall the life that life itself has hidden.

See also:

Friendship
I / *I* / "I"
Ocean
Other
Reading (Doubloon)
Reading (Water)
Repetition
Savage
Skin
Tattoo

SPECTACLES

The thinnest surface of the whale's skin can be removed with but a finger's strength. Left to dry it grows brittle and transparent, "and laid upon the printed page," Ishmael says, "I have sometimes pleased myself with fancying it exerted a magnifying influence. At any rate, it is pleasant to read about whales through their own spectacles, as you may say." Ishmael reads by the light of whale oil. He reads a text about whales through which the word whale is itself magnified by the thin whale skin laid upon it. One could hazard a guess that Ishmael wrote his book on whales by a similar light, and that the book he's reading about whales may be his own. There is in the image some bewildering self-reference—as if the whale were a creaturely force that makes possible its own study even after it ceases to exist as a creature. As much as Stubb, eating his whale steak by the light of the selfsame slain beast, participates in some "universal cannibalism" of the world, so Ishmael, reading by, through, and of the whale, participates in some universal tautology. What one pursues speaks not only of desire. What one desires also refers back to the self who does the desiring. We see by the light of what we want; we read, and interpret what we read, by the light cast by our desire. The eye is a desiring lens. Cannibalism and tautology share an identifying principle; the principle is not skepticism, though it ends in the self. Both imply that all consumption is also self-consumption. Both subject the one who desires to the cost of that desire. Both make the pursuer also the pursued.

See also:

Cosmogony
Eyes
Hunger
Reciprocity
Scroll
Skin

SPERMACETI

Tashtego, while perilously removing the spermaceti from the vast Heidelburgh Tun, drops into the head he was emptying. Then, adding to the mortal danger of drowning in the prized oil, the cables holding the whale's head snap, and the head with Tashtego enwombed within it begins to sink. Queequeg dives into the ocean, boarding-sword in hand. Queequeg cuts a hole in the head and reaches in:

> He averred, that upon first thrusting in for him, a leg was pre-
> sented; but well knowing that that was not as it ought to be, and
> might occasion great trouble;—he had thrust back the leg, and
> by a dexterous heave and toss, had wrought a somerset upon the
> Indian; so that with the next trial, he came forth in the good old
> way—head foremost.

Not only does Queequeg rescue Tashtego, he avoids a breach delivery in doing so. Underneath the wit is a philosophical speculation. Ishmael, with gradually increasing persistence, claims the sperm whale as a Platonic Leviathan. As he meditates on the demise narrowly avoided by Tashtego, he says:

> Now, had Tashtego perished in that head, it had been a very pre-
> cious perishing; smothered in the very whitest and daintiest of
> fragrant spermaceti; coffined, hearsed, and tombed in the secret
> inner chamber and sanctum sanctorum of the whale. Only one
> sweeter end can readily be recalled—the delicious death of an
> Ohio honey-hunter, who seeking honey in the crotch of a hollow
> tree, found such exceeding store of it, that leaning too far over, it
> sucked him in, so that he died embalmed. How many, think ye,

have likewise fallen into Plato's honey head, and sweetly perished there?

Given Ishmael's speculations, given his suspicions about the sperm whale's Platonic nature—"the Sperm Whale, a Platonian, who might have taken up Spinoza in his latter years"—it seems as if to die within the sperm whale's head is likewise to die within Plato's. Tashtego's oily crisis inside the whale grants him witness to the Forms that form the insensible world, grants him access to that soulful reality he forgot in being born and, in being born, embodied. Tashtego's rebirth, with Queequeg as midwife, headfirst out of a womb that is itself a head, is a philosophical passage paralleling a physical one. Socrates' philosophical method was maieutic. Aboard the Pequod, at least for a day, Queequeg is our Socrates, the whale our universe, and Tashtego the emblem of the human soul emerging again into the world. But Queequeg is not a propositional Socrates, he is an active one. He does not ask a question to reawaken knowledge forgot. He acts in fluent unconsciousness, the natural ease of one who need not speak. He acts, too, in the sorrow of one who cannot speak—his actions serve as his philosophy.

See also:

Babel
Crisis
Eyes
Flame
Hands
Plato
Reading (Epistemology)
Scroll
Skin

STARRY ARCHIPELAGOES

The stars shine from their distance, beacons bright across abyss. A habit of mind considers the stars unreachable, a sphere encompassing our earthly sphere, casting light benign or light malignant, influencing lives of which the stars have no part, save a glimmer in the eye. Not everyone thinks so. Queequeg's people "believe that the stars are isles, but that far beyond all visible horizons, their own mild, uncontinented seas, interflow with the blue heavens; and so form the white breakers of the milky way." The vision of the cosmos as a series of out-ringing orbs—a perfect order in which none connect, each sphere encompassing a lesser sphere, so that our earthquake life does not ripple a red star's light, nor does a star's collapse blow from its downward motion a single mote of dust in the room where one writes—gives way to a vision of the universe in which each part, however abysmally distant, is also connected, also one. A star's death, in this latter cosmology, does more than darken a portion of the sky—it also darkens the eye that gazed up at it, and removes it from the eye, and from the life behind the eye, as a destination.

Pip, too, sees the world in metonymic connection to the universe—to speak of a part is to imply the whole, and if language forges the sense of reality in us, to speak of one location (even of a coffin aboard a ship upon the ocean) connects one to the farthest edge of the universe. As the ocean touches every shore at once, so in this ocean existence one mote connects each to all: "A Universe in a Grain of Sand." Pip gives Queequeg a message to carry with him to the "sweet Antilles" in the stars:

> But if the currents carry ye to those sweet Antilles where the beaches are only beat with water-lilies, will ye do one little errand for me? Seek out one Pip, who's now been missing long: I think he's in those far Antilles. If you find him, then comfort him; for

he must be very sad; for look! He's left his tambourine behind;—
I found it. Rig-a-dig, dig, dig! Now, Queequeg, die; and I'll beat
your dying march.

What such a metonymic world allows, and Pip in his prophetic madness
understands this point in the most heartbreaking of ways, is the recovery
of everyone, and everything, that has been lost—including oneself. When
Pip says "I" he refers both to someone he is whom he does not know, a
phantom in the flesh, and a poor boy lost in the edges of existence, waiting
to be found. Death is a distant island that tricks the eye into thinking it a
star, "but Death is only a launching into the region of the strange Untried;
it is but the first salutation to the possibilities of the immense Remote, the
Wild, the Watery, the Unshored." The ocean prefaces death. The water
extending out indefinitely to every horizon, so that the eye nowhere finds
boundary or limit, suggests that the world is flat at the same time that it
is rounded. The living move forward and stay afloat upon the bending
surface. But the dead sail straight, released from gravity's grave pull, and
in their current-pushed keel connect the stars to the stars. Ishmael goes
to sea when contemplating suicide not to distract himself from his self-
destructive thoughts but because this ocean-life is also deathly. A whaler
dies just enough, by virtue of stepping aboard the ship, to sense that the
world is not simply a sphere contained by another sphere, inviolate and
blue, singing its own elegy as it daily turns its tune.

See also:

Coffin
Crisis
Death
Leg (Ghost)
Ocean
Prophet
Reading (Doubloon)

STORM

Two storms occur in *Moby-Dick,* one actual and an ominous warning, and one metaphorical but just as dangerous. Both storms occur at sea. The first rages outside the sailor suffering the gale and, simultaneously, another gale blows within him. The wind in both cases threatens to drive the ship against the land that seems to promise safety but instead harbors destruction:

> But in that gale, the port, the land, is that ship's direst jeopardy; she must fly all hospitality; one touch of land, though it but graze the keel, would make her shudder through and through. With all her might she crowds all sail off shore; in so doing, fights 'gainst the very winds that fain would blow her homeward; seeks all the lashed sea's landlessness again; for refuge's sake forlornly rushing into peril; her only friend her bitterest foe!

The storm—murkily metaphorical, murkily real—turns home hostile, makes of harbor a horror, because it removes the sailor from the indefinite ocean which has become his universal home. A whaler lives in unutterable danger; home is where you tell your story. Bulkington's silence is also his storm. A syllable of thunder on sea sounds out an infinite power; on land, it is but the worded echo of a power endured.

The second storm batters the Pequod before the final chase begins. Ahab enters as madly into it as Lear enters into his storm. Such a storm confuses the world with oppositions. The cloud is an ocean in the air; the gale is a current. The falling rain is a link that forges sky to sea and makes of them a single thing. The boundaries do not hold. Ahab's madness, like Lear's madness, reflects itself in the furious storm he faces. The exterior world and the interior world have lost—in storm—their opposition. A man at such a moment can hold lightning in his hand, flame on a harpoon blade's tip. The storm undoes the order of the world and returns it to its primal strife, in which each agent suffering the storm also acts within it, on it, of it.

The world is this stormy turmoil, defined only by the limits of its own enraged system. A world within a world. The storm does not reconcile opposites, it brings them into collision, into collusion—implicates the subject with the object, undoes the distance between one who sees, or thinks he sees, and the world seen. The storm connects all to all. Our daily life, our blue-sky life, offers the safety of knowing where sky begins and land ends, where I begin and you end, where the world is everywhere not me. The storm is the end of that safety. The storm offers no transcendental harmony, no redeeming sense of our mortal inter-indebtedness—it is the indescribable strife of self moving against other self, world tumbling into world (the same turmoil of clouds storming against clouds whose fury tears ions from atoms and explodes into lightning), in which we are both one and at war with each other, which is to say, self-hostile, self-thunderous, self-storming.

See also:

Cordelia
Death
Hands
Lightning
Nothing/ness
Starry Archipelagoes
Truth

SURPLUS

1. Moby Dick

Rumor and superstition radiate outward from Moby Dick, infecting most who hear of him with a fear that borders on repulsion, and others with a fear that draws them magnetically toward the object of their horror. The whaling life creates an atmosphere in which superstitions abound, not because whalers are weak minded but because "of all sailors, they are by all odds the most directly brought into contact with whatever is appallingly astonishing in the sea."

Of all such appalling astonishments, none is more appalling than the whale Ahab pursues. Whalers ascribe to Moby Dick impossible attributes, with "new terrors unborrowed from anything that visibly appears." Men believe the white whale is ubiquitous, "that he had actually been encountered in opposite latitudes at one and the same instant of time." Some whalemen go further, "declaring Moby Dick not only ubiquitous, but immortal." If one thinks one has struck with a harpoon his heart, it is but an illusion, and the white whale at the instant of its seeming death might, in opposite latitude, be found ramming the boat of a man trying to cast a lance into him. The white whale, whalemen say, is not a beast of dumb instinct but a creature of "unexampled, intelligent malignity." Whom Moby Dick kills, he means to kill. Whom Moby Dick wounds, he means to wound. Moby Dick is "truth with malice in it."

Moby Dick's horror emanates from the impossible peculiarity of his attributes. He is one and he is all. He is a single point and he is everywhere. He is living and he is dead at once. Moby Dick's physical characteristics identify him exclusively: a crooked jaw, a curious spout, a "pyramidical white hump" on his "snow-white, wrinkled forehead." Yet, the closer one comes to identifying the white whale, and in seeing giving

chase, the more that unique particularity widens, becomes more diffi-
cult to address, to see. The point of particularity (a point sharper than
any harpoon tip) is also, impossibly, a universal width. "[T]o chase and
point lance at such an apparition as the Sperm Whale was not for mortal
man"; to "attempt it would be inevitably to be torn into a quick eter-
nity." The whalemen who pursue Moby Dick, the men who feel Ahab's
"quenchless feud" as their own, chase a whale who embodies qualities
no body can contain.

The white whale exists in surplus. It lives within the indefinite reaches
of the ocean, but in its deeper existence overflows all boundary of self
and world. This surplus—this quality of the white whale being always
more than its singular existence—is the most significant aspect of Moby
Dick's lethal nature. The white whale is "fatal to the last degree of fa-
tality." He does not merely introduce you to the death he causes, he is
death's commencement and its depthless end. Moby Dick is the tangible,
material, creature whose nature unfolds into the intangible, the immate-
rial, the immortal, the eternal, the infinite. The men who chase the white
whale also chase these indecipherable qualities that overflow any pos-
sible comprehension. To hunt the white whale is also to hunt the evanes-
cent, malicious truth that refuses all definition, all boundary, all body, all
life—yet stores the force of its fatality in a singular being.

2. Ahab

Stubb dreams of Ahab as a pyramid, and of the whale as Ahab. Moby
Dick swims with a pyramid in his brow; Ahab's vital strength lurks in
his "Egyptian chest." Explicitly enough, Ishmael leads us to understand
that Ahab and Moby Dick are interconnected in the most harrowing of
ways—they share symbols, share a symbolic life, and so both participate,
unwittingly or unwillingly as it may be, in that to which they both refer.
Ahab's hate for the whale that wounded him also manifests a self-hatred,
for the chase is curiously, and horrifically, a work that occurs within him
as it occurs outside of him. Ahab also pursues himself as a man who

exists simultaneously outside himself and within himself. Ahab is a center and a circumference, and if we can ascribe to his mad pursuit motives deeper than mere revenge—a quest after dark truth, a quest not to die but a quest after death, a quest to witness, to know, the world past the world's margins—he exemplifies the terrible possibility that one chases after an answer that is always located within oneself, even as it swims to the knowable world's limit. Ahab's self, too, is in surplus. He does not end at his reach's end. His body is a broken boundary from which his rage gains continual momentum. He leaks out.

What occurred when Ahab struck the white whale with a six-inch knife, and the whale turned around at the glance and, "sweeping his sickle-shaped lower jaw beneath him," reaped away Ahab's leg "as a mower a blade of grass," exceeded the wounding of Ahab's body. Moby Dick wounds deeper—wounds the mind, wounds the spirit. The wounded mind isn't simply insane, nor the wounded spirit enraged with doubt. Moby Dick wounds actively, which is to say, wounds in surplus rather than wounds by lack. Moby Dick exasperates intellect, heightens doubt. The white whale wounds with the force of "that intangible malignity which has been from the beginning." The wound is the underside of the world.

Ahab is not weakened by Moby Dick. He is mortally injured, but that mortal wound sets loose in Ahab a force that allows him to abandon time and place, all constraints of the surface world on which Ahab works but does not dwell. His madness is the overflow of his intellect, not "one jot" of which has he lost. Far opposite, the wound gives Ahab "a thousand-fold more potency than ever he had sanely brought to bear upon any one reasonable object." Moby Dick, in wounding Ahab, also lends him the surplus of strength and purpose by which Ahab will chase him.

The intelligence with which Moby Dick acts leads one to suspect he wounded Ahab so that the pursuit we read of can begin. The wound does not warn, it beckons. If, as in Stubb's dream, it is an honor to be kicked by a man like Ahab (so says the Merman), what honor is it to be wounded by Moby Dick? It is the honor of being made more than oneself, made aware of how one always exists in excess of the limits of one's body and one's mind. The whale wounds Ahab to remind him, and so us, how one is born of the same mystery one pursues. The self in surplus of the self.

See also:
I / *I* / "I"
Justice
Magnet
Paradox
Pyramid
Reciprocity
Whiteness
Wound
You / Thou

Tablet

When Ishmael walks into Father Mapple's chapel, Queequeg turns and looks at him: "This savage was the only person present who seemed to notice my entrance; because he was the only one who could not read, and, therefore, was not reading those frigid inscriptions on the wall." Those "frigid inscriptions" are etched into "several marble tablets, with black borders" that serve as memorials to sailors lost at sea. Ishmael watches the worshippers reading, assuming (rightly or wrongly) that those reading a particular tablet are the mourners of the sailor—husband or son, father or brother—lost at sea. He notes each reader's isolation: "Each silent worshipper seemed purposely sitting apart from the other, as if each silent grief were insular and incommunicable." When a mourner visits the cemetery where a loved one eternally sojourns, when she reads the headstone, what little comfort remains is, in part, the sense that the name carved into the headstone refers to the body buried beneath it. Death seems not to deny reference; the name refers to the named.

The awful sorrow Ishmael witnesses in the reader-worshippers in the chapel has no such comfort. The names and brief narratives—"towed out of sight by a Whale, / on the Off-shore Ground in the / PACIFIC"— refer as much to the nothingness carved into the stone by which the letters appear as to the loved ones lost. What keeps open and causes "the old wounds to bleed afresh" is more than language's ghostlike ability to haunt the mourning mind with memory. Memory, after all, can be recompense for loss—to see the face the words evoke. The sorrowful isolation of those in the chapel emerges from the words carved on the tablets, words whose sense extends out toward a body that can never be reclaimed back into reference. The language pushes against a realm into which no word can pierce: the body drifting infinitely down within the infinite sea. Such a death refuses to divorce body from soul. The two merge and are lost together in death, each equally lost in the infinite realm to which they now belong, to which words may point, may suggest direction, may cast out the living mind along a thoughtful, pointed line—but the line attaches to nothing. The point widens, as if into a net through which, when pulled up, the indecipherable world escapes. Such words do not bring memory. Such words call out into the depths from which no sound can return, not in response or in echo. Such carved words bring the mind against the very blank they would name. One who reads such words moves her lips as she does so, seeming to speak as she reads, lending her whispered voice to etched words, but by her speaking she turns herself deaf. Silence is all that speaks back.

See also:

Death
Dictionary
Faith
Inscribe
Leg (Ghost)
Orpheus
Reading (Epistemology)
Silence
Starry Archipelagoes
Tzimtzum
Whale (Ghost)

Tattoo

A tattoo merges the act of writing with the act of etching, that act of ink put to vellum (a skin prepared for use as parchment) and engraving. The ink is inscribed beneath the skin and, through that thinnest epidermal layer, shows forth—often a symbol, a word of symbolic weight, a hieroglyph. The tattoo makes of the body a book, a library of lived experience, and the marks inked into skin serve both to communicate that experience emblematically as well as to remind the bearer of the tattoo of the event lived through. To bear the mark of such memory on the skin means that the memory cannot settle merely into the past tense, a matter of the mind. Rather, the lived experience is borne always in the living present—and, written on the body, such experience confronts all experience to come, establishes relation with what the body bears as its content, and fosters awareness of the apparent fact that we approach no new experience as a blank slate. The body actualizes translation.

Queequeg is heavily tattooed. Ishmael, hiding in the bed of their soon-to-be shared room, spies fearfully as Queequeg undresses and performs his rites:

> Such a face! It was of a dark, purplish, yellow color, here and there stuck over with large, blackish looking squares. . . . But at that moment he chanced to turn his face so towards the light, that I plainly saw they could not be sticking plasters at all, those black squares on his cheeks. They were stains of some sort or other. At first I knew not what to make of this; but soon an inkling of the truth occurred to me. I remembered a story of a white man—a whaleman too—who, falling among the cannibals, had been tattooed by them. I concluded that this harpooner, in

the course of his distant voyages, must have met with a similar adventure. . . . Meanwhile, he continued the business of undressing, and at last showed his chest and arms. As I live, these covered parts of him were checkered with the same squares as his face; his back, too, was all over the same dark squares; he seemed to have been in a Thirty Years' War, and just escaped from it with a sticking-plaster shirt. Still more, his very legs were marked, as if a parcel of dark green frogs were running up the trunks of young palms.

We see here Queequeg in a curious unveiling of text, but, just as importantly, we also catch Ishmael in the process of reading this other's text. Here is a book in the form of a person—not information he can gather, not a fact to insert into a treatise, but a text that bears the weight of actual mystery, that resists interpretation, that claims that some act other than cognition is required in order to read this book, this person. As Wallace Stevens writes, "The poem must resist the intelligence / almost successfully."

The wisdom here is in the nature of the failure of such resistance. Ishmael does not learn how to read the "text" Queequeg presents (for reasons to be revealed much later in *Moby-Dick*); Ishmael befriends—by his own description, becomes "wife of"—Queequeg. He does not learn the content of the body, but rather seeks to understand it, and with it the man who bears the content. In the morning, Ishmael prays to Queequeg's wooden god, Yojo, and finds Queequeg thumbing through the pages of a bible, reading a book he cannot read.

When, now long aboard the Pequod, Queequeg grows ill, "there seemed but little left of him but his frame and tattooing." Reduced to a spine (binding) and a marked skin (vellum), Queequeg asks for a coffin to be built, so sure he is he will die. These Nantucket coffins, which Queequeg much admired on first seeing them, are dark canoes in which sailors' bodies are placed and pushed out to sea. Queequeg places various sundries in the coffin-canoe for the trip to the afterlife, but he ends the preparations in remarkable fashion:

Many spare hours he spent, in carving the lid with all manner of grotesque figures and drawings; and it seemed that hereby he was striving, in his rude way, to copy parts of the twisted tattooing on his body. And this tattooing, had been the work of a departed prophet and seer of his island, who, by those hieroglyphic marks, had written out on his body a complete theory of the heavens and the earth, and a mystical treatise on the art of attaining truth; so that Queequeg in his own proper person was a riddle to unfold; a wondrous work in one volume; but whose mysteries not even himself could read, though his own live heart beat against them; and these mysteries were therefore destined in the end to moulder away with the living parchment whereon they were inscribed, and so be unsolved to the last.

Here the tattoo gains a kind of emblematic complexity—for the deep tenet of thinking in and of *Moby-Dick* is the fundamental belief that one can clarify complexity without reducing it, even as the complexity burgeons forth, obscuring itself in its own expansion. In the case of Queequeg's tattoo, the subjective self has no choice, no ability to even understand, what it is he signifies. A tattoo complicates issues of text, body, and time, but in this particular case the tattoo also complicates issues of self and self-knowledge, of cultural inheritance, of experiential epistemology.

The body here exists as a page permeable, though not transparent, to absolute exteriority and absolute interiority. Queequeg bears upon himself the knowledge of his entire culture. If he could learn how to read himself, the inherited knowledge of all his ancestors would be legible to him. One could say that every body bears in it this same promise; Queequeg is unique in that his body bears on it this graphical content that remains invisible, unwritten, unintelligible in the rest of us. Not that Queequeg's tattoos ease the difficulty of his non-knowledge for him. Quite the opposite. His tattoos only sharpen the point, the poignancy, of seeking answers in a world that seems to resist them, for his very body bears every possible answer to every possible question he could ask (if by epistemology we understand the whole reach of a particular culture's thinking).

To bear a treatise of truth, to bear an epistemology, is to bear all knowledge to the limits any such knowledge encroaches upon. That is to say, Queequeg does not have written upon him infinity but the limited whole that bears his culture's relation to infinity. It is by virtue of that relation—that living relation of a self with the world, and of the world with that Nothing from which the world sprang—that Queequeg carves his body into his coffin. For it is only in such relation that one can believe one's own illiteracy to be less important than the overwhelming faith that the world can read what you yourself cannot—that the world is literate, or that is literate which reads the world.

The tattoo presents the act of reading as such: a self without freedom to doubt the body, for the body bears truth. And that, in the act of reading itself, the body also reads the world, and the world beyond the world.

See also:

Coffin
Etching
Friendship
Hieroglyph
Inscribe
Line
Nothing/ness
Reading (Epistemology)
Savage
Skin
Starry Archipelagoes
Writing

Thought (Ahab)

The last day of the chase, before Ahab has unpuzzled Fedallah's prophecy, he speaks in reverie:

> Here's food for thought, had Ahab time to think; but Ahab never thinks; he only feels, feels, feels; *that's* tingling enough for mortal man! to think's audacity. God only has that right and privilege. Thinking is, or ought to be, a coolness and a calmness; and our poor hearts throb, and our poor brains beat too much for that.

Feeling the wind blow through his ashen gray hair, Ahab muses, analogizes, realizes and asserts:

> How the wild winds blow it; they whip it about me as the torn shreds of split sails lash the tossed ship they cling to. A vile wind that has no doubt blown ere this through prison corridors and cells, and wards of hospitals, and ventilated them, and now comes blowing hither as innocent as fleeces. Out upon it!—it's tainted. Were I the wind, I'd blow no more on such a wicked, miserable world. I'd crawl somewhere to a cave, and slink there. And yet, 'tis a noble and heroic thing, the wind! who ever conquered it? In every fight it has the last and bitterest blow. Run tilting at it, and you but run through it. Ha! a coward wind that strikes stark naked man, but will not stand to receive a single blow. Even Ahab is a braver thing—a nobler thing than *that*. Would now the wind but had a body; but all things that most exasperate and outrage mortal man, all these things are bodiless, but only bodiless as objects, not as agents.

Calm thought and the bodiless, maddening wind, Ahab's windswept hair (gray for having grown out the ash heap of his mind), and the mast that anchors the billowing sail—all become interwoven on this last day of Ahab's life. The force that drives Ahab and with him the crew of the Pequod shares much with the "nameless, inscrutable, unearthly thing" he chases. Wind and white whale. The sail fills with wind as a mind fills with thought—a strong enough gale will blow both to tatters, and a gale of less brutal force will push one around the world. But such thought comes as force, as a rage that must be collected, not countered. The thought-full mind, like the wind-full wave, reverberates with the element that fills it, thundering as the fabric snaps taut when the gust is caught. The sail billows and the mind pulses: one on mast of pine, one on spine. No object, but agent.

Ahab suspects that Moby Dick is of the same nature. Yet in the white whale, object and agency confuse their opposition. The white whale is thought embodied, wind calmed, breath contained. The other men aboard the Pequod think that Moby Dick is intelligent; Ahab knows differently. Ahab knows the white whale is intelligence: thought thinking itself. What better explanation can exist for the first sighting of dreaded Leviathan:

A gentle joyousness—a mighty mildness of repose in swiftness, invested the gliding whale. Not the white bull Jupiter swimming away with ravished Europa clinging to his graceful horns; his lovely, leering eyes sideways intent upon the maid; with smooth bewitching fleetness, rippling straight for the nuptial bower in Crete; not Jove, not that great majesty Supreme! did surpass the glorified White Whale as he so divinely swam.

On each soft side—coincident with the parted swell, that but once leaving him, then flowed so wide away—on each bright side, the whale shed off enticings. No wonder there had been some among the hunters who namelessly transported and allured by all this serenity, had ventured to assail it; but had fatally found that quietude but the vesture of tornadoes. Yet calm, enticing calm, oh, whale! thou glidest on, to all who for the first time eye thee, no matter how many in that same way thou may'st have bejuggled and destroyed before.

A thoughtful calm precedes an active terror. But even such silent, calm, self-thinking thought leaves a trace in the world. The white whale leaves behind it a white scroll, a wake that unrolls like an endless parchment.

Ahab may not care for dictionaries, and the worded world dictionaries define, but he cares for the page such nonsense is printed upon. "So that to this hunter's wondrous skill, the proverbial evanescence of a thing writ in water, a wake, is to all desired purposes well nigh as reliable as the steadfast land." The page writ upon water waits for no word to buck it down with meaning made explicit. Ahab reads the page on the water. It unfolds upon the waves as a blank page unfolds beneath ink: the meaning that must exist before meaning is possible. The blank before appearance. The thinking silence before the thoughtless word.

See also:

Brain
Breath (Thought)
Inspiration
Leg (Ghost)
Line
Pacing
Reading (Water)
Thought (Hunt)

THOUGHT (HUNT)

Epistemologies hide in sentences. *Moby-Dick* is littered not only with the odd detritus of leaky knowledge and failed fact, but with theories of knowledge that lurk like jettisoned ballast—a potential threat and a potential balance both. One such, from a meditation upon the sperm whale's forehead, and so also our own:

> Few are the foreheads which like Shakespeare's or Melancthon's
> rise so high, and descend so low, that the eyes themselves seem
> clear, eternal, tideless mountain lakes; and all above them in the
> forehead's wrinkles, you seem to track the antlered thoughts
> descending there to drink, as the Highland hunters track the
> snowprints of the deer.

The metaphor is telling in its effort at accuracy. The eyes are pools whose water is the seen world—the vaster one's attention, the deeper the water. The eyes are the pools the antlered thoughts drink in. The image makes a vast claim: that thoughts (note how the body of the deer is constructed by metonymy, as if the defining scope of the whole beast must be imagined in order to be seen) feed upon vision, thoughts slake their thirst in the perceptual.

The cost of thinking thoughts in the world is an embodiment in which they must survive in the world. To grasp these thoughts one hunts them. The hunter does not see the body of the deer, he sees only the footprints—the evidence of existence, not the existence itself. The antlered thoughts are vulnerable when they drink from the eyes' pools that nourish them in their animal form. Thoughts take form to dwell in the world and do not sustain that form themselves. Thus they drink, and can be hunted. The hunter is the same I from whose eyes the deer drink. The thinking self is divided in two. There is one who sees, whose attention deepens his own eyes into "clear, tideless, eternal mountain lakes," and there is one who watches the thoughts lap perception from his own eyes; he is also the one who kills them. They are the same one. "I think" is always being hunted by "I am."

See also:

Brain
Breath (Thought)
Imagination
Nothing/ness
Phrenology
Reading (Epistemology)
Truth
Whale (Ghost)

TIME

Time grants us the simple goodness of life, but also takes it away. We change and we witness change in the world, and both types of flux occur within time. While we live the world exists for us, and though none can say if the world ceases to exist when we've ceased to exist, there can be no doubt that when I die my world is gone. Time reminds us to look as all we love passes before us as we ourselves pass away. No instance of time diminishes Time, but in time we diminish. Add time to space, and we can near that which we love, we can cross distance to grasp that which has caught our affection—across time we can speak. A syllable contains a second. A word moves from mind to mouth, from mouth to ear, and then from ear into the other's mind. The spoken word and the word remembered exist differently in time. A word gathers meaning in memory as a bee gathers sweetness in a hive—the residue after the flight. Expression is a temporal activity before it is a linguistic one. Even approach is a form of evanescence.

~

Time is, as Kant notes, "nothing else than the form of the internal sense, that is, of the intuitions of self and of our internal state." Time gains reality within us. We cannot perceive time in the objects of the world, but we do perceive the objects of the world within time. Witness is a mortal activity; the mortal is he who sees. What he sees—the world's phenomena—may or may not be mortal. We witness the witness. But as we cannot know another's knowing, so we cannot see another's sight. We express what we see and listen to others express what they see, and so we unfold the interior reality in which we perceive and think into an outer world another recognizes, thinks of, participates in. The word carries forward world by virtue of language's inherent ability to transfer time as it transfers meaning.

We express something of our mortality when we speak of what we love, what we think, what we see. Those we speak to listen mortally. We do not recognize in each other time so much as we recognize time in ourselves. No person's life is as real to us as our own life is. If there is such a thing as the "suspension of disbelief," it is not a fictive quality so much as it is a quality of faith. To think another's life is as real as my own is to suspend my disbelief. Knowledge is not fact, but rather this stranger, less empirical, doubtful activity of such faith. I do not know the world, but in knowing myself know the world. Likewise of that other who is not me—my friend, my wife, my child. A transcendent moment may be a simple concept: the mutually creative point at which a world expressed and a world received coincide in time. I speak out the world within the reality of subjective time that makes my world possible, and you listen from your own time, from the depth and singularity of your own subjectivity. Transcendence occurs when my world becomes real for you and thus is no longer merely mine, while the perception of this world is no longer merely yours. In becoming real for you, my world gains from your otherness, from your not being me. You shape it as you listen to it.

Such moments betray the easy dichotomy of subject and object, self and world, self and other. Expression and perception merge into a single creative gesture, not timeless but partaking simultaneously of two times, blurring the inevitable confines of our impenetrable selves for a miraculous conjunction in which the world hovers between us, co-created, equally real for both. This world is not removed from time. Rather, like the moment of erotic consummation, it is the world that manages to fuse subjectivity and objectivity, cause and effect, into simultaneous rather than successive qualities. Socrates considers this intermediary space love. The loved world, the erotic world, requires a you and a me to exist—and to exist is to be in time.

Ahab is a man wounded by a whale who seems immortal. To be wounded by such a creature is not to receive a mortal wound so much as it is to receive an immortal one. Ahab's wound will never heal because it is only accidentally a damage to flesh. The immortal wound brings to crisis the dichotomy between exterior and interior, body and soul. Ahab's "quenchless feud" results from the substitution of a temporal reality for an eternal one. That Moby Dick removed Ahab's leg is far less a loss than the wound the whale opened in Ahab's nonbodied self. Ahab is a leaky vessel, not taking in water but leaking as a barrel of oil, the sperm escaping back into the ocean from which it was stolen. Except there is no end to Ahab's leaking, for he is not leaking substance. He is leaking essence; he is leaking soul.

The result of this damage is that Ahab's subjective self has lost its sense of time. Ahab is no longer a temporal man, which is not to say that he is eternal. Ahab no longer has the most basic of human abilities to lend reality to the world through the basic reality of his own subjective sense of time. If there can be an explanation as to why Ahab so willingly sails his crew toward certain death, it is not to be found in questioning his ethics. Ahab has been removed from ethical consideration, for he has ceased to belong to time. Such a cessation of time has removed him from his own humanity. Such a condition is what underlies the absolute honesty of asking, "Is Ahab, Ahab? Is it I, God, or who, that lifts this arm?" Ahab has lost the ability to distinguish between cause and effect, subject and object. There is no definition of agency because there is no end to it. Ahab is uncertain of himself. He has lost time. And this loss that underlies his lack of self-recognition also conditions his inability to recognize the human lives under his sway. Ahab doesn't hesitate to send all after the white whale because he cannot recognize their mortality. His own rupture from time removes him from the empathic understanding of others' being in time. He cannot see his own death, so how see that for others his mad chase is a mortal question? We cannot guess at a reality that does not emerge from the understanding of our own. Ahab is a man without a world because he is a man without time.

See also:

TONGUE

(The sperm whale's mouth is large enough that a man can live within it. Or so Ishmael claims.)

～

A sperm whale has no discernible tongue.

～

A sperm whale swallows a prophet who will not speak.

～

When the prophet leaves the whale's mouth, he speaks.

～

A sperm whale swallows a prophet for a tongue.

See also:
Expression
Jonah
Prophet
Scroll
Silence
Skin

Totem

Opposite the besooted oil painting in the Spouter-Inn, whose image Ishmael cannot stop attempting to decipher and so understand, stands a wall "hung all over with a heathenish array of monstrous clubs and spears. Some were thickly set with glittering teeth resembling ivory saws; others were tufted with knots of human hair; and one was sickle-shaped, with a vast handle sweeping round like the segment made in the new-mown grass by a long-armed mower." Ishmael stands between two walls—and in a sense, his position in the Spouter-Inn presents the difficulty of his position throughout the novel he narrates—unable to interpret a mimetic translation of the world and "shuddering to see" the implements of a totemic one. The horror he feels in seeing the barbarous tools (among which also hang old harpoons and lances, "storied weapons" with which a man fifty years ago killed fifteen whales in a day) is not an aspect of their appearance so much as a recognition of some darker meaning that radiates from the objects themselves.

Ishmael is caught in the chasm in his mind—a chasm whose walls, though deeper than any earthly canyon, are also the walls of the Spouter-Inn's main room. Ishmael is suspended above, by reason's mere plank, the abyss that forms between two competing approaches to understanding the world. It might be too simple to claim these two worldviews represent modern and archaic ways of thinking, for such an approach carries with it a judgment that *Moby-Dick* seeks to complicate (we must remember that Ishmael's allegiance is to none but the King of Cannibals). On one wall he finds the semiotic difficulty of the distance that occurs between any sign and any signified, the haunting arbitrariness of language's ability to evoke and connect to the world it names.

Interpretation—like the Pequod's chase that originates in Ahab's wound and terminates in the whale that gave the wound—always attempts to cross a distance. That distance, as Emerson speaks of it, seems at times "an innavigable sea [that] washes with silent waves between us and the things we aim at and converse with." At other times it seems we manage to skate artfully from surface to surface and can claim to understand what we feel we grasp—as Ishmael moves from the surface of soot on the painting to the surface of the painting itself. The looming sadness in such understanding is that one senses beneath the surface a depth that remains unexplained if not unexplainable. We come to recognize how a sign connects to a signified, and from that connection forms a world that seems almost solid enough to bear our own subjective weight alongside its objective meaning. But the work of interpretation finds no harbor in certainty. A fact is ice that's melting. A word is but a boat pushed by the waves ashore, grounded and true until the tide rises again and sweeps it back into the uncertain sea, floating on planks joined by nails—no more.

The other world resists interpretation. The totemic object speaks to us more than we speak of it. Meaning arises from some hidden essence within the material itself. It pronounces its own history—as if in the harpoon remains the deadly potency of the hand that used it to slay Leviathan. Such objects do not lend themselves to our hand to be used and, in being used, brought into meaning. The agency is peculiarly reversed. We are brought into meaning in the use of the powerful object whose reality is more fundamental, more essential, than our own. One senses the numen below the name, and the name is simply a cloak the indwelling spirit of the object can remove of its own volition and so be disclosed in its own power.

The Pequod—the ship that will be final abode for all save Ishmael—is a microcosm of these very issues:

> . . . this old Peleg, during the term of his chief-mateship, had built upon her original grotesqueness, and inlaid it, all over, with a quaintness both of material and device, unmatched by anything except it be Thorkill-Hake's carved buckler or bedstead. She was appareled like any barbaric Ethiopian emperor, his neck heavy

with pendants of polished ivory. She was a thing of trophies. A cannibal of a craft, tricking herself forth in the chased bones of her enemies. All round, her unpanelled, open bulwarks were garnished like one continuous jaw, with the long sharp teeth of the sperm whale, inserted there for pins, to fasten her old hempen thews and tendons to. Those thews ran not through base blocks of land wood, but deftly travelled over sheaves of sea-ivory.

The motion, purpose, and pursuit of the ship mimics a world whose meaning can be arrived at—and here, arrival of sign to signified is of a most literal potency—by bringing into encounter the subject that hunts its object. Indeed, the Pequod is dressed in the very bones of the animal it hunts, referring to that which it chases. But those very bones deny the semiotic value they seem to imply. They radiate out with their own totemic meaning, as if the Pequod itself were the whale god it chases.

See also:

Cosmogony
Dictionary
Etymology
Hieroglyph
Imagination
Jawbone
Pequod
Reading (Doubloon)
Reading (Epistemology)
Reading (Water)
Soot
Tattoo

TRUTH

When on Christmas Day the Pequod leaves the harbor, Ishmael sees at the ship's helm a man he first saw two weeks earlier at the Spouter-Inn: Bulkington. Along with the crew of the whale ship he worked on, Bulkington has just returned from a successful voyage and, entering the inn, they all go to the bar (carved to look like a right whale's head, from which the bartender, Jonah, pours drinks all around) to celebrate both their success at sea and now being back on mainland. Bulkington is described in a way that suggests he'll be a major character in the novel to follow:

> He stood full six feet in height, with noble shoulders, and a chest like a coffer-dam. I have seldom seen such brawn in a man. His face was deeply brown and burnt, making his white teeth dazzling by the contrast; while in the deep shadows of his eyes floated some reminiscences that did not seem to give him much joy. . . . When the revelry of his companions had mounted to its height, this man slipped away unobserved, and I saw no more of him till he became my comrade on the sea. In a few minutes, however, he was missed by his shipmates, and being, it seems, for some reason a huge favorite with them, they raised a cry of "Bulkington! Bulkington! where's Bulkington?" and darted out of the house in pursuit of him.

In a strange sense, his shipmates' cries of Bulkington's name hint at an impossibility *Moby-Dick* often seems to pursue—that a name is not enough to call back actual presence. For his shipmates' cries for him do nothing to call Bulkington back. He lives outside the call of his own name. Bulkington is a silent man.

Silence pervades, to a lesser degree, the entire crew from Bulkington's ship. When Ishmael observes the crew the next day at breakfast, prepared to be amazed at stories of adventure, he is surprised to find that "nearly every man maintained a profound silence." Such silence seems to originate in their experience on the ocean. The very condition that Ishmael believes leads to "a good story" results in the inability to speak at all. One could claim that the difficulty and horror of whale hunting has shocked these men past words—but such a guess hazards an easy psychological explanation to a symptom with deeper, if not depthless, sources.

Bulkington is mentioned again, memorialized really, in one of the oddest chapters in *Moby-Dick*: "The Lee Shore." Ishmael, breaking all narrative thrust, lets us know that the hulking brawn of the man he witnesses at the helm will go down with the Pequod. Bulkington's earlier and present silence function as a conduit to the silence in which the book ends, as if to hold one's tongue, far more than to sleep, is to prefigure death. Stranger still, Ishmael—beyond subverting the narrative's push toward climax and tragedy—calls attention to the book-as-a-book, the page-as-a-page: "Wonderfullest things are ever the unmentionable; deep memories yield no epitaphs; this six-inch chapter is the stoneless grave of Bulkington." The importance of this page, this chapter, is not in conveying information, not in speculation, not in furthering plot or unfolding character. Its importance is in its materiality, in its being a page bound in a book and, by existing materially, functioning as the grave marker for a man in no grave—a man buried in abyss. Ishmael seems to suspect, and in the audacity with which he writes the chapter seems to want to make us suspect, that a book's tale is but a surface to a deeper work language attempts—not to fill silence, not to end silence, but to mark it, to encompass it, to let us know that silence, despite infinite permutations of every word and letter with every other word and letter, still exists. It is the silence of the grave whose headstone is not granite, but etched upon a page.

This silence, though, is not without source, even if no source can be named. We glimpse it when we see Bulkington at the helm—and do so throughout *Moby-Dick,* remembering he is silently there, surely a favorite among these men, too, though we never read his name again.

> Know ye, now, Bulkington? Glimpses do ye seem to see of that mortally intolerable truth; that all deep, earnest thinking is but the intrepid effort of the soul to keep the open independence of her sea; while the wildest winds of heaven and earth conspire to cast her on the treacherous, slavish shore?

Truth, it seems, is a different thing upon shore than it is upon the sea. But "in landlessness alone resides the highest truth, shoreless, indefinite as God." What is true is so with or without our knowing it. To see it doesn't define it. Bulkington is a silent man because he is a truthful man, and because he is a truthful man he steers the ship. Truth is at the helm; truth is not the destination.

See also:

Chaos
Death
Description
Experience
Expression
Flame
Ocean
Saying / Said
Silence
Tablet
Thought (Whale)

Tzimtzum

Behind Creation another story lurks, explains, complicates. The first question of the world is Form. The question does not begin with "what," but with "how." What philosophical and theological theories may gloss when considering *ex nihilo* as a creative crux is that Nothing must first exist for creation to occur in it. *Tzimtzum,* in midrashic and kabbalistic thought, is this story.

God, in the absolute infinity of God's being, desired to create a world, a universe. God's own infinite nature, in some sense, the limitless expanse that defines, but overflows all definition, refused Creation's possibility, for no open space existed in which Creation could occur. All was full with All.

The first act of creation, before a word was spoken above the water, was divine contraction. God betrayed God's own infinite essence in order to create a space of Nothingness: mercy as a form of economy. As the microscopic self, so the Stoics would say, always reflects the macroscopic universe, creation operates along a parallel line within us. The first creative act is to remove the self that can only say "me," can only say "I," in order to open the possibility of a you. Within Nothing you can occur.

Upon that Nothing, God took the vessels of the first ten letters of the Hebrew alphabet, the *Sefirot* (imagined as hollow glass vessels), and with them etched on Nothing those words that unfolded into Being.

In order to write, God poured the infinite fecundity of God's creative essence into the letter-vessels. As when any finite object (a vessel to carry water, a vessel to carry life) is filled with infinite source, the finite shatters. The glimmering shards by which the world formed fell into the world, into all that makes up world—into us, our mind and skin. Although this original language is fallen and broken, it carries still within it an iota of that original, infinite, creative power.

To write is to contribute to the ongoing creation of the world.

To write one must withdraw from the page enough to allow the poem to exist.

To do so, one might put on a mask. "Call me Ishmael."

See also:

Aleph

Bet

I / *I* / "I"

Inscribe

Nothing/ness

Reciprocity

Tablet

You / Thou

Unwritten Entries

The epilogue is hidden inside the book, unlinked to any entry but swallowed inside them all, as the snake swallows its own tail, as the whale swallows a prophet, a speaking which makes a beginning of ends. Here floats an orphan entry, belonging to no other, awaiting within the little ocean of its own utterance a reader—as she or he wanders through pages searching for meaning suspected or meaning lost—to rescue it, to bring it, too, into mind. But this orphan speaks only of those it, too, has lost. Those words it did not, or I did not, have breath enough to warrant speaking, but leave to the reader's continued hunt on this ocean we now share:

ARISTOPHANES

BULKINGTON

DESIRE

ETERNITY

GOD

MASK/S

MEMORY

REPRESENTATION

SOUL

TEACHING

TRANSCENDENCE

USE

Vengeance

Ahab's revenge is a deeper blasphemy than Starbuck guesses:

> Vengeance on a dumb brute!" cried Starbuck, "that simply smote
> thee from blindest instinct! Madness! To be enraged with a dumb
> thing, Captain Ahab, seems blasphemous.

As Ahab, in response, suggests to Starbuck, so he suggests to us, that
we must, "Hark ye yet again,—the little lower layer." Revenge to Ahab,
which seems to Starbuck but a petty instinct toward a useless reciproca-
tion, represents a far different purpose. Ahab's wound does not merely
damage and call into question his mortal self; the wound damages Ahab's
world. Nothing falls outside the scope of Ahab's damage. The whale is
the agent that threatens the very universe it represents. For Ahab, "the
desire for vengeance is," as Simone Weil writes, "a desire for essential
equilibrium. We must seek equilibrium on another plane. We have to go
as far as this limit by ourselves. There we reach the void." Ahab does not
seek vengeance as a means of inflicting harm to right a previous harm.
He does not live in a world whose ethic is simply "an eye for an eye,
a tooth for a tooth." In pursuing revenge, Ahab seeks to create in the
white whale the same emptiness the white whale created within him. He
wants to inflict harm to bring balance to harm done. He wants to dam-
age the "inscrutable thing" of which the whale is but agent or mask to
the precise degree in which the inscrutable thing has wounded him. The
whale is the wall behind which the universe mockingly lingers whole. To
wound it, one must strike through the limit behind which it dwells.

See also:

VISHNOO

Ishmael retells a myth to further contextualize whaling in all its cosmic honor:

> That wondrous oriental story is now to be rehearsed from the
> Shaster, which gives us the dread Vishnoo, one of the three
> persons in the godhead of the Hindoos; gives us this divine
> Vishnoo himself for our Lord;—Vishnoo, who, by the first of
> his ten earthly incarnations, had for ever set apart and sanctified
> the whale. When Brahma, or the God of Gods, saith the Shaster,
> resolved to recreate the world after one of its periodical dissolu-
> tions, he gave birth to Vishnoo, to preside over the work; but
> the Vedas, or mystical books, whose perusal would seem to have
> been indispensable to Vishnoo before beginning the creation, and
> which therefore must have contained something in the shape of
> practical hints to young architects, these Vedas were lying at the
> bottom of the waters; so Vishnoo became incarnate in a whale,
> and sounding down in him to the uttermost depths, rescued the
> sacred volumes.

The waters still exist when the world does not. The whale exists in these waters unbound by world. The books to teach God how again to create the world must lie at the bottom of an incommensurable depth. The book is the bedrock of the world. God becomes a whale to retrieve the books. God is a power without limit. For God to read is to learn to limit God's own power. A word is a form into which God pours his power. To read divinely is to simultaneously create. Creation occurs within form, within limits. A word, like a whale, can be a godly, godlike, ungodly incarnation.

See also:

Hero
Idolatry
Letter
Ocean
Orpheus
Skin
Tzimtzum

Void

Ahab pursues the white whale across the ocean's void. He sails forward on the surface of abyss, but he thinks below the waves, in the "little lower layer" where the white whale dwells.

Ahab, too, is a man in whom void has opened. Moby Dick, in scything from the captain his leg, opens in Ahab a hellish wound which cannot heal:

> The very throbbing of his life-spot became insufferable anguish; and when, as was sometimes the case, these spiritual throes in him heaved his being up from its base, and a chasm seemed opening in him, from which forked flames and lightnings shot up, and accursed fiends beckoned him to leap down among them; when this hell in himself yawned beneath him, a wild cry would be heard through the ship; and with glaring eyes Ahab would burst from his state room, as though escaping from a bed that was on fire.

The description grasps into presence Jonathan Edwards' horrific account of the hellishly rent human heart that would "immediately turn the soul into a fiery oven, or a furnace of fire and brimstone." It frightens not only in suggesting the torment of the burning heart, its flame struggling to break through its confines and join the conflagration consuming the world entire, but also in one's imagining the flames died down, no fuel remaining in heart nor world, leaving the dark ash that is the world's final shroud. But before this final void, this void that but prefigures some ultimate null, exist other voids, other chasms, and each, to those wounded as Ahab is wounded, must be crossed. Between Ahab and the white whale exists an indefinite distance, metaphysical and physical, and when the

Pequod leaves harbor for the sea, its impossible task entails crossing unimaginable leagues.

A book, too, crosses the void. Language places a world treacherously above an abyss that threatens to swallow it at any moment. The blank page is a blank wall. The ocean is a blank page. The troubled waters but remind one of the seething soul that requires a crossing of impossible distance. Ishmael and Ahab, who seem never to talk to one another, never to meet, are involved in parallel difficulties. One chases across the void to gain a vengeance; one traverses the void with words that create the world in which the chase occurs.

The fury of Ahab's purpose shocks: "I'd strike the sun if it insulted me." For Ahab, all that insults him can be struck through with fury: "If a man will strike, strike through the mask! How can the prisoner reach outside except by thrusting through the wall? To me, the white whale is that wall, shoved near to me."

Simone Weil helps us understand the awful anger that so alarms Starbuck: "The tendency to spread the suffering beyond ourselves. If through excessive weakness we can neither call forth pity nor do harm to others, we attack *what the universe itself represents for us*. Then every good or beautiful thing is like an insult." One does not normally think of Ahab as weak, but a wounded man's strength comes from the sudden exertion that results from recognizing oneself as mortal. As Dickinson says, "A wounded deer leaps highest." Wound, too, is the creation of void—a void that occurs on the physical boundary between self and world. The nature of void erases the distinct line between an inner life and outer world, blurs them into a single, confused, indefinable admixture in which the self and world are maddeningly one. And yet this combination does not confirm the harmonious unity of self and world, for an order has been broken, a void has been created. Ahab, by virtue of his encounter with Moby Dick, does not feel himself to be part of the overarching order of the universe in which he plays his fated part. Ahab feels anguish, affliction, void. He hears no harmony but, hauntingly, the whale god's "silence, then, *that* voices thee." The sun insults Ahab because it represents to him one aspect of what the universe could be: that Platonic ideal that casts its intelligible light upon what's seen. But in order to see we must consider the light as the fundamental reality, and not the world which in the light shines. For Ahab the world is dark—beneath the waves, beneath vision, voiced by silence. He is in the void. His only escape to strike through what represents the universe to him: the white whale that dwells in the void it creates.

See also:

Experience
Expression
Jonah
Nothing/ness
Ocean
Silence
Surplus
Vengeance
Whiteness
Wound

WHALE (GHOST)

A sailor and a whale suffer from the ocean the same threat: both can drown. Both breathe on lungs. The whale's blood is warmer than a man's. Sailor and whale share a living principle, but in their lives, and in their deaths, differ almost completely. A whaler dies by falling into the ocean, pulled down by whale, grievous injury, or the gravitational wake of the sinking ship, and his body is forever lost, memorialized only by a carved stone in a chapel, before which his family never ceases mourning, never having a body to bury so mourning could end. A whale dies by being struck when it inspires and then pulled higher into the air, its skin stripped, its head emptied of spermaceti, its teeth yanked for scrimshaw. Then it is cast loose to the current, and as it floats away, "square roods of sharks and cubic roods of fowls" flock to it, raising a murderous din.

In death a sailor loses all proof of corporeality, and his soul seems to disperse through the whole watery element into which it's freed. A whale loses all proof of soul, all proof of the immaterial force that through its limbs drove its leviathanic wanderings, and all that remains is body. A sailor drowns and in diving down becomes soul; a whale rises and becomes body. From far away, the waves that crash against the carcass cast a white spray, and a captain sets down in his log, "*shoals, rocks, and breakers hereabouts: beware!*" For years afterward, "ships shun the place" so as not to be wrecked by a danger that doesn't exist. A human ghost haunts because the soul has retained its human guise when no body remains to shape it. A whale haunts because its ghost becomes a solid mountain, and when the mountain sinks, the mark on the map still says "*mountain.*"

See also:

Death
Faith
Fossil
Inspiration
Leg (Ghost)
Scroll
Skin
Tablet

WHITENESS

Ishmael fears Moby Dick. He wants all who read his work to understand the nature of his "vague, nameless horror." He wants to explain his revulsion, but he can begin only by saying, "It was the whiteness of the whale that above all things appalled me." At one level, Ishmael values himself as a man of reason, a man of accuracy. He begins his attempt to assay white's appalling hue by rationalizing: the color of the dead is pale ash, the dreaded polar bear is white, and likewise the white shark. The dead and these ferocious animals are fearful in and of themselves, but the "abhorrent mildness" of each changes the quality of the fear felt. Whiteness tames the wildness of the beasts, and the paradox frightens. Ishmael's fear isn't the simple reaction to the fact of one's mortality, nor the simple reaction to those creatures that threaten mortally. His fear arises in the recognition that "there yet lurks an elusive something in the innermost idea of this hue" that colors all the examples.

The failure in describing whiteness (a word, unlike "white," that hints at a deeper, more essential quality, speaking of more than color on a surface) occurs because Ishmael seeks to explain by example. The initial horror, and the first sense of the problem's appalling depth, becomes apparent when one sees that whiteness is not a quality that can be understood through comparison. Whiteness is not a representative horror, and in order to understand it, one must be willing to leave behind what objects manifest the color, to leave the perceptible world behind. As Ishmael intrepidly warns, "in a matter like this, subtlety appeals to subtlety, and without imagination no man can follow another into these halls."

Here, imagination does not function by widening probability into possibility, and possibility into impossibility, making a farce of verity. Here imagination is a focus, a meditation. Imagination must fuse itself to thought, must supply to the mind the substance by which this difficult thinking can occur—for nothing in the eye, nor in the perceivable world, will do. To speak about whiteness, one must risk abandoning the real world for a world underneath, a world whose certainty is imaginary, whose bedrock seems real when we imagine it as real, but whose actual solidity is ether.

Ishmael chooses a strange analogy to begin his imaginative work. He asks us to imagine a "strong young colt, foaled in some peaceful valley in Vermont, far removed from all beasts of prey." Then "shake a fresh buffalo robe behind him," and at the first scent of the "wild animal muskiness" the foal will "start, snort, and with bursting eyes paw the ground in phrensies of affright." As the buffalo robe to the colt, so, Ishmael says, is the nature of whiteness to him. The scenario, and the meaning Ishmael asks us to ascribe to it, is shocking. He claims that within us, as within the colt, lurks some quality of being or soul that knows to fear that which we have not consciously experienced. Such fear leaps into the muscle before the mind, shakes the mind, for no thinking can explain the reaction.

Whiteness appalls because it leaps from the world below experience, before experience—and we recognize it beneath the guise of our knowledge. Whiteness presents us with impossible witness: the a priori recollection of a world that remains submerged in us but affects us still, beneath intuition, beneath instinct, mute and universal. Whiteness relocates reality and, in doing so, brings our relation to that reality into question. Whiteness means we may be merely an appearance of ourselves. We find ourselves caught in a metaphysical crux. Below us whiteness "by its indefiniteness it shadows forth the heartless voids and immensities of the universe," while above we stare up into the "white depths of the milky way." The height and the depth of the real world remain above and below us—though even such relational terms, even the attempt to locate our existence spatially within the universal whiteness, betrays our inability to say anything true of it at all—and we remain as but a pip, a dot, upon a blank page that extends infinitely in every direction.

Light exasperates the world it reveals. A prism divides "white light" into the spectrum of every hue. Ishmael sees this Newtonian optics as speaking to the terror of the experienced world. The colors that paint with beauty the perceptible world, that stun the eye with the sense of living, derive from the invisible no-color white. "[T]he great principle of light," Ishmael says, "for ever remains white or colorless in itself." Whiteness convinces the eye, and whiteness occupies the mind, when through a prism split. But the nonsensuous self recoils. For in seeing the world the unspoken-self, the mute-self, recalls that every world is but the surface of a world, as a map torn from an atlas reveals a next land, and so on, from first page to last, until one finds oneself staring at the blank page at the end of the known world. At the end of the world, whiteness begins, and witness ends.

༷

When Ahab, struck mad in his sleep by the hellish fury of his purpose, awakes and runs screaming from his cabin, he is "for the time but a vacated thing, a formless somnambulistic being, a ray of living light, to be sure, but without an object to color, and therefore a blankness itself."

Ahab sees whiteness. He chases whiteness. Ahab is himself what he sees and chases: a whiteness that is a blankness.

See also:

Accuracy
Death
Fear
Imagination
Infinite / Indefinite
Nothing/ness
Surplus
Truth
Wonder
Writing

WONDER

With a first page that follows by some strange indeterminate time the event already lived—*Moby-Dick* opens with Ishmael justifying the motives for his trip:

> By reason of these things, then, the whaling voyage was welcome; the great flood-gates of the wonder-world swung open, and in the wild conceits that swayed me to my purpose, two and two there floated into my inmost soul, endless processions of the whale, and, mid most of them all, one grand hooded phantom, like a snow hill in the air.

Although it would be reductive to call *Moby-Dick* a novel of wonder, Ishmael and all aboard the Pequod suffer wonderment, enchantment, and spell, trancelike reverie balanced by horror's gravitational abyss. In fact, Ishmael claims the promise of such wonder as the deep-set basis for his decision to go whaling. His phrase, "the wonder-world," echoes mysteriously through all the pages to come, as a promise of new experience and new knowledge as much as a consequence of the same desires. Wonder values the world as mystery—and those who participate in its mystery become both complicated by, and complicit with, the entrancing difficulty that draws them toward the unfamiliar world. Wonder is its own risk.

Ishmael encounters this risk first in the most intimate and comical of ways. On his first night in the Spouter-Inn he is forced to share a bed with a "dark complexioned" harpooner who is late arriving, wandering through New Bedford trying to sell his last shrunken head. Ishmael, assured by the innkeeper that the harpooner, so late is the hour, has harbored elsewhere for the night, decides to make his way to bed. In the room, Ishmael sees some of the harpooner's belongings, "outlandish fish hooks" and a "tall harpoon," each object imbued with a sense of the danger and repulsion and curiosity Ishmael felt in hearing about the mysterious man. He goes so far as to try on one of his unseen bedmate's garments, "ornamented at the edges with little tinkling tags something like the stained porcupine quills round an Indian moccasin," and, seeing himself in a mirror, is so horrified at his own appearance that he tears the covering off. Such is wonder's work. Ishmael feels simultaneously attracted to and repulsed by the objects in the room—objects whose attraction is their aura of belonging to, and signifying, a life wholly different and darker than his own. When Queequeg does arrive, Ishmael says nothing. He watches from under the covers as Queequeg undresses, hardly daring to breathe as he examines with minute attention the markings upon and stature of the harpooner's body. He watches as Queequeg performs his religious rites, and Ishmael's mounting fascination is matched only by his expanding fear. Wonder cleaves. It produces paradoxical effects: creating fear in which one feels no impulse to run. Far from it, the greater the fear one feels, the more entranced by it one becomes—unable to speak, to move, or to act in any way that risks breaking the spell, that trespasses against the mystery of the other by "demand a satisfactory answer concerning what seemed inexplicable in him."

Dangers abound though—and not the dangers that compel Ishmael toward the "wonder-world" governed by "a snow hill in the air." The danger of being caught in a spell, which is also to say being caught in the wake of one's inexplicable interest in the other, is that wonder transforms either oneself or the fascinating other. Cortez's men, coming to the city of Tenochtitlán, felt they were encountering a city pulled from the pages of a fairy tale. Wonder bedazzled their eyes; they felt they had never seen anything so beautiful—and they destroyed it. What comes inexplicably, what dazzles and amazes, exists at a curious distance from the lives of those who experience it. Wonder creates the "wonder-world," which obscures the object of wonder in haze. We can destroy what creates wonder within the spell of wonderment. We act not as ourselves but in tumult of fear woven into fascination—and act against the dreamlike vision as if we ourselves were merely dreaming. But wonder is two-faced. There is another side, another momentum besides destruction, into which reverie can turn when reverie, inevitably, becomes action.

When, after being spellbound so long, Ishmael sees Queequeg preparing to get into bed, his tomahawk-pipe alight, he reacts: "I sang out." The choice of diction is curious. When Ahab appears for the first time upon the Pequod's quarterdeck, he grills his crew as to the proper behavior upon his whaling ship:

"What do ye do when ye see a whale, men?"
"Sing out for him!"

This overlap speaks to wonder's allure. One "sings out," and on board the Pequod, the next act of sighting wonder is to lower the boats and heave murderously toward it. But Ishmael's singing out at the sight of a person of wonder produces a far different effect. He beds down with wonder, and wakes with wonder's arm draped around him, almost as if "I had been his wife." In suffering wonder, Ishmael suffers reversal. He becomes wife (a joke, but not merely a joke); he becomes other.

The opposing effect of wonder is to destroy oneself, to shatter the nonwondrous sense of self-knowledge each person possesses and, by witnessing wonder, become a wonder oneself. The mystery of the I that cannot explain who "I" is—such as the narrator of our book—reveals himself as a wonder. This transformation makes of his story no event, no description, no explanation, but expands all impulses toward definitive answer into a more wondrous and inexplicable depth. Ishmael gives us the event so that we might learn to sing out when we sight the question.

See also:

Experience
Friendship
Hands

Imagination
Magic
Other
Paradox
Quest / Question
Savage
Tattoo
Totem

WOUND

Ahab is not driven by pride; he is a man guided by wound.

This wound is worth meditating on, for it can explain more than any-thing else the nature of the relationship between an I and a You. When Ahab lost his leg to Moby Dick's scythelike jaw, he simultaneously struck out with a dagger to wound the whale. The ferocity of Ahab—a man, Peleg reminds us early on, who "has his humanities"—is ridiculously palpable. Why, with harpoon lost and boat destroyed, floating in the turmoil of the white-frenzied froth of the depthless ocean, would a man try to kill a whale—a creature whose heart lies fathoms deep beneath its skin—with a six-inch blade? There is no simple answer, but there is one that sounds simple. For Ahab's I-self and Moby-Dick's You-being to enter into relation, a wounding contact has to be made that threatens Ahab's life entirely. The result of the wound is madness as much as it is pain. Ahab has a hell loosed inside him. He is described as a man whose soul is leaking out of him, and if it is true, his soul is leaking out through the wound that Moby Dick has given him.

Once bodily healed, he walks upon his jawbone leg that knocks upon the wood of the deck—a deck as wrinkled with Ahab's pacing as is his forehead furrowed with thought. Ahab is described as a man who walks half on death and half on life, and the description is as figuratively im-portant as it is literal. Ahab's courage, his fundamental approach to life, which is to say his understanding of how meaning comes to be mean-ing, is not in recovering from the wound, not in learning how to "heal," but rather in striving to stay absolutely wounded. He must return to his wound's source to do so. For the wound has given proof of the soul in place of belief in the body. Fact has been shattered, for fact is but a use of "truth," a body of truth, a knowledge that gains insight as profit. Thinking is no business venture; nor is faith. Ahab is a broken idol, a shattered image—and such shattering has given him the tremendous gift of his hatred, a hatred whose force thrusts him outside the prison of body, the prison of world, the prison of language, into inscrutable proximity with mystery.

By mystery I also mean something quite simple—the open possibility of meaning before meaning has taken form and, in taking form, has become but a mask of truth in which we read the mask as "meaningful." What is at stake is the nature of reality. Whatever the result of the first fulfilled prophecy in *Moby-Dick*—the prophecy that brought Ahab to the white whale to be wounded—the notion of the way in which the world is real altered irretrievably. The madness Ahab suffered in the bowels of his own ship, the very madness from which he's still recovering when Ishmael signs his name on the line, is the vertiginous result of having the world shattered, as if the world were but a hollow stone we mistook for the world, now broken, and we must confront the expanding absence it had contained. Ahab says, "Truth has no confines." He means so literally. Only a wounded man can speak so—and he can only be wounded by You. The futile stabbing of Moby Dick strangely parallels the wound Ahab himself suffers. Not that he wounds Moby Dick in any significant way. The point is simpler. For the I-Thou encounter, as Martin Buber describes it, to be a living relationship—this I that says You, and in saying You, says I—there must exist a reciprocity, even if that reciprocity is vastly unequal. It is in such relation, Levinas might say, that formal logic's ability to explain relation is overthrown. We can bring meaning to that unexplainable inequality. The nature of the I is to act positively in the world: the I wounds as an addition. As such, Ahab inscribes wound on the parchment-white skin of Moby Dick. (It's worth noting that Moby Dick's blood is described as inky black. As such, the mark with which Ahab wounds the whale fills with ink, a repetition of the very creation of the world. See *Tzimlzum*.)

The You of Moby Dick wounds oppositely. You wounds by increasing lack, by adding nothingness, and for that soul brave enough to confront that nothingness, to dwell in it, and then to refuse to leave it, there is no choice but to return to that which created the wound. For one cannot exist in two worlds at once—in the world where one walks on a living leg and, simultaneously, in the world where one walks on a ghost leg. In the world the wound is written, it sounds as positive as fact. The world is shattered when the wound itself is wounded—when our capacity to want to know, to want to make meaning, to want to write beautifully or think beautifully is amputated, and in its stead we sense the Nothing over which such hollow desires hovered. We tend to think of such capacities as art, science, philosophy—all of Ahab's "humanities"—as sufficient unto themselves, and we realize, once we've confronted You (if we ever confront a You), that they are not.

It is the wound that by harming us completes us. This completion is not perfection. Rather, the wound completes us with our imperfection. To bear the wound is also to bear the lack the wound opens. The physical wound cicatrizes, but the metaphorical does not. The wounded contain an emptiness, and desire leaps out of such emptiness, such lack. Desire propels one toward that which may fill the lack. Ahab pursues Moby Dick along such a desirous line. He does so, it seems, not to heal himself. Ahab lives the wound.

See also:

Ahab
Death
Hero
Iconoclasm
Leg (Ghost)
Nothing/ness
Paradox
Reciprocity
Surplus

Time
Truth
Tzimtzum
Void
Writing
You / Thou

WRITING

Ishmael's impossible task is to write about a world that falls outside the realm of experience. He suffers silence, that mute residue of genuine crisis, and he suffers in breaking his silence. Ishmael is an author. His work is to write a book. To do so he must make a mark on a blank page; he must mar silence and silence's fecund possibilities and, in picking up a pen, risk betraying the nature of what he wants to express. Martin Buber describes the dilemma:

> This is the eternal origin of art that a human being confronts a form that wants to become a work through him. Not a figment of his soul but something that appears to the soul and demands the soul's creative power. What is required is a deed that a man does with his whole being.

The authorial crisis is in speaking of that world whose livingness occurs beyond the grasp of language. One betrays deeply what one loves by pulling its silent life up into spoken experience. But this work is not merely accomplished by the will or imagination of the author—or, more accurately, it need not be. Writing—for an author such as Ishmael—is a soul-full work. It is not so for everyone who puts pen to paper. Aristotle speaks of the virtue of such work. For a whaler who is also a writer, for the man in whom both qualities are singular and fused, the work of writing about whaling is also the "being-at-work" of the soul. This writing life is Ishmael's active life, his ethical life. He does not do it, as Ahab does not chase the white whale, simply to accomplish the end of the activity. Rather, as Aristotle has it in the *Ethics,* "it is clear that being-at-work is something that happens, and not something that is present like some possession."

This work of the world and the word is also self-work. "One will be literate, then, only when one produces something literate, and does so in a literate way, that is, in accordance with the art of writing within oneself." The effort by which *Moby-Dick* exists (as narrated by Ishmael-as-author) arises out of the work of attempting to know oneself in a world of difficulty. One can hear the echo of Keats's world as the "vale of soul-making." One writes out of the glancing wounds that are the conduits and consequences of actual attention. The eye is also such a wound.

Yet writing calls into question, into doubt—and doubt that can reach down to torment as often as it reaches up to grace—both the self that dwells in the world and the world dwelt in. Buber gives shape to the difficulty:

> The deed involves a sacrifice and a risk. The sacrifice: infinite possibility is surrendered on the altar of the form; all that but a moment ago floated playfully through one's perspective has to be exterminated; none of it may penetrate into the work; the exclusiveness of such a confrontation demands this. The risk: the basic word can only be spoken with one's whole being; whoever commits himself may not hold back part of himself; and the work does not permit me, as a tree or man might, to seek relaxation in the It-world; it is imperious; if I do not serve it properly, it breaks, or it breaks me.

The work of the book may destroy both he who wrote it and the world he wrote. The book must find a way to express a world without destroying either the world or the one who writes of it. To do so, the book must fail, be open to failure; the book, too, must be wounded. Melville understood as much. He writes to Hawthorne of the courage to write books that fail. He speaks of the nature of this writing work: "My dear Sir, a presentiment is on me,—I shall at last be worn out and perish, like an old nutmeg-grater, grated to pieces by the constant attrition of the wood, that is, the nutmeg." The writer worn out by the work of the writing. The world endless, but the self a mortal limit.

Ishmael, Melville's other self or the mask he speaks through, also values failure: "For small erections may be finished by their first architects; grand ones, true ones, ever leave the copestone to posterity. God keep me from ever completing anything. This whole book is but a draught—nay, but the draught of a draught." Such failure allows one to put the formless into form without sealing off the infinite possibilities by which it can be continually expressed. The author is one who damages the work so as not to damage the world.

ﾉﾝ

Ahab pursues a whale; we catch a book. These outcomes are not unrelated.

The implication in Ishmael's work is that the activity of writing and the activity of whaling are parallel. From the masthead Ishmael watches fins emerge as thoughts spontaneously forming when they pass from watery depths to surface air.

When he classifies whales, he names them as books.

This is not simply wit.

The whale escapes and the book escapes, and they both flee along the same line by which we drew near their forms—almost comprehensible, almost tangible, almost legible. The book in our hand contains a depth and holds its breath. Reading and writing are impossible work. Buber writes: "The actualization of the work involves a loss of actuality." The impossibility of Ishmael's impossible task is that he must accomplish the work of form and the work of flight simultaneously. The book rises and dives back down.

See also:

Classification
Etymology
Experience
Expression

Inscribe
Line
Orpheus
Silence
Tablet
Tzimtzum

You / Thou

Silence and language function as pivot in *Moby-Dick*. In order to understand the connection and difference between our two protagonists—Ishmael and Ahab—we must understand the differing relation to silence and language that invests each character with such indelible uniqueness. Ishmael and Ahab do not maintain an oppositional relationship (as do, say, Ahab and Starbuck), nor do they maintain a friendship that incorporates difference into togetherness (as do Ishmael and Queequeg, Ahab and Pip). Throughout *Moby-Dick,* it seems Ishmael and Ahab never come into contact, never come into a personal relation at all. Ishmael observes Ahab. At times, he observes so closely it feels as though Ishmael has access to Ahab's thoughts, his mutterings, his fervid monologues, so much so that we begin to suspect that Ishmael shares in Ahab's access to himself. Normal explanations of such authorial access to a character's inner life reside in staid notions of point of view: Melville's omniscience exerting its force through Ishmael's subjectivity. Although at a certain level that explanation holds (and opens up the curious relation of Ishmael, as narrating "author," to Melville, who authors Ishmael), it holds by virtue of reducing the narrative complexity that makes of *Moby-Dick* a masterpiece resistant to totalizing critique. An equally valid claim: Ahab is Ishmael's character. As such, the question is not what Ishmael actually overheard, actually glimpsed, but rather the explanation Ishmael must give himself by explaining to himself, revealing to himself, Ahab's motives.

But *Moby-Dick* is not a selfish book. Ishmael understands Ahab in the way he does, hears conversations none can hear, sees Ahab when the captain is locked in his cabin, thinks Ahab's thoughts as Ahab thinks them, because Ishmael's quest and Ahab's quest are the same. They occur simultaneously, in parallel relation, but at different levels. Ishmael stays above the waves, and loses the whales when they dive down; Ahab dives down with the whale. Ishmael tells our You of what happened aboard and to the Pequod. Ahab tells nobody nothing. Ahab is chasing his Thou.

Understanding Ishmael's and Ahab's quests as parallel pursuits—though parallel on different planes—reveals important differences in the You-me, I-Thou relationships under consideration. Ishmael's work is the work of expression. Ishmael needs a You in order to unfold his interior life, the residue of witness whose weight becomes knowledge, before an exterior world. The humility of Ishmael—and perhaps at a broader and deeper level, the humility embedded in the archetype of the author—is in realizing that he is not large enough a vessel to contain the world he has seen, lived within, experienced. For it to exist, he must speak it out of him. This giving away of resource (and the world is resource entire) in order to realize it, this sense of emptying oneself of world in order to gain world, places Ishmael deep within the ethical concerns of the Other that marks Levinas's thought. Not only does Ishmael risk speaking over complete abyss (and so risk losing the world he's attempting to give, to gain) to our readerly You, but his innate understanding of the place of the Other in terms of expression allows Ishmael the strange access to Ahab and all the men aboard the Pequod. Within Ishmael's ability to listen to others, to dissolve, almost, into those others to whom he listens, he reverses the result of the crisis that birthed in him both silence and the necessity to speak into, and against, that silence. In turning to Queequeg, to Starbuck, to Pip, in turning back to the entire crew, he pulls them up from the deathbed ocean. Ishmael does not remember to memorialize; he is no engraver of stones to place in Father Mapple's chapel. Ishmael's work is the expression that makes possible relation. Expression is the work of the lungs and the mind: breath-inspired syllables. What is the difference between Ishmael and Ahab? Ishmael's work—or, I should say, the work his You-me relation requires of him—resuscitates the men who followed Ahab and drowned.

Ahab's work differs. Ishmael works against the silence he finds himself in; Ahab dwells in silence. At one level, this silence shares similarity with Ishmael's silence. Ahab dwells in the silent residue of his wounding encounter with Moby Dick. This silence is born of trauma, of crisis, of the face-to-face encounter with death that stuns one into blankness. Yet Ahab reacts oppositely of Ishmael. Ahab doesn't seek a means of expression. Ahab doesn't, as Ishmael does, discover a means of deepening silence, and so in creating anew that which he suffers, find a means of speaking into it, speaking against it. Ahab uses words, but he uses words as a magnet uses magnetism—not to convey information but to align in proper relation those elements he seeks to control. The difference, at the most fundamental level, between Ishmael and Ahab is in their relation to You. Whereas Ishmael, suffering as he suffered, lost a definition of self—the ability to say "I" and mean I, and has been reduced to a me— Ahab maintains this most intimate and powerful form of self-speaking, of self-recognition. That quality in Ahab variously interpreted as egomania, megalomania, monomania, or madness can, perhaps, be reduced to a far more simple psychological construct: Ahab still says "I." He says his I ferociously, vindictively, yes—but he also says it in relation to the Thou that attacked him, dismasted him, and almost annihilated him.

That annihilation is not merely a mortal condition. One can be destroyed and live—such a person, horrific as it is to imagine, is one who has neither I nor me as a resource, as a verbal means back to the self. Such a person is lost absolutely, as lost as the whalers aboard the Pequod— those figures caught in the moment of sinking, a last breath still in their lungs, a breath by which Ishmael's me would buoy them up to air again, a breath which Ahab's I will let escape as a bubble to the ocean's surface while the man who breathed it drowns.

Ahab's I, the I-Thou relationship in which he is obsessively enmeshed, doesn't let him recognize the members of his crew as others worthy of expression, of discourse. He speaks at them, not with them. Indeed, without the need to give orders, to convince, seduce, beguile, without the need to exert his will upon the will of his crew, Ahab might not speak at all. A valid argument contrary to my point can be found in pointing to those most famous of passages Ahab speaks, Shakespearian in their force. Part of what marks the power, the awful beauty of such passages is the way in which they slip between an outward speaking and an inward one. Ahab's ferocious language verges always into soliloquy, solidifying, self-speaking. "I" arguing *I* back into the obsessive cohesion of his own purpose, lest his purpose be swayed, lest he recognize a man of his crew as a man fully human, fully worth moral consideration and, in that moment of recognition, realize he cannot go on in his frenzied pursuit. (Starbuck, that most unworthy foil of Ahab, almost unhinges him so.)

If there is proof to my claim, it is scant, almost peripheral. When Ahab finally emerges aboard the Pequod, now in the sunny climes of the tropics, he emerges as if from some silent reverie. He asks his crew if they've heard of a white whale, and when Tashtego answers "Moby Dick," Ahab pauses, thinks, and answers, "Moby Dick?" Whatever his connection to Moby Dick is, it is not the name by which Moby Dick is known. Ahab is before the name—not kneeling in front of it, but existing ahead of it, before the name need be named to be known.

See also:

Death
Dictionary
Expression
Friendship
I / *I* / "I"
Other
Reciprocity
Savage
Saying / Said
Void
Wound
Writing

Endnotes

References throughout are to the following edition: Herman Melville, *Moby-Dick: Or, The Whale* (New York: The Modern Library, 1952).

Prefatory Material

John Keats, *Selected Letters,* ed. Robert Gittings (Oxford: Oxford World Classics, 2002), 232–233.

Friedrich Nietzsche, *Beyond Good and Evil: Prelude to a Philosophy of the Future,* trans. Walter Kaufman (New York: Vintage Books, 1989), 229.

Plato, *Timaeus and Critias,* trans. Desmond Lee (London: Penguin 1971), 42.

Apology

Henry David Thoreau, *Walden and Civil Disobedience* (New York: Penguin Classics, 1983), 52.

Adam

Augustine, *The Confessions of St. Augustine,* trans. Edward Bouverie Pusey (New York: Collier Books, 1961), 14.

Babel

John Donne, "Meditation XVII," *The Works of John Donne: With a Memoir of His Life,* ed. Henry Alford (Parker, 1839), 575.

Breath (Thought)

Chambers Dictionary of Etymology, ed. Robert K. Barnhart (New York: Chambers, 2001), 1037.

Coffin

Ludwig Wittgenstein, *Tractatus Logico-Philosophicus,* trans. C. K. Ogden (Mineola, NY: Dover Publications, 1999), 107.

CORDELIA

Charles Olson, *Call Me Ishmael* (Baltimore, MD: The Johns Hopkins University Press, 1997), 47–51.

Shakespeare, *King Lear* (New Haven: Yale University Press, 1956), I:1.

Martin Heidegger, "The Origin of the Work of Art," *Basic Writings,* trans. David Farrell Krell (San Francisco: Harper Collins, 1977), 170.

COSMOGONY

Ludwig Wittgenstein, *The Blue and Brown Books* (New York: Harper & Row, Inc., 1964), 121.

CRISIS

T.S. Eliot, "Little Gidding," *Four Quartets* (London: Faber and Faber, 1950), 42.

DEATH

Ludwig Wittgenstein, *Tractatus Logico-Philosophicus,* 106.

DICTIONARY

Ludwig Wittgenstein, *Tractatus Logico-Philosophicus,* 105.

DOUBLOON

Chambers Dictionary of Etymology, 865.

DUPLICATES

Simone Weil, "Human Personality," *Simone Weil: An Anthology,* ed. Sian Miles (New York: Grove Press, 1986), 67.

ETCHING

Herman Melville, "To Nathaniel Hawthorne [17] November 1851," *Tales, Poems, and Other Writings* (New York: The Modern Library, 2002), 43.

ETYMOLOGY

The Zohar: The Book of Enlightenment, trans. Daniel Chanan Matt (Mawah, New Jersey: Paulist Press), 47–50.

The Midrash Rabbah, trans. Rabbi Dr. H. Freedman, vol. 1 (London: The Soncino Press, 1977), 1–14.

EXPERIENCE

Martin Buber, *I and Thou,* trans. Walter Kaufmann (New York: Touchstone, 1970), 56.

EXPRESSION

Emmanuel Levinas, *Totality and Infinity,* trans. Alphonso Lingis (Pittsburgh: Duquesne University Press, 1969), 172.

Emmanuel Levinas, *Totality and Infinity,* 173.

Emmanuel Levinas, *Totality and Infinity,* 174.

Emmanuel Levinas, *Totality and Infinity,* 176.

EYES

Plato, *The Republic,* trans. G.M.A. Grube (Indianapolis: Hackett Publishing Company, Inc., 1992), 183.

FAITH

Jonathan Edwards, "Sinners in the Hands of an Angry God," *Early American Writing,* ed. Giles Gunn (New York: Penguin Books, 1994), 326.

Simone Weil, *Gravity and Grace,* trans. Arthur Wills (Lincoln, NE: University of Nebraska Press, 1997), 45.

FEAR

The Midrash Rabbah, 482–508.

Zohar: The Book of Enlightenment, 60–64, 72–74.

FOOL

Shakespeare, *King Lear,* IV:2

FREEDOM

Martin Buber, *I and Thou,* 102.

Martin Buber, *I and Thou,* 104–105.

FRIENDSHIP

Anne Carson, "Bittersweet," *Eros the Bittersweet* (Champaign, IL: Dalkey Archive Press, 2000), 3–9.

Plato, "The Symposium," *Selected Dialogues of Plato,* trans. Benjamin Jowett (New York: The Modern Library, 2001), 228–234.

Montaigne, "Friendship," *Essays,* trans. J.M. Cohen (New York: Penguin Books, 1958), 97–98.

Aristotle, *Nicomachean Ethics,* trans. Joe Sachs (Newburyport, MA: Focus Publishing, 2000), 176–177.

HERO

Mircea Eliade, *Rites and Symbols of Initiation: The Mysteries of Birth and Rebirth,* trans. Willard R. Trask (New York: Harper Torchbooks, 1958), 64.

I / I / "I"

Martin Buber, *I and Thou,* 78.

Martin Buber, *I and Thou,* 111.

Martin Buber, *I and Thou,* 115.

IDOLATRY

Plato, "The Phaedrus," *Selected Dialogues of Plato,* trans. Benjamin Jowett (New York: The Modern Library, 2001), 175.

ICONOCLASM

"Genesis," *Tanakh: The Holy Scriptures* (Philadelphia: The Jewish Publication Society, 1985), 12:1.

The Midrash Rabbah, vol. 1, 313–378.

Zohar: The Book of Enlightenment, 63–64.

Avivah Gottlieb Zornberg, *The Beginning of Desire* (New York: Doubleday, 1995), 89–93.

IMAGINATION

John Keats, *Selected Letters,* 41.

John Keats, *Selected Letters,* 63.

INFINITE / INDEFINITE

Martin Buber, *I and Thou,* 82.

Martin Buber, *I and Thou,* 83.

INSCRIBE

Jacques Derrida, "Plato's Pharmacy," *Literary Theory: An Anthology,* eds. Julie Rivkin and Michael Ryan (Oxford: Blackwell Publishing, Ltd., 1998), 429–450.

Plato, "Phaedrus," *Selected Dialogues of Plato,* 189–190.

Plato, "Phaedrus," *Selected Dialogues of Plato,* 194–195.

JONAH

Thomas Hooker, "A True Sight of Sin," *Early American Writing,* ed. Giles Gunn, 151.

"Jonah," *Tanakh: The Holy Scriptures,* 1037–1040.

KNOWLEDGE

Martin Buber, *I and Thou,* 90.

LINE

Euclid, *The Thirteen Books of Euclid's Elements,* trans. Johan Ludvig Heiberg (Cambridge: University Press, 1908), 153.

Ralph Waldo Emerson, "Compensation," *Essential Writings of Ralph Waldo Emerson* (New York: The Modern Library, 2000), 163.

LOOMINGS

Euclid, *The Thirteen Books of Euclid's Elements,* trans. Johan Ludvig Heiberg, 153.

MAGIC

Martin Buber, *I and Thou,* 131.

Martin Buber, *I and Thou,* 137.

MAGNET

Ralph Waldo Emerson, "Nominalist and Realist," *Essential Writings of Ralph Waldo Emerson,* 392.

NOTHING/NESS

Emmanuel Levinas, *Totality and Infinity,* 233.

Martin Heidegger, "The Origin of the Work of Art," *Basic Writings,* trans. David Farrell Krell (San Francisco: HarperCollins, 1977), 170.

OCEAN

Friedrich Nietzsche, *Beyond Good and Evil: Prelude to a Philosophy of the Future,* 229.

OMEN

Emily Dickinson, "To Colonel T. W. Higginson 1863," *The Life and Letters of Emily Dickinson,* ed. Martha Dickinson Bianchi (Biblo & Tannen Publishers, 1972), 249.

ORPHEUS

Maurice Blanchot, *The Space of Literature,* trans. Ann Smock (Lincoln, NE: University of Nebraska Press, 1983), 172–173.

OTHER

Ludwig Wittgenstein, *Tractatus Logico-Philosophicus,* 105.

Emmanuel Levinas, *Totality and Infinity,* 51.

PARADOX

Martin Buber, *I and Thou,* 143.

Martin Buber, *I and Thou,* 121–122.

PEQUOD

John Mason, "The Taking of the Fort at Mystic," *A Library of American Literature from the Earliest Settlement to the Present Time,* eds. Edmond Clarence Stedman and Ellen MacKay Hutchinson (New York: Charles L. Welsters & Co., 1890), vol. 1, 180–184.

PROPHET

Aristotle, *Nicomachean Ethics,* 177.

PYRAMID

William Blake, "The Marriage of Heaven and Hell," *Selected Poetry* (Oxford: Oxford University Press, 1996), 76.

RECIPROCITY

Martin Buber, *I and Thou,* 108.

TATTOO

Wallace Stevens, "Man Carrying Thing," *The Collected Poems of Wallace Stevens* (New York: Vintage, 1990), 350.

TIME

Immanuel Kant, *Critique of Pure Reason,* trans. J.M.D. Meiklejohn (Amherst, NY: Prometheus Books, 1990), 30.

TOTEM

Ralph Waldo Emerson, "Experience," *The Essential Writings of Ralph Waldo Emerson,* 309.

TZIMTZUM

Aryeh Kaplan, *Sefer Yetzirah* (Boston: Weiser Books, 1997), 14.

Zohar: The Book of Enlightenment, 33–39.

VENGEANCE

Simone Weil, *Gravity and Grace,* 50.

Void

Jonathan Edwards, "Sinners in the Hands of an Angry God," *Early American Writing,* ed. Giles Gunn, 323.

Simone Weil, *Gravity and Grace,* 50.

Wonder

Tzvetan Todorov, *The Conquest of America: The Question of the Other,* trans. Richard Howard (Norman, OK: University of Oklahoma Press, 1999), 127–130.

Writing

Martin Buber, *I and Thou,* 60.

Aristotle, *Nicomachean Ethics,* 175.

Aristotle, *Nicomachean Ethics,* 26.

Martin Buber, *I and Thou,* 60.

Herman Melville, "To Nathaniel Hawthorne 1851," *Tales, Poems, and Other Writings,* 39.

Martin Buber, *I and Thou,* 68.

Photo by Sergio Vucci

DAN BEACHY-QUICK is the author of five collections of poems, a novel, and several works of nonfiction, including *A Whaler's Dictionary* and *Wonderful Investigations*. His poems, criticism, and essays have been widely published in magazines and reviews, and frequently anthologized. A graduate of the Iowa Writers' Workshop, Beachy-Quick is an Associate Professor of Literature and Creative Writing at Colorado State University. He lives in Fort Collins, Colorado.

Milkweed Editions, a nonprofit publisher, thanks Joanne and Phil Von Blon for their generous underwriting support for this book.

Milkweed Editions also gratefully acknowledges sustaining support from Anonymous; Emilie and Henry Buchwald; the Patrick and Aimee Butler Family Foundation; the Dougherty Family Foundation; the Ecolab Foundation; the General Mills Foundation; the Claire Giannini Fund; John and Joanne Gordon; William and Jeanne Grandy; the Jerome Foundation; the Lerner Foundation; the McKnight Foundation; Mid-Continent Engineering; a grant from the Minnesota State Arts Board, through an appropriation by the Minnesota State Legislature, a grant from the National Endowment for the Arts, and private funders; Kelly Morrison and John Willoughby; an award from the National Endowment for the Arts, which believes that a great nation deserves great art; the Navarre Corporation; Ellen and Sheldon Sturgis; Target; the James R. Thorpe Foundation; the Travelers Foundation; Moira and John Turner; U. S. Trust Company; Joanne and Phil Von Blon; Kathleen and Bill Wanner; Serene and Christopher Warren; and the W. M. Foundation.

THE McKNIGHT FOUNDATION

Interior design by Wendy Holdman
Typeset in Sabon
by BookMobile Design & Publishing Services

Printed in the USA
CPSIA information can be obtained
at www.ICGtesting.com
JSHW022206140824
68134JS00018B/898